SOCIAL SECURITY IN THE BALKANS
VOLUME 1

Studies in Critical Social Sciences Book Series

Haymarket Books is proud to be working with Brill Academic Publishers (www.brill.nl) to republish the *Studies in Critical Social Sciences* book series in paperback editions. This peer-reviewed book series offers insights into our current reality by exploring the content and consequences of power relationships under capitalism, and by considering the spaces of opposition and resistance to these changes that have been defining our new age. Our full catalog of *SCSS* volumes can be viewed at https://www.haymarketbooks.org/series_collections/4-studies-in-critical-social-sciences.

SOCIAL SECURITY IN THE BALKANS

VOLUME 1

An Overview of Social Policy in
Croatia, Albania, Bosnia and Herzegovina,
Greece, Romania and Bulgaria

EDITED BY
MARZENA ŻAKOWSKA
DOROTA DOMALEWSKA

Haymarket Books
Chicago, IL

First published in 2021 by Brill Academic Publishers, The Netherlands
© 2021 Koninklijke Brill NV, Leiden, The Netherlands

Published in paperback in 2022 by
Haymarket Books
P.O. Box 180165
Chicago, IL 60618
773-583-7884
www.haymarketbooks.org

ISBN: 978-1-64259-795-0

Distributed to the trade in the US through Consortium Book Sales and
Distribution (www.cbsd.com) and internationally through Ingram Publisher
Services International (www.ingramcontent.com).

This book was published with the generous support of Lannan Foundation and
Wallace Action Fund.

Special discounts are available for bulk purchases by organizations and
institutions. Please call 773-583-7884 or email info@haymarketbooks.org for more
information.

Cover design by Jamie Kerry and Ragina Johnson.

Printed in the United States.

10 9 8 7 6 5 4 3 2 1

Library of Congress Cataloging-in-Publication data is available.

Contents

PART 1
Social Security: Overview of Reforms and Challenges

PART 2
Pension System: Scheme and Development

PART 3
Social Security Evolution and Economic Recession

Acknowledgements

The inspiration for writing this three-volume book was the experience gained during research begun by Marzena Żakowska in the Balkans in 2014. However, it could not have been written without the help of many people whom we wish to thank profusely.

Our gratitude goes to Professor Cezary Smuniewski for his encouragement to start the project and his guidance and constructive comments during the development process. We would like to thank Professor Jarosław Gryz and Professor Mark Juszczak for their insightful discussions during the research. We acknowledge the funding received from the War Studies University, Warsaw, Poland. Our thanks go out for the support we received from Professor Col. Tadeusz Zieliński, Professor Col. Andrzej Soboń, and Professor Jarosław Solarz, who authorized the project and offered us thoughtful advice. We owe thanks to Tomasz Żornaczuk from the Polish Institute of International Affairs and Marta Szpala from the Center for Eastern Studies for their valuable counsel.

We are thankful to Professor Ilona Urych, Col (res) Doctor Lech Drab, Doctor Adam Szynal and Shkëlzen Macukulli for believing in our work. We would like to thank the authors of all the individual chapters – without their expertise, patience, and dedication, this book would not have been completed. We extend our gratitude to Katarzyna Tarasewicz, Richard Koss, Marcin Lachowski, Debbie de Wit, and Judy Pereira, who supported forming the final shape of the book.

We are grateful to our Families, Friends, and all our Colleagues in the Balkan states. Without their support this endeavor would not have been possible.

A special word of thanks goes to the Editor of the Studies in Critical Social Sciences Series, Professor David Fasenfest, who offered constructive remarks and coordinated the study.

Figures and Tables

Figures

Tables

Abbreviations

AAI	Active Ageing Index
AEP	Active Employment Policy
AIC	Akaike's Information Criterion
AKAGE	Intergenerational Solidarity Insurance Account
ALL	Albanian Lek
ALMPS	Active Labor Market Policies
ANEL	Independent Greeks / Right-wing Party
AROPE	Indicator – At risk of poverty or social exclusion indicator
ATLAS	system that allows for cross-checks among social insurance funds
BGN	Bulgarian lev
BIC	Bayesian Information Criterion
CD	Coefficient of Determination
CEE	Central and Eastern Europe
CeMI	Centre for Monitoring and Researching
CES	Croatian Employment Service
CFI	Comparative Fit Index
CHIF	Croatian Health Insurance Fund
CMEA	Council of Mutual Economic Assistance
CPI	Consumer price index
DB	Defined benefit
DC	Defined contribution
DZS	Croatian Bureau of Statistics
EDU_enroll	Education enrolment degree
EFKA	Greek United Social Insurance Agency
EKAS	Greek Social Solidarity Pensioners Allowance
EKAV	Greek National Center for Emergency Social Assistance
EKKA	Greek National Center for Social Solidarity
EOKF	Greek National Social Care Organization
EOPYY	Greek National Health Service Organization
ER	Employment rate
ESKE	Greek National Strategy for Social Inclusion
ESKF	Greek National Social Care System
ESPN	European Social Policy Network
ESSPROS	European System of Integrated Social Protection Statistics
ESTIA	System that records the social insurance funds' real estate assets
ESY	Greek National Health System
ETEA	Greek Insurance System Support Fund

ETEAEP	Greek United Subsidiary Insurance and Single Benefit Fund
EUROSTAT	European Statistical Office
FBiH	Federation of Bosnia and Herzegovina
FRY	Federal Republic of Yugoslavia
GMB	Guaranteed Minimum Benefit
HANFA	Croatian Financial Services Supervisory Agency
HBS	Household Budget Survey
HDIKA	Computerized system of databases
HDZ	Croatian Democratic Union
HRK	Hrvatska Kuna (currency)
IKA	Greek Social Insurance Institute
ILIOS	System that records all pensioners and their characteristics
ILO	International Labor Organization
IMF	International Monetary Fund
INSTAT	Albanian National Institute of Statistics
IPA	Instrument for Pre-Accession Assistance
ISIL	Islamic State of Iraq and Syria
ISSH	Albanian National Social Insurance Institute
KAPI	Greek Elderly Care Centers
KEAO	Greek Social Insurance Debt Collector Center
KEPA	Greek Disability Certification Center
KM	The Bosnia and Herzegovina convertible mark
Life_expect	Life expectancy
MLE	Maximum Likelihood Estimation method
NCO	National Classification of Occupations
NDC	Notional Defined Contribution
NHS	National Health System
NIS	National Institute of Statistics
OD	Old-age dependency ratio
OGA	Greek Agricultural Insurance Agency
PASOK	Panhellenic Socialist Movement
PAYG	Pay-as-you-go system
PEDY	National Primary Healthcare Network
PENS_NE	Net pension replacement rate
PIKPA	Greek Patriotic Institute for Social Protection and Perception
PLMPS	Passive Labor Market Policies
PPS	Purchasing Power Standard
PSI	Private sector involvement
RA	Reform Agenda for Bosnia and Herzegovina 2015–2018

REGOS	Central Registry of Affiliates (responsible for all aspects of pension insurance based on individual capitalized savings)
RON	Romanian currency (Leu)
SEM	Structural Equation Modelling
SFRY	Socialist Federal Republic of Yugoslavia
SII	Social Insurance Institute
SILC	Survey on Income and Living Conditions
SRMR	Standardized Root Mean Residual
SSI	Social Solidarity Income
TEVA	Food Aid Fund for the Disadvantaged
TIC	Technology, information and communication
TLI	Tucker-Lewis index
UB	Unemployment benefit
UNDP	United Nations Development Program

Notes on Contributors

Predrag Bejaković
took his doctorate at the Economics Faculty in Zagreb and now works full time as a senior researcher in the Institute of Public Finance, Zagreb. His main fields of scientific interests are labor economics, the pension system, welfare policy and public administration. He received the Croatian annual award for science on 12 December 2009. He achieved a Fulbright fellowship at the University of Madison, Wisconsin, USA in 1995–1996, and a British Council Scholarship at the Universities of Essex and Bath in 2000–2001. He publishes in scientific and professional journals and he is the author and co-author of a number of books on economics, the pension system, education (particularly VET and adult education), policy planning, public finance and labor economics. He was a member of the working group responsible for Strategy of Education, Science and Technology. He is now a member of the working groups for the development of the Strategy Croatia 2024 and is responsible for social policy and the pension system. He is a member of the working group for defining the minimum wage in Croatia. His recent articles include "The importance of digital literacy on the labour market" (co-author with Željko Mrnjavac, Employee relations, 42(4), 2020), "How to achieve efficiency and equity in the tax system?" (Revija za socijalnu politiku, 27(2), 2020), and "Fully funded pension system in six non-EU Balkan countries" (co-author with Željko Mrnjavac, Ekonomska misao i praksa, 29(1), 2020), "Determinants of tax morale in Croatia: an ordered log it model" (co-author with Slavko Bezeredi, Business systems research, 10(2), 2019). He has also authored numerous chapters in books. His ORCID is https://orcid.org/0000-0002-4164-8220 and his e-mail address is: predrag.bejakovic@ijf.hr.

Mirela Cristea
is a professor at the University of Craiova (Romania), Faculty of Economics and Business Administration, Department of Finance, Banking and Economic Analysis, and the Center for Economic, Banking and Financial Research. Her main research directions and teaching activities are insurance and private pension funds, banking administration, and interdisciplinary research in economics. She obtained the scientific title of Ph.D. in Economics at the University of Craiova and graduated from the Post-Doctoral School in Economics and Applied Sciences in Economics at the Romanian Academy of Bucharest, on the subject of the private pension system in Romania. She received two national awards from the Faculties on Economics Association

in Romania, in 2007 and 2013, for two books on life insurance and the pension system. In addition, she is co-editor, reviewer and member of the scientific and organizational committees for numerous journals and conferences. She has written over 60 articles, books and chapters. She is author of the following recent book chapters: "Challenges and Perspectives of International Migration in Europe within the Brexit Framework" (Emerald, 2020), "Digital Transformation & the EU labour markets" (Academic Conferences and Publishing, 2019), "Pension Systems in a Competitive Economy, in Terms of Equality between Women and Men" (Peter Lang, 2016). She has written over 20 articles indexed in Web of Science database, such as "Population ageing, labor productivity and economic welfare in the European Union" (Economic Research-Ekonomska Istraživanja, 33(1), 2020); "The impact of population ageing and public health support on EU labor markets" (International Journal of Environmental Research and Public Health, 17(4), 2020); "Global Ageing: Do Privately Managed Pension Funds Represent a Long Term Alternative for the Romanian Pension System? Empirical Research" (Romanian Journal of Political Science, PolSci, 16(1), 2016). Her ORCID is https://orcid.org/0000-0002-6670-9798 and her e-mail address is: mirelas.cristea@gmail.com.

Dorota Domalewska

is an assistant professor at the National Security Faculty, War Studies University, Warsaw, Poland. She is the Head of the Department of Security Education. During the years 2012–2015, she was a lecturer at Stamford International University and Rangsit University in Thailand and, in 2019, a research fellow at Rangsit University, Thailand. She carries out interdisciplinary research blending the field of security, communication and education. She is the author of "Multidimensional communication from a security perspective. Communication in crisis situations and strategic communication" (Warsaw: War Studies University, 2020, in Polish), and "Determinants of the modern security environment" (co-editor with Radosław Bielawski, Warsaw: War Studies University, 2020, in Polish). She has published numerous articles on security education, immigrant integration processes, strategic communication in social media, and societal security. Since 2016, she has been an Associate Editor and, since 2020, Editor-in-Chief of Security and Defence Quarterly, ISSN 2300-8741. Her ORCID is https://orcid.org/0000-0002-1788-1591 and her e-mail address is: d.domalewska@akademia.mil.pl.

Nikos Kourachanis

is an assistant professor of Social Policy and Housing in the Department of Social Policy at Panteion University of Athens. His research interests are social integration policies with an emphasis on the homeless, immigrants and refugees. He is the author of five books (four in Greek and one in English) and many scholarly articles in international peer-reviewed journals related to citizenship, social policies, migration and housing. His ORCID: https://orcid.org/0000-0001-9034-7902 and his e-mail address is: n.kourachanis@gmail.com.

Effrosyni E. Kouskouna

is an actuary from Greece, Fellow of the Hellenic Actuarial Society (FHAS), holding a BSc in Mathematics (National & Kapodistrian University of Athens), an MSc in Statistics of Insurance Organisations (Athens University of Economics & Business). She is currently the Chairperson of the National Actuarial Authority (since 2009), working on social and occupational pensions issues. Formerly, she has worked as a chief actuary in insurance companies. She has many years (since 1988) of experience in a variety of fields that cover a wide range of issues related to social, occupational and private insurance. She participates in a group conducting actuarial studies for the financial evolution of the Greek pension system and in the rule-making team on the activities and supervision of the Occupational Funds (IORP II). As an actuarial pension expert, she is a representative of Greece at the article 83 group of Eurostat (actuarial issues of the EU staff pension scheme) and she has co-operated for many years with the ILO. Effrosyni is a teaching fellow on actuarial issues at courses of the Hellenic Actuarial Society (since 1996) for candidates to achieve a fellowship of this Society. Her research interests and scientific publications include actuarial, fiscal and social issues.

Christos Koutsampelas

is an assistant professor in the Department of Social and Educational Policy of the University of Peloponnese. His research focuses on socio-economic inequalities and, in particular, on identifying, measuring and understanding differences in human achievements and opportunities as well as in assessing public policies which might contribute to reducing these differences in an efficient and sustainable way. He has been involved in several research programs, published articles in peer-reviewed academic journals and collective volumes and co-authored a large number of policy reports. He has participated as an independent expert in the European Network of Independent Experts on Social Inclusion (2011–2014) and in the European Social Policy Network (ESPN) (2015–2018). His recent work on social protection included Financing Social Protection in Cyprus (Brussels: European Commission, 2019) and "The Social Protection System in Cyprus: Recent Initiatives and Labour Market

Implications" (Cyprus Economic Policy Review, 13(2), 2019). His e-mail address is: ch.koutsamp@uop.gr.

Velibor Lalić

is an Assistant Professor at the Faculty of Security Studies, University of Banja Luka, Republika Srpska, Bosnia and Herzegovina. His main research interests are hate crimes, ethnic and religious violence, radicalisation, terrorism, and migration, mainly focusing on Bosnia and Herzegovina and the Western Balkans. He is a managing editor of the Journal of Security and Criminal Sciences, ISSN 2637-3076, which is published in collaboration with the Faculty of Security Studies, the University of Banja Luka, and the University of Criminal Investigation and Police Studies, Belgrade. His recent articles include "Policing Hate Crimes in Bosnia and Herzegovina" (co-author with Slađana Đurić, Policing and Society, 28(9), 2018), "Fear of Terrorism – An Emerging Research Agenda in BiH" (co-author with Mile Škiman, In Criminal Justice and Security in Central and Eastern Europe – From Common Sense to Evidence-based Policy-making. Conference Proceedings, edited by Gorazd Meško, Branko Lobnikar, Kaja Prislan, Rok Hacin, Maribor: Faculty of Criminal Justice and Security, 2018); "Securitization of Migration in European Union and the Role of Private Security Firms" (co-author with Predrag Ćeranić, Security Dialogues, 10(1), 47–61), "Security in the Western Balkans – Current State and Prospects" (co-author with Predrag Ćeranić, in Security challenges and the place of the Balkans and Serbia in a changing world, edited by Ana Jović-Lazić, Alexis Troude, Institute of International Politics and Economics, Faculty of Security, University of Belgrade, 2020). His ORCID is https://orcid.org/0000-0001-8633-0470 and his e-mail addresses are: velibor.lalic@fbn.unibl.org and lalicvelibor@gmail.com.

Shkëlzen Macukulli

is an Albanian diplomat born in Durrës, Albania. He has served for many years as Counsel of the Albanian Embassy to Warsaw, Poland. Macukulli holds a master's degree in International Business and International Relations. He is a Ph.D. candidate in Political Sciences - and has represented Albania at various conferences on international relations, security and human rights. His research interests are related to international issues, security issues, and European integration. Currently, Macukulli works at the Ministry for Europe and Foreign Affairs of the Republic of Albania. His ORCID is https://orcid.org/0000-0002-2858-1199 and his email address is: dr_shkelzen8@hotmail.com.

Irina Mindova Docheva
is an associate professor at the Faculty of National Security and Defence, Department of National and International Security, "G.S. Rakovski" National Defence College, Sofia, Bulgaria. Her research interests are national and international security, privatization of security and diplomacy. Recent publications include "Privatizing security" (Journal of Defense Resources Management 7(1), 2016) and "Spodelyaneto nainformatsiya v konteksta na otvetnite deystviya za borba s terorizma (Information sharing in the context of counter-terrorism responses)" (in Evropaprez 21 vek: Regionalnata sigurnost ineobhodimite reformi v Evropeyskiya sayuz, 2017). Her email address is: irina_mindova@abv. bg.

Graţiela Georgiana Noja
is an associate professor at the West University of Timisoara, Faculty of Economics and Business Administration, Department of Marketing and International Economic Relations, from Timisoara, Romania. She currently holds the Vice-Dean position at the Faculty of Economics and Business Administration and was the director of the East European Center for Research in Economics and Business (ECREB) (2018–2020). Her main research and teaching activities are developed within the framework of Economics and International Business area, with a focus on the world economy, globalization and European economic integration. She is Manager of the Erasmus+ Project 2019-1-RO01-KA203-063214 entitled "Coordinated higher institutions responses to digitalization", implemented during 2019–2021 by the lead partner (applicant organization) West University of Timisoara, having as partners other four prestigious European universities and an institute specialized in prospective studies and analyses. She is also co-editor, reviewer and member of the scientific board of numerous top tier journals and international conferences. Her scientific outputs cover over 50 publications, out of which 20 articles are indexed in the Web of Science database, such as: "Flexicurity models and productivity interference in CEE countries: a new approach based on cluster and spatial analysis" (Economic Research-Ekonomska Istraživanja, 31(1), 2018); "Population ageing, labor productivity and economic welfare in the European Union" (Economic Research-Ekonomska Istraživanja, 33(1), 2020); "The impact of population aging and public health support on EU labor markets" (International Journal of Environmental Research and Public Health, 17(4), 2020). Her ORCID is https://orcid.org/0000-0002-9201-3057 and her e-mail address is: gratiela.noja@e-uvt.ro.

Teuta Nunaj Kortoci

holds a Ph.D. in Economic Science. She is a lecturer and researcher at Barleti University in Tirana, a member of Academic Senate at Barleti University. She is the Head of the Admissions Office at Barleti University. She is a member of General Assembly of the Western Balkan Alumni Association founded by the European Union and co-founder of Albanian Forum for Economic Development in Serbia. Nunaj Kortoci holds a Ph.D. from the European University of Tirana with a thesis entitled "The Public Administration Reform in Albania", which was evaluated with a maximum number of points. She joined the University of Warsaw as an Erasmus Ph.D. scholar. Her current research interests are related to management, international economy, public administration and higher education. Nunaj Kortoci has authored several peer-reviewed articles such as: "Relationship between number of employed students with number of students that perceive themselves as brands" (European Journal of Economics, Law and Social Sciences IIPCCL Publishing, 3(2), 2019), "Universities and public administrations' institutions in Albania: The cooperation between them from the point of view of students" (Mediterranean Journal of Social Sciences, 7(6), 2016), "The training of Albanian public administration: An analysis of training policies and their impact in the professional development of civil servants" (Journal of Education and Social Research 6(3), 2016), "Personal Branding perception by Albanian students" (International Journal of Global Business, 9(1), 2016). She has written over 80 analytic articles in the daily press in Albania, Kosovo, North Macedonia, Montenegro, Great Britain, Norway and has given over 50 TV professional interviews. Her ORCID is: https://orcid.org/0000-0002-5449-2915 and her email address is: teuta.nunaj@gmail.com.

Mile Šikman

is Head of the Department for Police Training, Ministry of the Interior Republic of Srpska. He earned his Ph.D. from the Law Faculty, University of Kragujevac. He is an associate professor at the Faculty of Security Studies and Law Faculty, University of Banja Luka, Republika Srpska, Bosnia and Herzegovina. His main research interests are organized crime, terrorism, corruption, and other serious crimes. He is a managing editor of the Journal of Security, Police and Citizens, ISSN 1840-0698, which is published by the Ministry of Interior Republic of Srpska. His most important book is "Criminal Law Reaction on Serious Crimes" (co-author with prof. dr Miodrag Simović, Law Faculty Univerity of Banja Luka, 2017). His recent articles include "Certain Manifestation Forms and Proving Money Laundering in the Emerging Market" (co-author with Miloš Grujić, Policing and Society, Acta Economica, 18(32), 2020); "Adequacy of Penal Policy in Criminal Cases of Organized Crime" (co-author with prof. dr Miodrag

Simović, Teme 43(4), 2019) and "Fear of Terrorism – An Emerging Research Agenda in BiH" (co-author with Velibor Lalić, In Criminal Justice and Security in Central and Eastern Europe – From Common Sense to Evidence-based Policy-making. Conference Proceedings, edited by Gorazd Meško, Branko Lobnikar, Kaja Prislan, Rok Hacin, 2018, Maribor: Faculty of Criminal Justice and Security). His ORCID is https://orcid.org/0000-0003-1485-8916, and his e-mail addresses are: mile.sikman@pf.unibl.org and milesikman79@gmail.com.

Aspasia Strantzalou
is an economist from Greece and is currently on the scientific staff at the Hellenic Parliamentary Budget Office (2018-today), working on social policy issues. Formerly (2003–2018), she has worked at the Greek Ministry of Labor, Social Security and Social Solidarity on social security issues, mainly on the pensions system. As a pension expert, she has been a representative of Greece at the Social Protection Committee (SPC) of the European Committee (2006–2018) and has contributed to the reports published by this Committee. She has also been vice chair of the ad-hoc group on Efficiency, Effectiveness and Financing of Social Protection and a member of the Indicators Sub-Group of the Social Protection Committee and of its Working Group on Age (2004–2008), having contributed to the Pensions Adequacy Reports and also a member of the Mutual Information System on Social Protection (MISSOC) (2004–2009). She has been a teaching fellow (on economics and mathematics for economists) at the economics department of the University of York (1997–2002) and a teacher of economics at the Greek School of Pedagogical and Technological Education (ASPAITE) (2004–2006). Her research interests and scientific publications lie within the area of fiscal and social policy.

Nevenko Vranješ
holds PhDs in Law and Political Sciences. He earned his first PhD from the Faculty of Law, University of Niš, Republic of Serbia and the second from the Faculty of Political Sciences, University of Belgrade, Republic of Serbia. He is an assistant professor at the Faculty of Political Sciences, University of Banja Luka, Republika Srpska, Bosnia and Herzegovina. His main research interests are public administration, local self-government, administrative law, European administrative space and EU administrative law. He also researches political systems, European integration processes, Euro-Atlantic integration processes focusing on Bosnia and Herzegovina and the Western Balkans. His areas of expertise include public administration reform, strategic planning, civil service and local self-government, and is engaged in the delegation of European Union to Bosnia and Herzegovina and other international organizations. He

is a member of the group of independent experts of the Council of Europe for local self-government. He has published a book entitled "Civil Service Systems and transition reform of public administration" (Banja Luka: Grafid, 2017); "The origins, genesis and nature of the secessionist rhetoric in the Republic of Srpska" (co-author with Aleksandar Savanović, Aleksandar Vranješ, and Željko Budimir, Zagreb: Politička misao, 57(1), 2020); "Challenges of the implementation of European administrative space in General administrative procedure in Bosnia and Herzegovina" (Usaglašavanje pravne regulative sa pravnim tekovinama (Acquis Communautaire) Evropske unije – stanje u Bosni i Hercegovini i iskustva drugih) (Banja Luka: Research Centre Banja Luka and Institute for Comparative Law, 2020); "Protection of national minorities at the local level in Croatia and Bosnia and Herzegovina" (co-author with Dana Dobrić Jambrović, Zagreb: Croatian Academy of Legal Sciences, 2019). His ORCID is http://orcid.org/0000-0003-0006-9449 and his e-mail address is: nevenko.vranjes@fpn.unibl.org.

Marzena Żakowska
is an assistant professor at the National Security Faculty, War Studies University, Warsaw, Poland. She is Director of the Global Affairs and Diplomacy Studies - and Chair of the War Studies Working Group at the International Society of Military Science. Her main field of expertise includes war and armed conflicts, Balkan states' security, migrations and social security. She is the author of such publications as "The roots of armed conflicts – multilevel security perspective" (Security and Defence Quarterly 3 (30), 2020), "Strategic challenges for Serbia's integration with the European Union" (Security and Defence Quarterly 2(11), 2016); "Mediation in Armed Conflict" (Security and Defence Quarterly, 4(17),2017); "Determining Polish parliamentarians' tweets on migration: A case study of Poland" (co-author with Dorota Domalewska, Czech Journal of Political Science 3, 2019); "Migration from war-torn countries -an analysis of parliamentarians' tweets" (co-author with Dorota Domalewska, Przegląd Europejski, no. 2 (2019), in Polish). Her ORCID is https://orcid.org/0000-0002-32457684 and her e-mail address is: m.zakowska@akademia.mil.pl.

Abstracts

Chapter 1

Pursuing sustainable economic development yet being riddled with the challenges of an ageing society, the pressures of globalization and widespread technologization, Croatia has undergone major structural changes and legislative reforms. Faced with numerous pressures and ongoing changes, Croatia is committed to implementing a comprehensive employment policy and social inclusion. The purpose of this chapter is to analyze the challenges and to assess the effects of the reforms in the areas of education, employment, social security and welfare, healthcare and housing. More specifically, the current study focuses on addressing the research question: how can the social security system in Croatia be improved? To meet the objectives of the study and answer the research question, a thorough literature review has been carried out with mixed research techniques. The analysis shows that long-term unemployment, poverty and social exclusion remain major challenges for sustainable development. However, the implementation of measures aimed at governance enhancement, human capital investment as well as fighting corruption and protectionism can improve the social security system in Croatia without a significant increase in expenditure.

Chapter 2

Bosnia and Herzegovina is a post-conflict country that was formed following the breakup of the former Socialist Federal Republic of Yugoslavia. The consequences of the tragic conflict (1992–1995), the problems of transition and the consequences of neoliberal policies have created numerous social problems in society. In the existing social environment, the planning, organization and implementation of any form of security, including social security, presents a significant problem. The aim of this chapter is to examine the problems pertaining to social security in the broad conceptual framework of social security and their implications for the current security threats, challenges and risks faced by Bosnia and Herzegovina (BiH). The analytical basis of this research is a review of sociological and security-related literature, including a secondary data analysis of public policy documents and media reports. The research results indicate that BiH has a very inefficient and dysfunctional social security system. BiH is faced with a number of security threats, challenges, and risks indirectly resulting from problems in the economic and social sphere of society, primarily depopulation, poverty and social exclusion, unemployment, migration, vulnerable social groups, as well as the issues of radicalization and terrorism. The existing institutions are unable to efficiently respond to the current threats and challenges faced by Bosnia and Herzegovina today.

Chapter 3

Albanian pension schemes have faced numerous challenges since the post-communist transition: the increasing elderly dependency ratio; the increasing number of pension beneficiaries in rural areas; the low number of direct contribution receipts compared to higher pension expenditures, which requires a special directive for financing pensions from the state budget; and the dominance of the public pension marketing relation to the private pension market. This chapter aims to analyze the current pension scheme as well as the factors and indicators that affect its functioning and could lead to its failure. The following research question guided the study: which factors ensure the stability of the Albanian pension scheme? The results of the study show that the 2014 pension reform that took place in Albania was partially successful. One positive aspect of the reform is that it has led to an increase in the number of contributors and direct contributions to the pension scheme. On the other hand, contributors in urban and run-down areas have been burdened with additional payments, which has led to the failure of this reform. Although the number of pensioners and private pension fund assets in Albania has doubled, the private pension market represents only 1.7% of the financial markets in Albania, which makes it limited, undeveloped and without any contribution to the pension scheme.

Chapter 4

Given the fragile fiscal situation since 2010, the Greek social security pension system has undergone numerous structural reforms in an attempt to safeguard its sustainability. The aim of this chapter is to analyze the pension system in Greece in terms of its structural development and changes since the reforms introduced in the last decade. What was once a multi-fund and multi-tier system with numerous rules determining pension benefits and eligibility for them has become a system that operates with the same rules for all and provides main and auxiliary pension benefits from two separate funds that operate on the basis of clearly specified rules. Statistical data will be used to present the challenges the system is facing in terms of fiscal sustainability and its ability to provide adequate pensions in the long term. The research has shown that long-term sustainability of the system seems attainable, but there are certain parameters that should be carefully monitored and reviewed to meet the needs of all the insured.

Chapter 5

Pay-As-You-Go (PAYG) pension systems around the world are based on the social security contributions of the labor force; as such, they are unfavorably influenced by demographic factors such as ageing of the population and the increasing phenomenon of migration in developing countries. On this basis, the purpose of this chapter is to highlight the organizational path of the Romanian pension system (the most important component of social security) and the influence of the demographic changes that will occur in the coming years. The study used Structural Equation Modelling (SEM) and integrative assessment (direct, indirect and total) of specific pension indicators and demographic data from Romania for the period 1990–2017. The results reveal that the working population (through social security contributions paid) is unable to sustain the PAYG public pension system in Romania in the face of demographic shortcomings. Thereby, adequate integration strategies and policies on the labor market, in particular relating to people aged 55–64, have become a policy priority in Romania. Therefore, it is essential to supplement public pensions with private ones, at least the mandatory component (by the authorities maintaining this pillar) for a sustainable pension system in Romania.

Chapter 6

Bulgaria has been implementing radical structural reforms to ensure economic stability and equitable growth since the end of 1989. However, a significant fall in wages, rising unemployment, a worsening old-age-dependency ratio, a decline in fertility rates, and high emigration outflows have put the social security system in Bulgaria under increasing strain. The Bulgarian authorities have responded to these trends by implementing a series of reforms designed to maintain the sustainability of the system. The aim of this chapter is to investigate broad issues concerning the pension system in Bulgaria and the economic, demographic, and social determinants that affect its sustainability. The contemporary model of the Bulgarian pension system is based on two main legislative acts: the Social Insurance Fund Act, adopted in 1996, and the Social Insurance Code, implemented in 2003. Social insurance is based on the principles of general and obligatory insurance, solidarity among the people insured, equal rights of insured people, social dialogue in the management of the social insurance system, and a fund-based organization of resources. This study employs desk research and a descriptive analysis of data to investigate the economic, demographic, and social dimensions of pension reform in Bulgaria. The findings suggest the need to further reform retirement policies because they need to be based on a cost-effective, multi-faceted policy that encompasses both pension schemes and a wider system of social protection. Furthermore, the fiscal risks resulting from demographic developments need to be considered in order to ensure the long-term sustainability of the pension system.

Chapter 7

Over time, Greece's public policy has created an unequal and ineffective social security system. Until the Great Recession, the social insurance system was the main target of funding, organization and operation. The social assistance system was a poor relative, and its role was overwhelmed by elements of fragmentation and social inadequacy. The purpose of this chapter is to investigate the effects of the Great Recession on Greece's social security system. In particular, it is argued that cuts in social spending are in line with worsening problems of poverty. As a consequence, social benefits are directed to groups that have reached the limits of impoverishment. Drawing on Social Citizenship Theory, it has been argued that these reforms are in line with modern trends in social policy. These trends, among others, focus on the privatization of social services and the management of extreme poverty. This study shows that alongside the significant increase in poverty due to the crisis, the social security system is experiencing a race to the bottom. The residual welfare system that has been established in line with the wider modern aspirations of neoliberal social policy has been limited to helping the extremely poor to survive.

Chapter 8

During the period from 2009-2015, Greece experienced one of the longest and deepest recessions that any western economy endured in the 20th century; its real GDP fell by over a quarter and all social and employment indicators deteriorated at an unprecedented rate. The ensuing fiscal consolidation measures not only relied on increased taxation but also on significant retrenchment of social security benefits, as well as on extensive reforms of several branches of the social security system, thereby altering its shape and capacity. The aim of this chapter is to provide an overview of the Greek social security system in the aftermath of the economic recession; emphasis is placed on the more important branches of the system such as pensions, healthcare and minimum income support. The analysis is based on a document analysis of legislative acts, official reports and research papers regarding national social policy; it utilizes a variety of statistical indices and quantitative information available from national and international agencies. By offering a snapshot of the system that crystallized in the aftermath of the recession and succinctly analyzing a selection of recent pivotal reforms, this chapter addresses the most important policy challenges that lie ahead in relation to building a sustainable and equitable social security system. The study shows that although austerity in general harmed social policy, several structural reforms were positive. However, in the coming years, considerable policy effort is needed to address the challenges of population ageing, tight public budget constraints and striking a balance between efficiency and equity.

Social Security in the Balkans

Marzena Żakowska and Dorota Domalewska

The Balkan region encompasses many ethnic, cultural groups, languages and religions. Although a striking dissimilarity is evident between the states in the region, numerous affinities are shared – a similar history, cultural and social legacy, recent political and economic crises, and integration processes with the European Union, which significantly affected the development of social security in the Balkans states. History (e.g., Ottoman domination) has had a profound impact on the region's culture and social structure, a state centralization, and the quest for national emancipation. All Balkan countries except Greece have experienced communist-era legacies on their economies, societies, and policies, including social policies. In the past 30 years, the Balkans have undergone many changes. Apart from Greece, the other states have transitioned from communism to post-communism and the formation of nation states. The armed conflicts in the 1990s chiefly affected the Western Balkan states' transition to an open-market economy and democracy. Despite the recent period of stability, the Balkan region was hard hit by the global financial and economic crisis in 2008. The impact of the crisis was much more severe in the Western Balkans and Greece than elsewhere in Europe. The Balkan states beset with numerous structural deficiencies were unable to elicit an effective response in ameliorating the effects of the economic downturn.

A new chance for sustainable growth for the Balkan states has accelerated the integration process with the European Union. While some countries have already joined the EU, like Greece (1981), Bulgaria and Romania (2007), and Croatia (2013), others are still on the path. In March 2020, the EU gave formal approval to begin accession negotiations with Albania and the Republic of North Macedonia. Montenegro and Serbia are the most advanced candidates working on closing the remaining negotiating chapters. In turn, Bosnia and Herzegovina and Kosovo are potential EU candidate countries. The speed with which the countries are moving to EU integration depends on the extent and direction of their reform processes, which is determined by political legacies from the communist period. The major impediments to the trajectories of reforms include inter-linked legacies of deeply rooted vertical power structures, power relations, ethnic collectivism, pervasive clientelism, corruption, and organized crime.

Nowadays, all countries in the Balkans are facing new political, economic, and social challenges, which have become a serious threat to the stability of the Balkan region and the security of Europe. High-risk problems include crises of democracy, a revival of national aspirations and ethnic tensions, hybrid threats, migration from war-torn countries, pervasive economic insecurity, unstable access to energy resources as well as risks of secession (e.g., Bosnia's Republika Srpska; Macedonia's Albanian-majority northwest). The major social problems embrace high unemployment, widespread poverty, brain drain, aging population, and falling birth rate. These put a heavy strain on the national and regional security.

The social security systems in the Balkan states are based on a mix of complex but intertwined schemes that have undergone major transformations in the past 30 years. In the communist Balkan states, Yugoslavia, Albania, Bulgaria, and Romania, social welfare was characterized by a mix of contributory and non-contributory universal provision of cash benefits and benefits in kind. By the 1990s the cost of escalating welfare spending had become unsupportable. The fall of communism, the breakup of Yugoslavia, the uncertain path towards the consolidation of individual states while launching wide-ranging political and economic reforms brought about growing instability and uncertainty that eventually erupted into civil wars. Another problem was weak executive leadership, lack of expert knowledge, and ineffective public administration. Therefore, the transition of the Balkan region to an open market economy and pluralist democracy is burdened by the consequences of wars and ethnic tensions. It also needs to be remembered that the post-Soviet Balkan states were not at the same level of development as each other. On the one hand, fully isolated Albania called itself a 'dictatorship of the proletariat' with rigid Marxist-Leninist political ideology and economic practice. On the other hand, former Yugoslavia enjoyed considerable autonomy, including economic freedoms and the freedom to travel. A different political path than other Balkan states was followed by Greece, which did not fall under communist control. Nonetheless, Greece also had an expanded state sector that was highly fragmented and inefficient. The 2008 financial and economic crisis hit hard in the Balkan region. To make matters worse, the governments were not effective in mitigating the effects of the global crisis. In Greece, the crisis led to welfare deregulation. Furthermore, poverty, deprivation, and income inequality increased, and social welfare was blamed for the mounting public debt. Undoubtedly, rising unemployment, salary cuts and a growing number of pensioners put a heavy strain on the Greek welfare system. Despite this, Greece is finally achieving the financial sustainability of its social security system. All in all, structural reforms in social protection launched in the Balkan region in the past 30 years have been patchy and not remarkably effective.

Persistent political and economic challenges impede development in the Balkan region placing unrelenting pressure on the national labor markets and social welfare. In this situation individuals cannot deal with economic risks on their own. Instead, the minimum standards of social security have to be provided by the state, in particular medical care, sickness benefit, unemployment benefit, old-age benefit, employment injury benefit, family benefit, maternity benefit, disability benefit, and survivor's benefit. Finding effective measures to resolve these problems ensures the sustainable development of social security, which may positively influence public opinion in the Balkans about continuing their political course towards full European integration. This is especially important when the Balkans have become a key area on the geopolitical chessboard, in which the European Union, NATO and Russia are competing to expand their political and military influence. In recent years China has also entered into economic competition with the West.

This three-volume book is the outcome of a four-year project (2016-2020) coordinated by Marzena Żakowska, funded by the Faculty of National Security at the War Studies University, Warsaw, Poland, and carried out by an appointed international team of scientists and experts. It aims to present a multifaceted analysis of the social security systems of the Balkan states and make recommendations for competitive and sustainable social security system development. Hence, it examines social security system development and the functioning of governance at the local and regional administration level from a historical, economic, political, sociological, and security perspective; describes the challenges and presents the prospects for social security including its impact on the region's competitiveness and economic growth. Therefore, the study seeks to answer the following research questions: What are the current problems of social security development in the Balkan states? What measures should be undertaken to ensure the development of social security in those states and sustained stability of social security in the Balkan region?

Consequently, the book follows a case study design to achieve an in-depth analysis of the social security systems in individual Balkan states. It analyzes various fields of public policy, including social policy, pension systems, health care systems, disability insurance, poverty, labor policy, and unemployment. The framework of this study is built on the understanding of social security as a mechanism for both meeting human needs and providing protection against social risks. The right to social security is a fundamental human right that was first proclaimed in the Universal Declaration of Human Rights (Articles 22 and

25) adopted in 1948 by the United Nations General Assembly, the International Covenant on Economic, Social and Cultural Right (Article 9), and in the national constitutions of all Balkan states. In broad terms, social security systems aim to meet human and social needs resulting from social risks, such as unemployment, poverty, illness, or accidents. Hence, these assistance measures guarantee access to sufficient social and health services, promote the welfare of the population at large, and help potentially vulnerable groups such as children, the elderly, the sick, and the unemployed. The choice of instruments and mechanisms for delivering social security may differ in various states as multiple measures achieve the same goals: on the one hand, protection from poverty to satisfy individual needs; on the other hand, development of the nation and stable state security. Thus, social security supports state development and social cohesion, affects social justice, and maintains social peace. Therefore, it is a fundamental component of ensuring the stability of the state on a sustainable basis. This same state security cannot be attained by the political, military or law enforcement domains alone; particularly in regions torn by conflict and instability. Thus, social security systems play a key role in enabling the conditions to develop sustainable peace, stability, and prosperity.

Furthermore, the study adopts a country-level analysis to provide comparative information on the different approaches for establishing social security and the implementation of social policy in varied political, social and economic conditions. The results are presented in a three-volume publication which reflects progressive stages of building social security systems in the Balkan countries based on EU guidelines.

Volume One, entitled "Social Security in the Balkans. An Overview of Social Policy in Croatia, Albania, Bosnia and Herzegovina, Greece, Romania and Bulgaria" is dedicated to examining the challenges and reforms facing social security, with chapters drawing on case studies from Croatia, Bosnia and Herzegovina, and Albania. Elaboration is also included on the pension systems in Greece, Romania, and Bulgaria. The closing part of the volume is a broad case study of the social security system in Greece, which emphasizes the evolution of the system and its functioning during the economic recession. Thus, the first volume presents a contrast between six Balkan states, each individually struggling with a wide range of social, economic, and political problems and adopting different means and methods of solving them.

This volume opens with Predrag Bejaković's study "The Social System in Croatia: Challenges and Reforms", which is an in-depth analysis of the Croatian path towards sustainable economic development involving major structural changes and legislative reforms of the pension system, healthcare, employment policy, housing policy, and education. These wide-ranging reforms aim to enhance a comprehensive social policy, reduce poverty, and promote social inclusion. The major challenges that hinder effective and efficient social policy implementation in Croatia are poverty and breaking the poverty cycle. Nevenko Vranješ, Velibor Lalić, and Mile Šikman in the chapter "Security Threats, Challenges and Risks in Bosnia and Herzegovina: Social Security Perspectives" present a case study of Bosnia and Herzegovina, an ethnically divided state beset with numerous social problems resulting from lingering post-socialist tension and a rocky road of neoliberal reforms and civil war. An inefficient and dysfunctional social security system does not alleviate many problems in the economic and social spheres of society. The main challenges the country faces include migration and depopulation, poverty and social exclusion, unemployment, vulnerable social groups, radicalization, and terrorism. Teuta Nunaj Kortoci and Shkëlzen Macukulli in the chapter "The Functionality of the Social Security Scheme in Albania: Challenges and Perspectives" recount the evolution of social security in Albania. The authors investigate the factors determining the stability and efficiency of the Albanian pension system and analyze the interrelationships between the dynamics in contributions and the number of pensioners. In the chapter "The Pension System in Greece" Effrosyni E. Kouskouna and Aspasia Strantzalou critically review the pension system in Greece. They elaborate on the reforms implemented within the pension system and assess their impact on social and economic development in Greece following the 2008 economic crisis and the years of austerity. The authors argue that the long-term sustainability of the Greek pension system is attainable; however, certain processes need to be slowed down or reversed, in particular ageing of the population, undeclared work and low labor market activity rates. Mirela Cristea and Grațiela Georgiana Noja in the chapter "The Current and Future Consistency of the Pension System and Social Security in Romania in the Face of Demographic Changes", outline pension system reform in the face of the socio-economic and political changes in Romania. With the help of Structural Equation Modelling (SEM) specific pension indicators and demographic data were investigated to prove the need to make changes to the pay-as-you-go public pension system to improve its efficiency. The recommended changes include among others maintaining privately managed pension funds and promoting the concept of active aging. In turn, Dorota Domalewska and Irina Mindova Docheva in the chapter "The Pension System in Bulgaria: The Complexity of Socioeconomic Development towards Sustainable Social Security", describe some general and specific pension reform strategies that have been implemented since the post-Soviet transformation. The reforms were introduced to mitigate the pressure caused by neoliberal economic restructuring as well as social and demographic challenges. The study offers recommendations for the long-term sustainability of the pension system to improve the economic feasibility of the reforms.

Subsequently, the following chapters provide a far-reaching analysis of social security problems in Greece. Nikos Kourachanis in "The Evolution of the Social Security System in Greece" reviews the evolution of social policies in Greece. The focal point of this is the re-shuffling of social security programs resulting from the 2008 fiscal crisis, in particular budgetary cuts in social spending. The financial crisis revealed the inefficiency of Greek social policy: the fragmentation of institutions and services, inequalities in access to social benefits across different professional and social groups, social inequalities, the inefficiency of social spending in tackling poverty, and the distorted and financially unstable structure of the insurance system and social assistance structures. As a result of the reforms implemented during and after the crisis, Greece suffered from rising poverty and social exclusion. Christos Koutsampelas in the chapter "Social Security in Greece in the Aftermath of the Economic Recession: Policies and Challenges Lying Ahead" discusses in detail post-crisis structural reforms in the field of healthcare, pension system, and the minimum income system. The author also reviews the most important policy challenges to achieving the social security goals of efficiency and equity and addressing demographic challenges.

Volume Two, entitled "Social Security in the Balkans. Overview of Social Policy in the Republic of North Macedonia and Montenegro", and Volume Three, entitled "Social Security in the Balkans. Overview of Social Policy in Serbia and Kosovo", consist of chapters providing in-depth analyses of the social security problems in specific Balkan states. The Balkan countries have been grouped in the volumes based on the status of their relationship to the European Union, for which the development of social security is a fundamental issue. The other factors taken into consideration were bilateral relations and socio-political problems they have to overcome to gain EU membership. Volume Two focuses on the Republics of North Macedonia and Montenegro as the most advanced EU candidates. The issue of social security policy is examined from the perspective of reform, opportunities and future perspectives; social protection, pension system, health care system, insurance, and analysis of main social risk – poverty and unemployment. Volume Three is dedicated to examining social security in Serbia, which is already well advanced on the EU membership on the negotiation path, and social security in Kosovo as a potential EU candidate country. It captures issues of social policy, social protection, and social care services and investigates unemployment and its influence on furtherance. Moreover, the issue of social cohesion, which is becoming one of the more challenging factors for developing comprehensive and sustainable social policy, is examined.

This three-volume study fills a gap in the existing literature by providing a comprehensive analysis of social security systems in the Balkan region, examining both their legacy and the contemporary challenges facing the sustainable development of individual countries and the region as a whole. We hope that the volumes stimulate public discussion of social security problems in the Balkan states and offer valuable guidance to policy makers and other experts in the fields of social policy and security.

Bibliography

Backer, Berit. "Self-Reliance under Socialism. The Case of Albania". Journal of Peace Research 19, no. 4 (1982): 360–361. https://doi.org/10.1177/002234338201900405.

Bideleux, Robert, and Ian Jeffries. The Balkans: A Post-Communist History. New York, London: Routledge, 2007.

Cruise, Rebecca J., and Suzette R. Grillot. "Regional Security Community in the Western Balkans: A Cross-Comparative Analysis". Journal of Regional Security 8, no. 1 (2013): 7–24.

Dessus, Zephyr, Albana Rexha, Albana Merja, and Corina Stratulat. Kosovo's EU Candidate Status: A Goal within Reach? Accessed March 25, 2020. http://aei.pitt.edu/88155/.

Destremau, Blandine. "Overview of Social Protection in Southern and Eastern Mediterranean Countries". In Social Security : A Factor of Social Cohesion: Euro-Mediterranean Conference, ed. Council of Europe and International Labour Organisation Belgium: Council of Europe Publishing, 2005.

Dixon, John E. Social Security in Global Perspective. Westport, Connecticut: Praeger, 1999.

European Commission. Commission Opinion on Bosnia and Herzegovina's Application for Membership of the European Union. Accessed April 18, 2020 https://ec.europa.eu/neighbourhood-enlargement/sites/near/files/20190529-bosnia-and-herzegovina-opinion.pdf.

European Commission. Commission Welcomes the Green Light to Opening of Accession Talks with Albania and North Macedonia. Accessed April 20, 2020. https://ec.europa.eu/commission/presscorner/detail/en/IP_20_519.

European Western Balkans. Will Serbia and Montenegro Open Any New Chapters This Month? 2019. Accessed March 25, 2020. https://europeanwesternbalkans.com/2019/06/03/will-serbia-montenegro-open-new-chapters-month/.

Gökay, Bülent. "The Global Financial Crisis and Its Impact on the Balkans and the Near/Middle East". Journal of Balkan and Near Eastern Studies 12, no. 2 (2010): 123–124. https://doi.org/10.1080/19448951003791765.

Gómez, Heredero, Ana. Social Security: Protection at the International Level and Developments in Europe. Belgium: Council of Europe Publishing, 2009.

Gorup, Radmila. After Yugoslavia: The Cultural Spaces of a Vanished Land. Stanford: Stanford University Press, 2013.

Heenan, Patrick, and Monique Lamontagne. The Central and Eastern Europe Handbook. London, Chicago: Fitzroy Dearborn, 2014.

Lampe, John R. Balkans into Southeastern Europe, 1914–2014. A Century of War and Transition. London: Palgrave Macmillan, 2006.

Lory, Bernard. "The Ottoman Legacy in the Balkans". In Entangled Histories of the Balkans. Vol. 3, ed. Roumen Daskalov and Alexander Vezenkov. Leiden: Brill, 2013. https://doi.org/10.1163/9789004290365_006.

Mitrovic, Miroslav. "The Balkans and Non-Military Security Threats - Quality Comparative Analyses of Resilience Capabilities Regarding Hybrid Threats". Security and Defence Quarterly 22, no. 5 (2018): 20–45. https://doi.org/10.5604/01.3001.0012.7224.

Prelec, Marko. New Balkan Turbulence Challenges Europe. Accessed April 13, 2020. https://www.crisisgroup.org/europe-central-asia/balkans/macedonia/new-balkan-turbulence-challenges-europe.

Samokhvalov, Vsevolod. "Russia in the Balkans: Great Power Politics and Local Response". Insight Turkey 21, no. 2 (2019): 189–210.

Thomas, Margo, and Vesna Bojicic-Dzelilovic. Public Policy Making in the Western Balkans: Case Studies of Selected Economic and Social Policy Reforms. Dordrecht: Springer, 2015.

Todorova, Maria. Imagining the Balkans. Oxford: Oxford University Press, 2009.

Tonchev, Plamen. China's Road: into the Western Balkans, European Union Institute for Security Studies. Brussels: European Union Institute for Security Studies, 2017. https://doi.org/10.2815/565207.

Visar, Xhambazi. China Buying Balkans Influence, Competing with West. Accessed March 17, 2020. https://balkaninsight.com/2020/01/28/china-buying-balkans-influence-competing-withwest/#gsc.tab=0.

Wagener, Hans-urgen. "The Welfare State in Transition Economies and Accession to the EU". West European Politics 25, no. 2 (2002): 152–174. https://doi.org/10.1080/713601579.

PART 1

Social Security: Overview of Reforms and Challenges

∵

CHAPTER 1

The Social System in Croatia: Challenges and Reforms

Predrag Bejaković

1   Introduction

Croatia is a relatively small country in South-Eastern Europe, surrounded by Slovenia, Hungary, Serbia, Montenegro, Bosnia and Herzegovina and Italy (sea border). According to the 2011 census, Croatia has 4.3 million inhabitants. From 1945 to 1990, it was a part of the Yugoslav Federation (SFRY). The leaders of the all-Serbian nationalist movement stood for the unification of the Serbs in one state, irrespective of the attitudes of other nations and republics within the federation. In such a political climate, particularly bearing in mind the changes that were sweeping Eastern Europe, many Croats believed that the time had come to attain complete autonomy. Many political parties were established, and the Croatian Democratic Union (HDZ) achieved an undisputed victory in the first free multi-party and democratic election in 1990. Based on a referendum in which more than nine-tenths of voters expressed their desire for a break with Yugoslavia, on June 25, 1991 the Croatian Parliament adopted a constitutional decision about sovereignty and independence. The Serbs in Croatia reacted by organizing a political boycott and they then openly rebelled, demanding full territorial autonomy. They declared that an area with a majority Serbian population ('Krajina') was independent from Croatia. With the aid of the Yugoslav National Army, the Serbs occupied more than one third of the country. The military conflict lasted until 1995, when the Croatian armed forces and police entered occupied western Slavonia to the east of Zagreb and seized control of the previously occupied region. The Dayton agreement, signed in Paris in December 1995, recognized Croatia's official and traditional borders and enabled the return of eastern Slavonia, which was fully integrated with the legal and administrative system of Croatia at the beginning of 1998.

Recent Croatian history has been marked by three political events: the fall of socialism, the declaration of independence and the Homeland War. The war had severe consequences in human losses and material damages. Therefore, in Croatia transitional problems, interlinked with the adverse consequences of the war, caused a slower democratization process as well as a longer post-transitional recovery than in many other post-communist countries. In the context of the war, the early years of the transition in Croatia were characterized by a fall in economic output, a huge drop in GDP, hyperinflation, increased unemployment, and a widespread unofficial economy. Croatia became a member of the Council of Europe in 1996, and with the signing of the Stabilization and Association Agreement it established relations with the EU in 2001. It achieved candidate status in 2004 and the negotiation process with the EU commenced in October 2005. Croatia became a full EU member state in 2013.

Croatia has faced many similar major structural changes to those experienced in other EU Member States. These changes include restructuring of the labor market as a precondition to achieving long-term and sustainable economic development in the face of globalization pressures and an ageing population. This also encompasses rapid growth of a knowledge-based society and broad acceptance of information and communication technologies. For the fulfilment of these demanding tasks related to economic and social progress, there is a need to create an adequate legal framework and efficient market institutions that allow job creation and social inclusion. Simultaneously, there is a need to reduce the vulnerability of those unable to adapt. Such a task was given to social welfare institutions that target policies in areas such as education, employment, social security and welfare, healthcare and housing policy.

The aim of this chapter is to analyze the challenges and the results of the aforementioned policies in Croatia. The purpose is to review the advantages and problems of various public policies and to propose measures for their improvement. The main hypothesis is that the social security system in Croatia can be improved with better targeting and more efficient use of available resources, without a significant increase in expenditures. After this introduction, the first section explains the mutual links between various social policies and provides a short history of their development in Croatia. The second part analyzes the situation, the problems and the possible solutions for each of the mentioned policies, from education, employment and healthcare to the pension system. The paper ends with a conclusion.

2   Social Policies in Croatia

There are multiple complex links between various social insurance and policies. Large allocations for social protection and care are likely to limit investment in education and technological development, which could in the long-term cause adverse consequences for economic growth and development.

A successful employment policy greatly reduces the risk of poverty and social exclusion and contributes to easier financing of pension and healthcare insurance systems. Enhancing the effectiveness of social policy has a number of side effects on the overall economy. For example, employment promotion measures do not have an effect solely on employment, but also affect an increasing number of active insurers and contributors, thus reducing welfare expenditures. Poor health status prevents and/or discourages education, training and the seeking of employment, thus increasing the risk of poverty. Through different types of interventions, or through the actions of well-meaning but largely incompetent politicians, or because of the narrow and short-term interests of individual groups, the state could be an obstacle to social development and social policy. Consequently, the expectations of citizens and the tax burden have also increased, which had undesirable consequences and contributed to the slowdown in economic growth.[1]

The modern social welfare system in Croatia was developed after the Second World War and the social legislation was established in 1946 and 1947. It primarily protected state sector employees, while many people in rural areas who were active in agriculture remained outside the main forms of social security. Along with the gradual abandonment of administrative socialism at the beginning of the 1960s, greater attention was paid to social issues and a network of social welfare centers was established. Later, social problems – above all poverty, open unemployment and forms of socially deviant behavior – caused the need for the development of a comprehensive, modern social policy. Due to the transition to a market economy, new conditions and demands in social policy and social welfare were erased in the 1990s when Croatia underwent a painful post-socialist political and economic change and had to overcome the difficult consequences of the War of Independence.[2]

In recent years, social policy systems in the wider sense (pension and health insurance, employment and unemployment protection and social welfare) have placed enormous pressure on Croatia's national budgets. At the same time, a significant part of the population has been exposed to the risk of poverty and/ or unsatisfactory access to appropriate public services. Most authors agree[3] that current social policies are in a broad sense largely far from succeeding in their

1   Nicholas Barr, Economics of the Welfare State (Oxford and New York: Oxford University Press, 2012), 34.
2   Nino Žganec, "Social Welfare in the Republic of Croatia, on the Road Towards Reform", in Employment Policies and Welfare Reform, ed. Ljiljana Kaliterna Lipovčan and Svenn-Åge Dahl (Zagreb: Institute of Social Researches Ivo Pilar, 2002), 177–220.
3   Zoran Šućur, "Poverty and Social Transfers in Croatia", Financial Theory and Practice 29, no. 1 (2005): 17–38.

primary tasks (reducing social inequalities and mitigating conflicts between social groups) and in reality, they reinforce existing social differences.[4]

Since the bulk of social transfers are pensions, weaknesses of the welfare system in Croatia in helping the poor can be linked to problems of the pension system. One can argue that this is not a failure of the pension system *per se* because this social insurance system has other objectives, primarily intertemporal social transfers or saving while of working age for future retirement income. However, public pension expenditures rose from 11.5 percent of GDP in 1996 to 12.8 percent of GDP in 2003, since when they have fallen slightly.[5] The existing deficit in the public pension system has been covered by the central budget, thus reducing the financial resources that could be otherwise redirected towards the poor. The incidence analysis shows that pensions represent a transfer to the relatively well-off and fail to adequately protect the elderly and disabled from falling into poverty.[6]

3   The Current State, Problems and Changes

3.1   *Poverty and Inequality*

Absolute poverty rates in Croatia have been relatively low, less than 5% of the population according to the international poverty standard of US$4.30 a day per person at purchasing power parity.[7] Given the EU official poverty line (60% of median equivalent income), the at-risk-of-poverty-rate in 2001 was about 17.1% with income in kind (just one percentage point higher than the average for the EU25) or 20.5% without income in kind.[8] The data is not fully comparable due to a slightly different methodology of the Survey on Income and Living Conditions, instead of the Household Consumption Survey. In 2011 an at-risk-of-poverty rate of 21.3% was recorded (Table 1.1).

4   Zdenko Babić and Danijel Baturina, "Poverty in Croatia", in Poor Europe. The Problem of Poverty in Chosen European Countries, ed. Grzegorz Libor and Dorota Nowalska-Kapuścik (Katowice: University of Silesia, 2015), 59–87.

5   International Monetary Fund – IMF, Government Finance Statistics Yearbook (Washington: International Monetary Fund, 2014).

6   Predrag Bejaković, "The Croatian Pension System and Challenges of Pension Policy", in Policy-Making at the European Periphery: the Case of Croatia, ed. Zdravko Petak and Kristijan Kotarski (Cham: Palgrave, 2018), 229–245.

7   Zdenko Babić and Danijel Baturina, "Poverty in Croatia", in Poor Europe. The Problem of Poverty in Chosen European Countries, 59–87.

8   Croatian Bureau of Statistics, Poverty indicators, 2001 – 2002, First Release 13.2.2. (Zagreb: Croatian Bureau of Statistics, 2014), https://www.dzs.hr/Eng/publication/2004/13-2-2e2004.htm (accessed May 4, 2019).

TABLE 1.1   Indicators of poverty for the Republic of Croatia 2001–2017 [in %]

Year	2001	2002	2003	2004	2005	2006
Risk-of-poverty rate	17.1	18.2	16.9	16.7	17.5	16.3
Year	2007	2008	2009	2010	2011	2012
Risk-of-poverty rate	17.4	17.4	18.0	20.6	21.3	20.5
Year	2013	2014	2015	2016	2017	
Risk-of-poverty rate	19.5	19.4	20.0	19.5	20.0	

SOURCE: CROATIAN BUREAU OF STATISTICS, INDICATORS OF POVERTY AND SOCIAL EXCLU-
SION (ZAGREB: CROATIAN BUREAU OF STATISTICS, 2018).

Poverty has remained stable or decreased slightly since 2011, and according to the latest available data the at-risk-of-poverty rate in 2017 was 20.0%. The at-risk-of-poverty rate by age and sex in 2017 was highest for persons aged 65 years or over and amounted to 28.6%. The difference by gender was highest in this age group and amounted to 31.7% for women and 24.1% for men. The lowest at-risk-of-poverty rate was recorded for persons aged 25 to 54 and amounted to 15.6%. In this age group, it was 16.3% for men and 14.9% for women. Employment in Croatia represents relatively secure protection against poverty, therefore the at-risk-of-poverty rate for employees was 4.8% (5.6% for men and 3.9% for women), while the same rate for the unemployed and inactive was 45.6% and 30.5%, respectively.[9] Education level is also significant: members of families in which the main earner had completed only primary education (or in some cases even less) made up nearly three-fourths of the poor.

These individuals have limited opportunities to find a job, therefore they are often unemployed; if they do find employment, they receive low wages and salaries. The risk of poverty is particularly high when low educational attainment is linked with inactivity or joblessness. Families in which household heads

9   Croatian Bureau of Statistics, Indicators of Poverty and Social Exclusion, 2017, First Release no. 14.1.1, (Zagreb: Croatian Bureau of Statistics, 2018), https://www.dzs.hr/Hrv_Eng/publication/2018/14-01-01_01_2018.htm (accessed May 4, 2019).

are inactive or unemployed are approximately three times more likely to be trapped in poverty than the total population.[10]

Poverty in Croatia is stagnant: those who are poor have reduced opportunities and need a long period to escape poverty. There is no recent data on the duration of poverty, but according to a survey by Šućur,[11] the average duration of receiving benefits is very long (almost five years). To put it briefly, the unemployed and inactive in Croatia are very vulnerable to poverty, while permanent and particularly full-time employment represent relatively secure protection against the dire problems of poverty.

Inequality indicators from 2003 to 2009 were also acquired from the Household Budget Survey (HBS), while those since 2010 have been calculated from the Statistics on Income and Living Conditions (SILC) by the Croatian Bureau of Statistics. The main inequality indicators include a quintile share ratio (S80/S20), which was 4.5 in 2004, and the Gini coefficient, which had a value of 0.29 in the same year. This is not a significant increase of the Gini coefficient in comparison to 0.28 in 1988. These values are slightly above the EU25 average, but they are not extreme values. While there was a relatively noticeable increase of quintile ratio to 5.1 in 2014, the Gini coefficient has stayed almost the same since (0.29 or 0.30).[12] Nestić[13] emphasizes that since 1998, there has been a conspicuous rise of wages and pensions share in the total income. This could be related to the progress in the political and economic transition towards a market economy, in which work efforts are more rewarded than in the socialist system that existed previously.

3.2   The Social Welfare System and Measures for Reducing Poverty

The government of Croatia adopted the Social Program in March and passed amendments in August 1993, while the Homeland War was being fought. The difficult conditions caused by the war made a program of this kind a necessity, when many people were drastically impoverished, and their subsistence was at risk. Victims of the war were in the most difficult position, primarily refugees and displaced persons. In 1992, there were more than 700,000 displaced

---

10   Predrag Bejaković, "The Role of Economic and Political Measures in Alleviating Poverty in the Republic of Croatia", Financial Theory and Practice 29, no. 1 (2005): 97–118.

11   Zoran Šućur, Siromaštvo: Teorije, koncepti i pokazatelji (Zagreb: Pravni Fakultet, 2001), 207.

12   Sebastian Leitner and Mario Holzner, Inequality in Croatia in Comparison. Research Reports 355n (Vienna: The Vienna Institute for International Economic Studies, 2009).

13   Danijel Nestić, "Economic Inequality in Croatia in 1998: Lower than Expected", Croatian Economic Survey 5, no. 1 (2003): 11–52.

persons and refugees, which was more than 15% of the total Croatian population. These persons received special support from the state. The new types of assistance that the Social Program provided represented an expansion or variation on those that were already in existence. To identify those entitled to obtain the assistance provided by the Social Program, the use of 'social cards', as they were called, was introduced. In 1993, social cards were issued to 5.4% of the population of Croatia.[14]

Even during the Homeland War and particularly after it ended, the Croatian Government has entirely respected the idea that reducing poverty is an important ethical and moral imperative, and it has been dedicated to its eradication in Croatia. This has been demonstrated by numerous strategic and political documents such as "The Joint Inclusion Memorandum of the Republic of Croatia" from 2007, "The Joint Assessment of the Employment Policy Priorities of the Republic of Croatia from 2008", "The Regional Development Strategy of the Republic of Croatia for the period 2017–2019", "Strategy for Combating Poverty and Social Exclusion in the Republic of Croatia for the period 2014–2020", and "The National Reform Program" for different years.

The present social welfare protection system in Croatia is a combination of old and new programs and consists of three important components: cash aid, benefits and services in kind, and a variety of foster care and residential programs. It has undergone fairly frequent modification owing to the changes in social and economic circumstances. The aim has been to improve the efficiency of the provision of social transfers and the services that are required. According to statistics kept by the Ministry of Demography, Family, Youth and Social Policy, there are various financial transfer benefits (like the Permanent Subsistence Benefit and Compensation for Heating) and numerous types of in-kind assistance are provided (preparation and/or delivery of meals to homes; housekeeping, dishwashing, water supply and similar; supply of medicines and other necessities; assistance with personal hygiene, dressing and bathing). Furthermore, the majority of local government institutions and bodies as well as many NGOs provide financial aid and a range of services for various groups of citizens like the poor, disabled and infirm persons, the elderly and so on.

For families whose income was below the "means of subsistence" prior to 2014, there was financial social welfare aid called the Permanent Subsistence

---

14   Nino Žganec, "Social Welfare in the Republic of Croatia; on the Road Towards Reform", in Employment Policies and Welfare Reform, 177–220.

Benefit.[15] This was a means-tested benefit the aim of which was to satisfy the basic needs of the living standard. The basic needs are a sum of individual benefits depending on the characteristics of the members of a household. Urban, Bezeredi and Pezer[16] state that the poorest decile benefited the most from the subsistence benefit. On the other hand, the introduction of a maximum limit to this benefit, defined as the amount of the gross minimum wage, had an adverse impact on the income of the second decile. The Guaranteed Minimum Benefit (GMB), introduced in a law which came into effect at the beginning of 2014, amended in September 2015, replaced this subsistence benefit. The GMB merged the basic social assistance benefit with two smaller schemes. The GMB is a national means- and asset-tested social welfare scheme. Croatia spends about 0.4% of GDP annually on this scheme. Anyone is entitled to the GMB providing his or her revenue is not sufficient to assure their subsistence. The structure of beneficiaries of permanent subsistence benefit and GMB in the period 2005–2017 is shown in Table 1.2. Presently, this social welfare scheme reaches only about 12% of those at risk of poverty. The amount that leaks to those with higher income is very low and it seems that the targeting has improved over time.

There are some other local social welfare forms of aid, such as a housing benefit and lump-sum assistance intended to aid poor citizens. The housing benefit is envisioned for covering the costs of electricity, gas, heating, rent, water, and other housing bills. Local self-government finances and distributes these benefits and defines income tests and benefit amounts. The maximum amount is equal to 50% of the Guaranteed Minimum Benefit (previously called the Subsistence Benefit). An explicit stipulation that went into effect in January 2014, is that recipients must also be beneficiaries of the Subsistence Benefit (now called the Guaranteed Minimum Benefit). A relatively broad scope of social benefits is provided by lower levels of government.[17]

Social welfare benefits may cause work disincentives due to the fact that certain payments are stopped when individuals (re)enter employment; this is usually

15   Ivica Urban and Slavko Bezeredi, EUROMOD Country Report Croatia (Colchester: University of Essex, 2016), https://www.euromod.ac.uk/sites/default/files/country -reports/year10/Y10_CR_HR_Final.pdf (accessed January 5, 2018).

16   Ivica Urban, Slavko Bezeredi and Martina Pezer, EUROMOD Country Report Croatia 2015–2018 (Colchester: University of Essex, 2018), https://www.euromod.ac.uk/sites/ default/files/country-reports/year9/Y9_CR_HR_Final.pdf (accessed January 5, 2018).

17   Ministry of Social Policy and Youth of the Republic of Croatia, Structure of social benefits, expenditures and beneficiaries of social protection in the Republic of Croatia: The Report within the Project "Synergistic Social System" (Zagreb: Ministry of Social Policy and Youth of the Republic of Croatia, 2016).

TABLE 1.2 The structure of beneficiaries of permanent subsistence benefit and GMB [%]

	2005	2006	2007	2008	2009	2010	2011	2012	2013	2014	2015	2016	2017
The share of beneficiaries in Croatia's total population	2.7	2.5	2.3	2.1	2.1	2.3	2.3	2.6	2.7	2.4	2.4	2.4	**2.0**
By gender													
M	49.6	49.4	50.7	50.0	50.5	50.3	48.4	55.1	51.8	52.9	52.2	50.0	**52.9**
F	50.4	50.6	49.3	50.0	49.5	49.7	51.6	44.9	48.2	47.1	47.8	50.0	47.1
Age 60+	16.0	15.9	17.2	17.4	16.8	16.4	16.5	16.0	14.4	14.5	15.1	16.4	16.3
Adult unable to work	14.8	15.6	17.2	18.1	18.1	17.2	16.1	15.2	14.8	15.0	15.1	14.5	17.1

SOURCE: FOR THE NUMBER OF BENEFICIARIES, THE STATISTICS ARE MAINTAINED BY THE MINISTRY OF DEMOGRAPHY, FAMILY, YOUTH AND SOCIAL POLICY (VARIOUS YEARS). FOR THE TOTAL POPULATION, STATISTICS ARE MAINTAINED BY THE CROATIAN BUREAU OF STATISTICS (DZS, 2017).

called the unemployment trap. In order for earning wages to be worthwhile, financial measures are important to enhance the employment prospects for marginal
groups in the labor market. With such measures it is possible to increase earned
income and the motivation to work in the official economy for those for whom
social welfare transfers are their sole source of income. In the last few years, more
research attention and political discussion have been focused on the "work does
pay" model. According to the assessments completed, vulnerable families in
Croatia are those in which an employed member earns a low income, families
that obtain all types of available social welfare benefits and aid, families in which
only one adult member works, and families with more than two children.

Total social expenditures in Croatia at the beginning of 2000s were around
21% of GDP and were significantly lower than the EU average. Nonetheless,
expenditures in Croatia were higher than in other transition countries (with
the exception of Hungary and Slovenia), and comparable to those in the Czech
Republic and Poland. In Croatia, there was a noticeable gradual reduction of
total social expenditures after 2001 (to 19% of GDP in 2008). This was possible primarily due to relatively strong economic growth until 2009. Since 2009,
because of the prolonged and deep economic crisis as well as a serious deterioration of the situation on the labor market, there was an opposite growth trend
in the absolute amount of these expenditures and an increase of their share of
GDP (to 21.5% in 2010). Comparing the latest data from 2016 on the share of
social protection outlays in the national GDP with the share of such outlays in
the GDP of other EU member states, Croatia ranks 21st, lagging by 6.2 percentage points behind the average of the EU-28 (Figure 1.1).

In 2001, social transfers reduced the poverty rate by 26.0% (from 47% to
21%); this was one of the strongest rates of reduction in comparison to the EU
or other candidate countries.[18] Regarding the level of poverty reduction due to
pensions and social transfers in 2017 (column 6 of Table 1.3), countries can be
divided into four groups:
–   countries with a poverty reduction rate of more than 30% (the highest, in
     Hungary is 33.3 percentage points, followed by Finland, France and Greece);
–   countries where the poverty reduction rate ranges between 25% and
     30% (Austria, Belgium, Czech Republic, Denmark, Italy, Netherlands,
     Luxembourg, Germany, Poland, Portugal, Romania, Slovak Republic,
     Slovenia, Sweden and the United Kingdom -data for 2016);

18   Dubravka Jurlina-Alibegović, Miroslav Mastilica, Danijel Nestić and Paul Stubbs, Social
      Protection and Social Inclusion in Croatia (Zagreb: The Institute of Economics, 2006),
      https://enil.eu/wp-content/uploads/2012/07/Social-Protection-Social-Inclusion-in-
      Croatia-Report-for-the-European-Commission.pdf (accessed June 7, 2019).

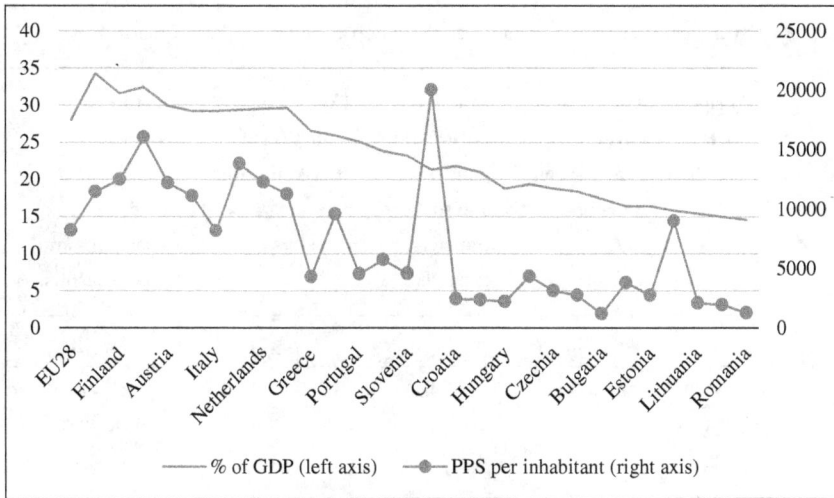

FIGURE 1.1   Social protection expenditure in the EU and Croatia (2016)
Note: PPS (Purchasing Power Standard) is the name of the artificial
currency used by Eurostat. Theoretically, one PPS can buy the same
amount of goods and services in each country.
SOURCE: EUROSTAT, HTTPS://EC.EUROPA.EU/EUROSTAT/DATABROWSER/
VIEW/SPR_EXP_SUM__CUSTOM_514905/DEFAULT/TABLE?LANG=EN
(ACCESSED JUNE 7, 2019).

– countries with a poverty reduction rate of between 20 and 25% (Bulgaria,
  Croatia, Cyprus, Netherlands, Romania and Spain);
– countries with a poverty reduction rate of less than 20% (Estonia, Latvia
  and Lithuania).

3.3   *Education*

Significant changes in Croatian education policy have been underway since
2000. This process has been reinforced by the exogenous influence of the EU
during the accession period.[19] Generally speaking, the level of education of
society in Croatia is relatively low, although this is much better for the younger
generation as compared to the population as a whole. According to the 2011
Census, the whole population consists of 31% of people with elementary
school and less, 53% with secondary education, 6% with college, and 10% with
university and art academy degrees (Table 1.4).

---

19   Tihomir Žiljak and Teodora Molnar, "Croatian Education Policy in the EU Context", in EU
      Public Policies Seen from a National Perspective: Slovenia and Croatia in the European
      Union, ed. Damjan Lajh and Zdravko Petak (Ljubljana: Faculty of Social Sciences, 2015),
      279–298.

TABLE 1.3   Poverty indicators, comparison between EU countries and Republic of Croatia, 2017

Country	At-risk-of-poverty rate, %	At-risk-of-poverty rate, before social transfers, %	At-risk-of-poverty rate, pensions and social transfers excluded, %	The rate of reduction of at-risk-of-poverty rate due to social transfers, %	The rate of reduction of at-risk-of-poverty rate due to pensions and social transfers, %
1	*2*	*3*	*4*	*5=3-2*	*6=4-2*
EU-28	16.9	25.0	43.9	8.1	27.0
Austria	14.4	24.9	43.4	10.5	29.0
Belgium	15.9	26.3	43.8	10.4	27.9
Bulgaria	23.4	29.2	44.8	5.8	21.4
Cyprus	15.7	24.5	37.5	8.8	21.8
Czech R.	9.1	15.8	35.2	6.7	26.1
Denmark	12.4	25.3	40.5	12.9	28.1
Estonia	21.0	28.9	39.2	7.9	18.2
Finland	11.5	26.7	43.7	15.2	32.2
France	13.3	24.1	45.4	10.8	32.1
Greece	20.2	24.0	50.8	3.8	30.6
Croatia	**20.0**	26.6	43.2	6.6	23.2
Italy	20.3	25.2	45.4	4.9	25.1
Latvia	22.1	28.3	39.9	6.2	17.8
Lithuania	22.9	29.8	42.3	6.9	19.4
Luxembourg	18.7	29.0	47.0	10.3	28.3
Hungary	13.4	25.0	46.7	11.6	33.3
Malta	16.8	23.7	37.5	6.9	20.7
Netherlands	13.2	21.9	37.9	8.7	24.7
Germany	16.1	24.1	42.1	8.0	26.0
Poland	15.0	24.0	43.6	9.0	28.6
Romania	18.3	23.6	45.2	5.3	26.9
Slovakia	23.6	28.3	47.5	4.7	23.9
Slovenia	12.4	17.5	37.4	5.1	25.0
Spain	13.3	24.0	41.5	10.7	28.2
Sweden	21.6	28.4	45.0	6.8	23.4
United Kingdom	15.9	28.1	42.7	12.2	26.8

SOURCE: CROATIAN BUREAU OF STATISTICS, INDICATORS OF POVERTY AND SOCIAL EXCLUSION, 2018, REVISED DATA, FIRST RELEASE NO. 14.1.1 (ZAGREB: CROATIAN BUREAU OF STATISTICS, 2018), HTTPS:// WWW.DZS.HR/HRV_ENG/PUBLICATION/2018/14-01-01_01_2018.HTM (ACCESSED JUNE 7, 2019). DATA FOR UNITED KINGDOM IS FOR 2016. UK IS NOT INCLUDED IN THE EU-28 AVERAGE.

TABLE 1.4   Educational attainment by the whole population 2001–2011 [%]

Year	2001	2011
Total	100	100
Primary school or less	41	31
Secondary school	47	53
College	4	6
University faculties and art academies	8	10

SOURCE: CROATIAN BUREAU OF STATISTICS, STATISTICAL YEARBOOK OF THE REPUBLIC OF CROATIA, VARIOUS YEARS, WWW.DZS.HR (ACCESSED JUNE 10, 2019).

These are quite positive figures, which show that the share of those without any education has decreased in comparison with 2001, while the share of those with post-secondary and tertiary education degrees has increased. However, those who have completed upper secondary education represent the highest share of the Croatian population. More than one quarter of the population in the 25–39 age group have completed tertiary education.

The labor force shows a better educational structure than does the population as a whole. Important changes in the educational structure of the labor force can be observed only over a longer period, namely 1981–2016 (Table 1.5).

While in 1981 two-fifths of employed persons had only completed elementary school or less, in 2016 this group represented only 9% of all employed. While the share of persons with secondary school grew by 11 percentage points from 48% in 1981 to 59% in 2016, the share of employed with university and art academy education increased by more than three times. In the structure of unemployed persons, the share of jobless people with primary school or less decreased, while the share of persons with college or university or art academy education significantly increased.

The main challenges for the educational system are not only to improve the level of educational attainment of the population and the labor force, but also to adjust the outcomes of the educational system to be closer to the needs of the labor market and to enhance life-long learning. Matković[20] analyzed the

20   Teo Matković, Obrasci tranzicije iz obrazovnog sustava u svijet rada u Hrvatskoj [Patterns of Transition from Education System to the World of Work in Croatia] (Zagreb: Faculty of Law – School of Social Work, 2011). Report on the Implementation of the Joint

TABLE 1.5   Educational attainment by employment and unemployed persons

	Employed					Unemployed	
	1981	1986	1996	2003	2016	2003	2016
Total	100	100	100	100	100	100	100
Primary school or less	40	37	30	17	9	30	26
Secondary school	48	49	53	59	59	63	60
College	5	6	7	8	9	3	6
University and art academy education	7	8	10	16	23	4	8

Note: 1981 and 1986 only include workers in the public sector; 1996, 2003 and 2016 include those employed in legal entities in public and private sector.
SOURCE: CROATIAN BUREAU OF STATISTICS' STATISTICAL YEARBOOK OF THE REPUBLIC OF CROATIA, VARIOUS YEARS, WWW.DZS.HR (ACCESSED JUNE 10, 2019).

vertical and horizontal dimensions of the mismatch. The vertical mismatch shows that attained education level is inadequate to that required for a particular occupation. Such an indicator means that an employee is overeducated or undereducated for their job. The horizontal dimension of mismatch shows that an employee does not work in the field of his/her major education program and/or university studies. Only 2% of youth are underqualified for their present job, while 18% are overqualified. 26% of employers required a lower educational attainment level than that acquired by interviewed candidates, while in 5% of cases young people were hired for jobs which required a higher educational level.

Croatia has had considerable experience in lifelong learning over more than 100 years: the participation rate in education and training (last four weeks – 2018) is higher than in the EU (for Croatia it is 18.6%, whereas the EU average is 11.1%).[21] However, there is a need to accelerate the integration of labor and learning, particularly for the older population (50+), by creating

Inclusion Memorandum of the Republic of Croatia in 2009, https://mdomsp.gov.hr/UserDocsImages//arhiva/files/42094//HR-JIM_REPORT_15_06_2009_ENG.pdf (accessed June 10, 2019).

21   Eurostat, Adult Learning Statistics, https://bit.ly/3fMn3ww (accessed June 10, 2019).

a strong link between the two, instead of the traditional separation between formal education and lifelong learning and adult education. Therefore, Croatia should promote adult learning and education as a right and obligation for all citizens.

It is of great importance that Croatia ensure this process of ongoing educational reform, but it also should pay more attention to school system drop-outs and successful completion of tertiary education. In collaboration with social partners, the government should adjust education output according to the needs of the market. Its goal is to create a new list of up-to-date occupations within the National Classification of Occupations (NCO) since the existing NCO contains a large number of obsolete occupations. It is also necessary to supplement the NCO with new occupations that have emerged on the labor market (primarily various occupations related to the IT industry).

4   Labor Market

Participation in the labor market plays the most significant role in determining citizens' standard of living and quality of life in every society. Over almost the whole past 30 years of independence, the Croatian economy has been characterized by U-shaped GDP trends, a strong and persistent decline in employment rates and, until recently, high unemployment, despite the rapid structural changes. In the regulation of labor relations and related policies, more attention has been dedicated to preservation of existing firms and jobs than to the creation of new employment opportunities. Legal regulations and the political measures implemented have been more oriented to preserving the existence of unprofitable companies instead of stimulating the establishment of new and profitable entities. This policy has led Croatia to achieving the opposite outcome than what was originally desired; it has resulted in a long-term decrease in the number of existing jobs and simultaneously limited the space for new employment opportunities. Therefore, there is a polarization of society into insiders (the relatively safely employed) and outsiders (until recently this was a significant number of the unemployed), who are often without jobs for a long period (more than one year) and have almost no chance of finding work.

In the observed 1991 to 2017 period (Table 1.6), due to the negative natural growth rate of the total population and relatively high emigration abroad since the start of EU membership, the total population in Croatia fell by 374,000 (8.3%), but the working-age population increased by 267,000. Simultaneously,

TABLE 1.6   The demographic structure of Croatia, 1991–2017, in thousands

Year	1991	2001	2013	2017	Difference 2017–1991
Total population	4,499	4,198	4,285	4,125	-374
Working age population	3,279	3,514	3,846	3,546	267
Labor force	2,040	1,746	1,682	1,830	-210
Persons in employment	1,811	1,469	1,387	1,625	-186
Unemployed persons	229	277	295	205	-24
Inactive population	1,711	1,769	2,164	1,712	1

SOURCE: CROATIAN BUREAU OF STATISTICS, CROATIA IN FIGURES (ZAGREB: CROATIAN BUREAU OF STATISTICS, 2018), HTTPS://WWW.DZS.HR/HRV_ENG/CROINFIG/CROINFIG_2018.PDF (ACCESSED MAY 22, 2019).

the activity rate (the share of the labor force in the working-age population) fell from 62.2% in 1991 to 51.6% in 2017. This reduction was mostly the consequence of a fall in the number of employed persons (by 186,000), which was accompanied by a slight decrease in the total number of unemployed persons (24,000).

According to the latest available data at the end of January 2019, 159,000 unemployed persons were registered with the Croatian Employment Service, which is 37,000 less than in January 2018.[22] The registered unemployment rate in January 2019 was 10.3% for the total population and 11.7% for women.[23] In some counties, the unemployment rate is significantly higher. Until recently the youth unemployment rate was exceptionally high (for example, for the 15–24 age group the rate was 42.3% in 2015).[24] Croatia shows a range of

22   Croatian Employment Service, Monthly Statistics Bulletin XXXII (Zagreb: Croatian Employment Service, 2019), http://www.hzz.hr/content/stats/0119/stat_bilten_01_2019.pdf (accessed June 2, 2019).

23   Croatian Bureau of Statistics, Persons in Paid Employment by Activities February 2019, First Release 9.2.1/2 (Zagreb: Croatian Bureau of Statistics, 2019), https://www.dzs.hr/Hrv_Eng/publication/2019/09-02-01_02_2019.htm (accessed June 2, 2019).

24   Croatian Employment Service, Monthly Statistics Bulletin XXXII (Zagreb: Croatian Employment Service, 2019), http://www.hzz.hr/content/stats/0119/stat_bilten_01_2019.pdf (accessed June 2, 2019).

characteristics when it comes to labor flexibility. There is a high proportion of people who are newly employed and have fixed-term contracts. A fairly high share of those currently employed work either shift work or on the weekend, while the portion of those in employment work nights or evenings. The number of fixed-term contracts had been decreasing until the economic crisis, but since the beginning of the crisis it has increased.[25] Flexibility in working hours is particularly weak with respect to part-time, non-agricultural work. Wage flexibility is relatively limited.[26]

The previous Job Placement and Unemployment Insurance Act (OG 16/17)[27] provides that unemployment insurance in Croatia is included as part of other unemployment benefits (UB). Unemployed persons have the right to UB provided they have worked nine out of the 24 months prior to the termination of their employment contract and that this was not caused by their own will or fault. An unemployed person may claim UB for a period of 90 to 450 days, as determined by the total number of years previously employed. The basis for determining the UB amount is the average salary earned in the three-month period preceding the end of employment, minus any statutory contributions. For the first 90 days, the amount of UB is equal to 60% of the base amount defined by the Government. Thereafter, the recipients get 30% of the base amount. During the first 90 days, UB may not exceed 70% of the legally defined base amount, which is equal to the average salary paid in the Croatian economy in the previous year. In the remaining period, it may not exceed 35% of this base amount. In 2017, the maximum benefit amounted to HRK 3,979 (€534), whereas the average unemployment benefit was HRK 2,028 (€272).[28] Thus, the net replacement rate (the share of the average unemployment benefit in the wage before unemployment) was 33.9%, which is one of the lowest in the EU, while the coverage rate (the number of the unemployment benefit recipients in the total number of unemployed persons) in 2017 was 17.5%.[29] In comparison with other EU

---

25   Jasminka Kulušić, Isplati li se fleksibilnost: hrvatsko tržište rada (Zagreb: TIM Press, 2009).

26   Predrag Bejaković, "Povećati fleksibilnost zaposlenosti", in Zaposlimo Hrvatsku, ed. Davorko Vidović (Zagreb: Hrvatska Gospodarska Komora, 2015), 107–120.

27   Current Zakon o tržištu rada (The Act on the Labour Market, OG 118/18) came into the force at the beginning of 2019. It has slightly changed some rules for the unemployment benefits, but there are yet no statistical data on its effects.

28   Croatian Employment Service, Godišnjak 2017 (Zagreb: Croatian Employment Service, 2018) http://www.hzz.hr/content/stats/0119/stat_bilten_01_2019.pdf (accessed April 4, 2019).

29   Ibid.

Member States, UB in Croatia has a relatively low replacement rate and a very low coverage rate.[30]

To make it easier to reenter the workforce and to increase the employability level of those who are more likely to become long-term unemployed, active employment policies (AEPs) are implemented. The Croatian Employment Service (CES) finances various measures such as the training of unemployed people, jobs training alone, incentives for employment or creating a start-up for self-employment, public work etc. Although such measures have a limited and/or almost no direct impact on total employment, they can redistribute employment opportunities so that fewer people become long-term unemployed (looking for a job more than one year). In approximately the last ten years, there has been a positive and significant increase in the number of participants, although this still does not suffice considering the total number of long-term unemployed. While the coverage rate (the number of newly included participants in AEP measures divided by the average number of the unemployed people registered by the Croatian Employment Service) in 2009 was 2.5%,[31] in January 2019 it was 16.8%.[32]

Although there are some ongoing public discussions and opinions whereby it is thought that unemployment could be resolved if sufficient financial resources were allocated for active employment policies, it is much more important to stress the quality of implemented measures than to strive to broaden their quantity and coverage. From a cost-benefit perspective, and when the efficient use of limited public resources is considered, it is crucial to target active employment policy measures at those with the lowest employability and with the lowest chance of entering the open labor market.

5   The Pension System

The pension system in Croatia is a popular topic and is regularly discussed in public debates. Although there are many reasons for this, two could be the

---

30   Ingrid Esser, Tommy Ferrarini, Kenneth Nelson, Joakim Palme and Olaf Sjöberg, *Unemployment Benefits in EU Member States*, European Commission, Employment, Social Affairs & Inclusion, Brussels, 2013.

31   The Croatian Employment Service and Ipsos, *External Evaluation of Active Labor-Market Policy Measures 2010–2013*, Summary Evaluation Report, The Croatian Employment Service and Ipsos, 2016.

32   Croatian Employment Service, *Monthly Statistics Bulletin* XXXII (Zagreb: Croatian Employment Service, 2019), http://www.hzz.hr/content/stats/0119/stat_bilten_01_2019. pdf (accessed June 2, 2019).

most important. The first is related to how the public as a whole is dissatisfied with the benefits from the pension system, which for the majority of retirees are very low and in many cases do not protect against poverty. The second has to do with the fact that the system is highly inconsistent internally, which results from a succession of partial reforms. This has caused different positions for pensioners who have started to receive their pension in different years and/ or whether these are regular or privileged pension benefits. The universal discontent with the pension system also has a gender dimension.

After the proclamation of independence in 1991, the Croatian pension insurance system followed the Bismarck continental Pay-As-You-Go (PAYG) model. The Homeland War at the beginning of the 1990s and the political and economic transition had a detrimental influence on the Croatian pension system. In the circumstances of bankruptcy of many big state firms, early retirement was used as a measure to solve the adverse social consequences of open unemployment. The pension system was a buffer for redundant or unemployed workers, the displaced, and a means to award merit (privileged) pensions,[33] quite often under questionable conditions. Thus, the number of retirees increased significantly, while the number of employees who paid pension contributions dropped. Even with the relatively small size of pensions (the average pension is around 39% of the average wage), the huge number of retirees caused constant growth of pension outlays (more than 11% of GDP). The government budget also took over responsibility for the previous federal obligations and the newly established merit pensions. All this caused a permanent need for transfers from the central budget, which led to budget deficits and contributed to the growing public debt. Croatian policymakers attempted, without success, to reform the pension system until a serious discussion on the restructuring of the system began in November 1995.[34]

The Croatian pension system has passed through many reforms: one systemic reform in 1998–2002, which resulted in the establishment of the three-pillar pension system, and numerous parametric reforms, the last of which included all three parts of the pension system (2013–2018).[35] The public pension system of unfunded pensions at the beginning of 2002 was replaced by

33 Marijana Bađun, "Pension Beneficiaries who have been Granted Pensions under More Favorable Conditions", Newsletter 44 (Zagreb: Institute of Public Finance, 2009), http://www.ijf.hr/eng/newsletter/44.pdf (accessed May 21, 2019).

34 Zoran Anušić et. al., Mirovinska reforma – druga i treća razina mirovinskog osiguranja (Zagreb: Inženjerski Biro, 1999).

35 Predrag Bejaković, "The Croatian Pension System and Challenges of Pension Policy", in Policy-Making at the European Periphery: the Case of Croatia, ed. Zdravko Petak and Kristijan Kotarski (Cham: Palgrave, 2018), 229–245.

a combined system of PAYG public unfunded (the First pillar) and mandatory (the Second pillar) and voluntary funded (the Third pillar) pension saving systems that are privately managed. New institutions were set up in the pension system, such as pension funds, pension insurance companies, REGOS and HANFA. The duty of REGOS is to maintain the system of individual capitalized savings, while the Croatian Financial Services Supervisory Agency (HANFA) is a supervisory authority responsible for monitoring financial markets, financial services and controlled institutions that provide these services. In this way, HANFA safeguards the interests of members of mandatory and of voluntary pension insurance.

In Croatia, there are three main types of pensions: old-age retirement pension, survivor benefits or family and disability pension. A person retiring at the age stipulated by law who has been insured for at least fifteen years (the insurance period or *mirovinski staž*) receives a full old-age retirement pension (*starosna mirovina*). The amount of wages earned and the associated contributions over the entire period of employment determine how much the pension will be. In 2019, men who have at least 35 years of employment history and women who are 57 years and 4 months of age and have 32 years and 4 months of an insurance period can obtain an early retirement pension (*prijevremena starosna mirovina*). The amount of this pension is also based on previous wages and related pension contributions, but a penalizing factor is applied. The widow or widower of an insured person is entitled to a family or survivor pension (*obiteljska mirovina*) if he or she is 50 years of age or older, or under 50, if he or she is incapable or work or is providing care for children. Children of the deceased insured person can receive the benefit if they are in secondary or tertiary education up to age 26, or if they are incapable of work. Individuals partially or fully unable to work may receive a disability pension (*invalidska mirovina*), with the condition of the person having been employed for a particular period as determined by their age. A person is eligible for a disability pension if he or she has a disability preventing work generally or for an occupation, as well as having the required period of participation in pension insurance.[36]

There are also other types of so-called privileged pensions that are not related to the prior pension insurance period and paid contributions. The privileged pension beneficiaries include veterans of the National Liberation War; employees performing certain activities within Internal Affairs and

---

36   Ivana Vukorepa, "Lost Between Sustainability and Adequacy: Critical Analysis of the Croatian Pension System's Parametric Reform", Revija za socijalno politiku 22, no. 3 (2015): 279–308.

Justice; members of the Croatian Home Guard Army 1941–1945; former political prisoners; members of the former Yugoslav National Army; full members of the Croatian Academy of Science and Art; members of the Parliamentary Executive Council, Federal Executive Council and administratively retired public servants related to the former Yugoslavia; members of the Croatian Parliament and others. In total there are 17 different groups of beneficiaries of the privileged pension, which represents about 15% of all pensioners. The size of their pension is generally significantly higher than the amount of the regular pension.[37]

At the end of 1990, there were 1.97 million insured persons, while 668,500 persons received a pension. At the end of 2018, there were 1.51 million insured persons and at the same time there were 1.24 million pensioners.[38] The number of pensioners in Croatia in the period 1990–2018 more than doubled. By contrast, the number of insurees under the PAYG system fell from almost 2 million in 1990 to 1.4 million in 2000, but it rose again to 1.6 million in 2008. During the economic crisis in the period 2009–2014, the number of employed and actively insured persons in Croatia fell by more than 200,000 and has just recently began to increase. This means that the System Dependency Ratio (the total number of actively insured persons in comparison to the total number of beneficiaries), which was almost 3.00 (or there were 296 active insured persons on 100 pensioners) in 1990, fell to a very unfavorable 1.22 in 2018.[39]

In the Croatian pension system, there are relatively weak relations between contributions paid for pension insurance and the future amount of pensions, which motivates payments to be issued in the form of an envelope wage (employees are given part of their salary in cash). Furthermore, the reduction of benefits for early retirement that was introduced in 1999 has been subject to constant changes and is relatively mild, thus it is a motivating factor that increases early retirement. While the average life expectancy was 77.9 years (male 74.9 and female 80.9),[40] the average effective exit age for retirement is around 62 for women and 63 for men. The average insurance period for old-age pensions is less than 31.5 years, while for a family pension it is 31 years and

37   Marijana Bađun, "Pension Beneficiaries who have been Granted Pensions under More Favorable Conditions".

38   Hrvatski zavod za mirovinsko osiguranje. Statističke informacije Hrvatskog zavoda za mirovinsko osiguranje 16, no. 6 (2019): 11, http://www.mirovinsko.hr/default.aspx-?id=17932 (accessed May 21, 2019).

39   Ibid., 32.

40   Eurostat, Life Expectancy by Age and Sex, https://ec.europa.eu/eurostat/web/products-datasets/-/sdg_03_10 (accessed May 19, 2019).

1 month. Therefore, the average female retired person receives her pension for more than 28 years, while a male pensioner benefits for almost 19 years.[41]

With the intention of improving the situation in the pension system, the government proposed, and the Parliament passed a set of six pension reform bills at the end of 2018. The reform, which entered into force as of January 1, 2019, foresees extending working life to age 67 as of 2033, penalizing early retirement by 0.3% for each month or 18% for five years, as well as allowing pensioners to continue working part-time for 4 hours a day and retain their pensions. The initiative proposes that an insured person be entitled to an old age pension upon reaching 65 years of age and having completed 15 years of qualifying periods. It also proposes that an insured person be entitled to early age pension at 60 years of age and 35 years of qualifying period. In March 2019, three trade unions started collecting signatures from citizens in order to call a referendum because they believe that people in Croatia should not work until they are 67. Trade unions also believe that the penalty for early retirement is too high (it should be 0.2% for each month) and that the equation of the retirement age for men and women had accelerated too much. Within two weeks they collected the signatures of at least 10 percent of voters, or about 370,000 people. Hence, the future of the pension system is unknown, particularly its financial long-term sustainability. Greater pension expenditures could endanger macroeconomic stability or increased pension outlays in the circumstances of limited public revenues or could lead to a necessary reduction of the average pension.[42]

6   Health Care

The health system is one of the most complex systems in the country. Health is one of the essential foundations of quality of life and full participation in society. Poor medical conditions and illness reduce the quality of life of patients and burden the family, thus causing loss of labor productivity and immediate and indirect losses for society and the state. Health can be preserved and improved, and many diseases can be cured. Measures to preserve health and treat disease are mostly through the healthcare system, for which each country allocates substantial resources.

---

41   Hrvatski zavod za mirovinsko osiguranje: 67.
42   Danijel Nestić and Iva Tomić, "Primjerenost mirovina u Hrvatskoj: što mogu očekivati budući umirovljenici" (The Adequacy of Pensions in Croatia: What Could Expect Future Retirees), Privredna kretanja i ekonomska politika 22, no. 130 (2012): 61–100.

TABLE 1.7   Expected longevity in years at birth in Croatia in the period 1991–2018

Year	Both sexes	Male	Female	Difference female –male
1991	70.9	66.0	76.2	10.2
1995	73.3	69.3	77.2	7.9
2000	73.0	69.1	76.6	7.5
2005	75.4	71.1	78.9	7.8
2010	76.7	73.4	79.9	6.5
2015	77.4	74.3	80.4	6.1
2018	77.9	74.9	80.9	6

SOURCE: EUROSTAT: HTTP://APPSSO.EUROSTAT.EC.EUROPA.EU/ (ACCESSED MAY 4, 2019); CROATIAN BUREAU OF STATISTICS, YEARBOOK OF THE REPUBLIC OF CROATIA, VARIOUS YEARS, WWW.DZS.HR (ACCESSED MAY 4, 2019).

Croatia has inherited a tradition of being well-organized but rather inefficient in managing public health care costs; this has contributed along with other measures, to a constant increase in life expectancy in years from birth (Table 1.7). Life expectancy for the population is just slightly below the EU average, estimated in 2016 at 81 years. Improvement in the quality of the health care system and general welfare in Croatia is reflected both by increased life expectancy (for 17 years in the period 1991–2018) and in a smaller gender-based difference. While in Croatia this difference was more than ten years in 1991, it had decreased to six years by 2018, which is slightly higher than the EU28 average of 5.4 years (2016).[43]

Since independence, Croatia's health care system has undergone a series of health reforms[44] that attempted to transform into a financial sustainable health care system the fragmented and relatively inefficient health system that was inherited from the former country and was worn out by the five years of hostilities in the region in 1991–1995. In the years before EU accession in 2013, Croatia implemented a number of important reforms in the health care sector, including changes in the payment mechanisms, pharmaceutical pricing and reimbursement, as well as health care provision, particularly emergency care reform.[45]

---

43   Eurostat, Mortality and Life Expectancy Statistics, https://ec.europa.eu/eurostat/statistics-explained/index.php/Mortality_and_life_expectancy_statistics (accessed May 19, 2019).

44   Siniša Zrinščak, "Zdravstvena politika Hrvatske: u vrtlogu reformi i suvremenih društvenih izazova", Revija za socijalnu politiku 14, no. 2 (2007): 193–220.

45   Dubravko Mihaljek, "Kako financirati zdravstvo u doba financijske krize?", in O zdravstvu iz ekonomske perspektive, ed. Maja Vehovec (Zagreb: Ekonomski Institut, 2014), 28–50.

The financial reform to address long-standing problems of hospital deficits was the most important of these. However, the reforms have not been completed or fully implemented, so there is a significant need for further improvements.[46]

Croatia's social health insurance system is based on the principles of solidarity and reciprocity. Therefore, citizens pay mandatory health insurance contributions (usually 16.5% of gross wages) and all insurers receive basic health care services. Contributions are collected by the state authorities (the Tax Administration) and transferred to the only public insurer, the Croatian Health Insurance Fund (CHIF), which further distributes resources to institutions (including private doctors) with which the Fund has contracts. The Fund provides universal health insurance coverage for almost the entire population. The right to health care includes primary health care, consultative specialist services and hospital care. Insured persons are entitled to orthopedic and other devices, dental-prosthetic care and devices and prescriptions for allowed medications. Insured persons have a right to sick pay, paid maternity leave and paid extended maternity leave, to have travel expenses reimbursed if these are incurred for medical treatment, support in the purchase of items for a newborn child (layette) and funeral expenses.[47]

Insured persons include employees in paid employment, the self-employed, farmers, pensioners and the beneficiaries of professional rehabilitation, unemployed persons registered with the Croatian Employment Service and members of their families, insured persons covered by conventions signed between Croatia and other countries, residents of Croatia who work abroad (if they are not insured through any other foreign carrier of health insurance), children up to the age of 18, children in regular schooling, and members of the Croatian armed forces. Family members and dependents of employees are defined as the spouse, non-marital partner, children, parents, grandchildren, brothers, sisters, and grandparents, if these are supported by the insured person. There is no minimum qualifying period in the case of cash benefits and medical services for health care insurance. Eligibility for the monetary benefit for illness is determined by a designated doctor in a primary health care institution.[48]

About 98% of Croatian citizens are covered by the public health insurance system. The remaining 2% lack coverage in many cases because of the failure to

---

46   Tanja Broz and Sandra Švaljek, "Financiranje zdravstva u Hrvatskoj: od reforme do reforme", in O zdravstvu iz ekonomske perspektive, ed. Maja Vehovec (Zagreb: Ekonomski Institut, 2014), 51–75.

47   Luka Voncina et. al., "Croatia: Health System Review", Health Systems in Transition 8, no. 7 (2006): 1–108.

48   Aleksandar Džakula et. al., "Croatia Health System Review", Health Systems in Transition 16, no. 3, (2014):1–162.

register before set deadlines. This is an achievement which has not been achieved in many significantly richer countries. However, citizens often complain about the quality of healthcare services and particularly the long waiting lists. Furthermore, the contributions collected are not sufficient for all health care expenditures, so the balance is covered by transfers from tax revenues (on national and county levels), donations, voluntary health insurance and direct user payments.[49]

In last few years, Croatia has spent about 8–9% of GDP annually on health care; about 80–82% of health care spending comes from public sources and 18–20% comes from private sources. Within the public sector, the CHIF accounts for around 95% of general government spending on health care. The CHIF and the Health Ministry have an important role in the supply aspect by setting health care delivery standards and negotiating volumes and prices of health services with providers. Private resources for health care financing are almost entirely patients' out-of-pocket expenditures and are almost negligible. Health care expenditures represented around three quarters of total health insurance outlays. Almost half was spent on hospital care. Less than a fifth of the total expenditures was spent on different types of compensation and allowances (for sick leave compensation, maternity leave and extended maternity leave, reimbursement of funeral expenses) and aid (childcare assistance).[50]

By the end of 2017, Croatia's health care system had a permanent work force of 69,841. Of these, 42,903 were employees in hospitals, 2,145 were GP doctors and 9,549 were specialized employees.[51] Others are administrative-technical and auxiliary staff. Of almost 3,800 dentists, around 600 work in state health institutions, 200 in private health institutions, and 3,000 in private dental practices.

Although the basic trend in the transition period since the early 1990s has been towards privatization of health care, the State actually increased its control of the health sector during that time.[52] The majority of primary care

49   Katarina Poturica Gerić, Nikolina Smajla and Ksenija Klasić, "Analysis and Comparison of Health Insurance Systems in Croatia and Germany", American International Journal of Contemporary Research 6, no. 3 (2016): 32–46.

50   Tanja Broz and Sandra Švaljek, „Financiranje zdravstva u Hrvatskoj: od reforme do reforme", 51–75.

51   Croatian National Institute for Public Health, Croatian Health Service Yearbook 2017, Croatian National Institute for Public Health, Zagreb, 2018, https://www.hzjz.hr/periodicne-publikacije/hrvatski-zdravstveno-statisticki-ljetopis-za-2017-tablicni-podaci/ (accessed May 21, 2019). The Croatian Bureau of Statistics, Statistical Yearbook of the Republic of Croatia, The Croatian Bureau of Statistics, Zagreb, various years, https://www.hzjz.hr/periodicne-publikacije/hrvatski-zdravstveno-statisticki-ljetopis-za-2017-tablicni-podaci/ (accessed May 22, 2019).

52   Aleksandar Džakula et. al., "Croatia Health System Review", 1–162.

physicians' practices have been privatized, and the remaining ones were left under county ownership. Private GPs and dentists who have contracts with the CHIF mostly perform primary care. The counties (21 in total) own the secondary health care facilities, while tertiary health care institutions (teaching hospitals, clinical hospitals centers and state institutes of public health) are state-owned. One of the biggest problems of the Croatian health system is that the role of primary care has been reduced, so more than a half of all consulting-specialist services are performed by clinical hospitals, which among other things, contributes to long waiting lists. There is a huge concentration of health institutions in the big cities, particularly Zagreb. Consequently, citizens who live a long way from the biggest cities have greater problems in gaining access to adequate health care. In some parts of Croatia (rural, island and mountain regions, or regions bordering Bosnia and Herzegovina), the transport infrastructure is underdeveloped, which seriously limits access to health care institutions for the population in these areas. Thus, in these areas, the number of primary care units must be increased in order to both shorten waiting times and improve the quality of emergency medical care.

A serious problem regarding health in Croatia is the people's generally risky behavior and reckless attitude towards their own health (especially poor nutrition, smoking, alcohol consumption, drug addictions, obesity, insufficient physical activity and similar lifestyle factors). For example, according to the European Commission (2019),[53] in 2017 around 64% of the population had a habit of the daily consumption of fruit, while in Croatia this is only 46%. Regarding vegetable consumption in the EU Member States, Ireland and Belgium had the highest proportion of the population who ate vegetables at least once a day (both 84 %), while in Croatia the share was 54%. In Croatia, 37% of the population have high blood pressure.[54] Croatia has the third highest number of smokers in the EU, as smoking is still accepted as a normal mode of behavior.[55] More than a quarter of citizens are smokers, while even more are obese. Furthermore, in the younger generation (up to 29 years of age), almost

---

53   European Commission, Do you Eat Fruit and Vegetables Daily? European Commission, Brussels, 2019, https://ec.europa.eu/eurostat/web/products-eurostat-news/-/DDN -20190401-1?inheritRedirect=true (accessed April 4, 2019).

54   Novi list. Ubojica broj jedan: Trećina ljudi u Hrvatskoj ima povišen tlak, Novi list, Rijeka, 2017, http://www.novilist.hr/Zivot-i-stil/Zdravlje-ljepota/Zdravlje/Trecina-ljudi-u -Hrvatskoj-ima-povisen-tlak, (accessed April 4, 2017).

55   Croatiaweek, Croatia has 3rd Highest Number of Smokers in EU (Croatiaweek, Zagreb, 2015), https://www.croatiaweek.com/croatia-has-3rd-highest-number-of-smokers-in-eu/ (accessed April 4, 2019).

one quarter never engage in sports, suggesting an underdeveloped conscious-ness of the importance of physical activity in health maintenance and quality of life.[56] Thus, it is important and necessary to ensure a constant campaign to change public attitudes towards health and disease.

7   Housing Policy

More than four-fifths of Croatian citizens own an apartment or house due to the tradition of private home ownership and to the mass privatization of the formerly state-owned housing stocks at the beginning of the 1990s, when they could buy apartments for well below the market price. Thus, Croatia has higher share of homeowners without mortgages than the EU 28 and similar to that of the EU 12.[57] The majority of homeowners do not have a mortgage and, as a result, housing costs do not create additional or particular financial pressure on the limited financial resources of many Croatian households. However, tenants paying rent in social, voluntary or municipal housing are nearly non-existent, as less than 3% of citizens lived as tenants in 2007, which henceforth decreased to less than 1% in 2012 (Figure 1.2).

The Government is trying to resolve the housing problems, in particular those of less affluent groups. The most important measure is the Program of Socially Stimulated House – Building (POS).[58] Through the co-operation of incentive state subsidies and local government bodies, the program allows a lower apartment-building price and more favorable opportunities for paying housing loans. Local government units compile a preference list based upon a completed survey and by identifying the housing needs for a particular area, which then leads to the construction of apartments.

Only in some major Croatian towns were social flats built in last 20 years (one should bear in mind that they are not social flats in the usual Western-European meaning) according to the Program of Socially Stimulated House Building. In the 2000–2009 period, a total of 4,619 apartments were built in 54 locations. Since the beginning of the economic crisis in 2009, such activities

---

56   The Institute for Social Research, Youth Study Croatia 2018 / 2019, The Institute for Social Research, Zagreb, 2019.

57   Eurofound, Trends in quality of life – Croatia: 2007–2012, Eurofound, Dublin, 2014, https://www.eurofound.europa.eu/sites/default/files/ef_publication/field_ef_document/ ef1438en.pdf (accessed April 10, 2019).

58   Ministry of Health and Social Welfare, Joint Memorandum on Social Inclusion of the Republic of Croatia (Zagreb: Ministry of Health and Social Welfare, 2007), https:// mdomsp.gov.hr/print.aspx?id=130&url=print (accessed May 17, 2019).

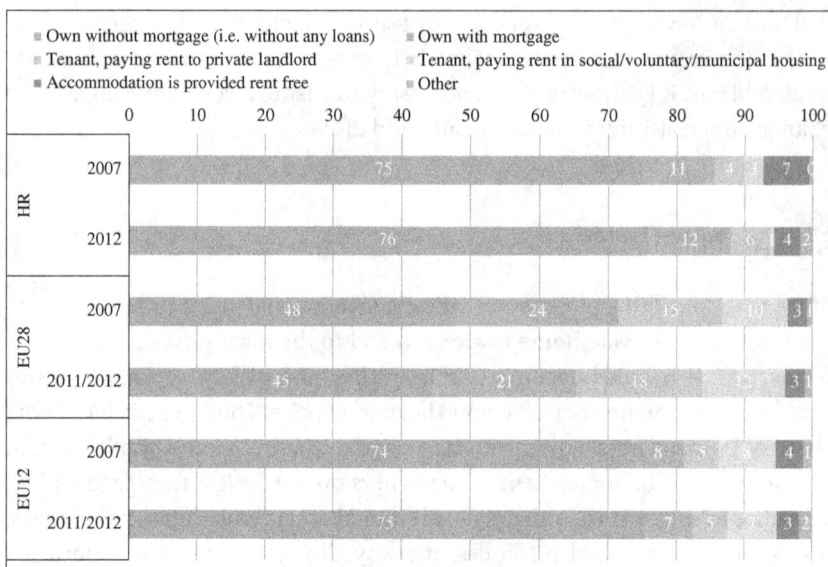

FIGURE 1.2   Housing tenure in 2007 and 2011/2012, Croatia, EU28 and EU12
SOURCE: Q18: WHICH OF THE FOLLOWING BEST DESCRIBES YOUR
ACCOMMODATION? (IN %), HTTPS://WWW.EUROFOUND.EUROPA.EU/SITES/
DEFAULT/FILES/EF_PUBLICATION/FIELD_EF_DOCUMENT/EF1438EN.PDF
(ACCESSED APRIL 10, 2019).

have almost totally ceased.[59] Tica[60] considers the main disadvantages of the
stated model to be the inadequate beneficiary targeting process. The reason is
that public funds are used to assist relatively better-off households, while even
though the loans are subsidized, many poor families are not able to compete
for these financial resources due to relatively high down payments and debt-
servicing costs. Therefore, Tica believes that there were significant inefficiencies and wrong signals sent to citizens regarding the housing policy.

There is an obvious need to formulate a housing strategy for Croatia, particularly a social housing concept, which has not been developed to date. One way
of implementing a new housing policy could be through public-private part-
nership because public sources are limited, and private funds are necessary.

---

59   Ministry of Health and Social Welfare, Report on the Implementation of the Joint
     Inclusion Memorandum of the Republic of Croatia in 2009 (Zagreb: Ministry of Health
     and Social Welfare, 2010).
60   Josip Tica, "The Macroeconomic Aspects of the Croatian Market", Ekonomski Pregled 55,
     no. 7–8 (2004): 641–659.

8   Conclusion

The position on the labor market (employment or unemployment) is a crucial factor in poverty and social exclusion in Croatia. Households in which the main primary breadwinner is either inactive or unemployed are at particularly high risk of poverty. For the majority of the long-term unemployed, it is difficult to escape poverty and related social exclusion, so they are often forced to be long-term recipients of social assistance benefits. The growth in numbers of those who are unemployed in the long-term and poverty among those who depend on the social security benefits and welfare in a time of economic recovery constitutes a threat that results in social policy exclusion, and has the potential to disrupt the sense of social solidarity and cohesion. On the labor supply side, there is a need to strengthen and improve employment policies and the effectiveness of intermediation in the labor market. On the labor demand side, it is important to further increase competitiveness, while also enabling new segments in the labor market to develop.

Croatia must address the challenges in developing and improving human capital, and in providing economic freedom and equality of opportunity, if the country is to overcome the problems it currently faces with poverty and avoid long-term and persistent poverty, policies should be implements that seek to improve governance, combat the problems with corruption and protectionism, and to invest more in human capital. A successful employment policy and a high level of employment are the most important factors in measures against poverty and social exclusion for two reasons. First, a high level of employment (particularly full-time) is the best way to ensure an adequate standard of living. Second, it is from the taxes and social contributions of the working population that the authorities collect the public revenues needed to finance social welfare programs. Furthermore, the activation of the unemployed and inactive is particularly important in the current conditions that exacerbate labor force shortages in Croatia.

This also applies to remaining longer in the world of work and postponement of retirement because most people in Croatia retire when they are relatively young, and they use their pension rights for a long period. With the intention of increasing their current small average pensions, steps have been taken to reform the pension system, which should decrease poverty among pension beneficiaries. The potential lowering of the legal retirement age could endanger the long-term financial sustainability of the pension system and cause further degradation of the amounts allocated by the existing pension fund.

There are possibilities of immediate improvement and the attainment of the necessary system integration of various forms of assistance and rights,

improved synergies of various systems and the optimal targeting and allocation. At the same time, a nominal larger social security allowance and total
outlays for social welfare do not automatically mean improving the well-being
of the population, as everything depends on how the funds are spent, how they
are distributed between individual areas and activities, and how well they are
targeted for the groups which need them. There are three conditions which
must be met if equitable growth is to be achieved. The first, is the building
of an environment that supports private entrepreneurship and increases the
level of investment in human capital. This would require a redefinition of the
state-market boundary for reasons of efficiency: the state should pull back from
its involvement in activities that are inherently part of the market. An apparent paradox is that rather than *decreasing*, the state's responsibilities should
increase. This does not entail a state that is larger than the private sector, nor
that the state should seek a dirigiste role, but rather state activity and intervention in areas that are critical, and the market is not able to allocate resources
efficiently or where there is significant inequity in access to basic assets and
opportunities to earn a livelihood. An equally key public policy activity is to
monitor the effects of employment and social programs.

Education and the earning of qualifications may be relatively easy to measure, but it offers only a poor proxy for human capital. Bearing in mind the
only available data on educational qualifications that have been formally
earned, without consideration of the quality of those programs and courses
of study in practice, and the share of those with these achievements who are
employed may quite easily produce conclusions that are misleading or mis-
taken. Furthermore, human capital is increasingly important, but it is not *per
se a guarantee* of competitiveness and economic development. Curriculums
are currently still focused on subjects and teaching methods that are highly
teacher-centered, and these put a great emphasis on knowledge of facts
learned passively. This does not foster the development of the kinds of high-
level technical, technological and social skills that the contemporary and
highly competitive economy demands. In Croatia, programs tend to demand
more rote memorization of the material provided than any kind of independent, critical or analytical thinking, deductive reasoning or innovation. This
is certainly a barrier to other educational approaches as well as to possibilities in future work. Put briefly, the education system in Croatia suffers from
a lack of emphasis on developing analytical and problem-solving abilities,
and there are weak links between education and the professional world.
Employees have to be capable of creating, analyzing and transforming information, communicating effectively, and organizing and coordinating business
activities. Furthermore, they have to develop communication skills, computer

knowledge, and the ability and willingness to engage in further education and training. The Croatian educational system should be made more flexible so as to become a navigable system.

The purpose of health care and health insurance reform in Croatia is, among others, to adjust the financing of health care to a model that is sustainable in the long term. This means balancing different sources of health care financing and enhancing competition between public and private institutions that provide health services and protection. This new model of health care financing has many advantages. Because of the potentially lower contributions for health insurance, labor costs could be reduced, which would increase the competitiveness of the Croatian economy. Additionally, citizens would have the opportunity to participate in buying higher-quality health services. To reduce the consumption of health care, it is also necessary to check the interventions, diagnostic and therapeutic services provided. Therefore, it is necessary to establish a unified system of cost lists that would incorporate five important categories: hospitals, prescription drugs, diagnostic procedures, the costs of care and the costs of home care. Apart from reform of the financing of the health care system, it is also important to implement a successful national information strategy that would allow data exchange and adequate valorization of provided health care services in particular institutions. Although the reform of health care and health insurance is not an easy or cheap task, there is a good chance that it could achieve improvements in health and the health care system. Reform of health insurance towards a greater role for private insurance and strengthening of market factors is a necessity for the long-term sustainability of the system. These reductions in the role of government also reduce the possibilities of paternalistic behavior and produce the conditions for higher wages. Reaching a national consensus on health care reform is rare; more common is consensus on specific corrections to address specific problems. However, it is crucial to explain and eliminate the general illusion that health care is a free service and simultaneously inform about and consider moral hazards, cream skimming, etc. In the long run this could contribute to an increase in personal responsibility. Directly bearing some of the costs of health care (via pay-roll deduction of premiums or out-of-pocket expenses) could induce individuals to adopt healthier lifestyles and take responsibility for their own health. For most citizens, after all, health care is far too important to be left to the state.

This contribution has confirmed the main hypothesis that the social security system in Croatia can be improved without a significant increase in expenditures. Croatia has to establish and develop legal and institutional arrangements that best suit its own economic and social situations, and its cultural and historical conditions and traditions. Croatia should develop clear and diverse pathways to encourage learning and increase employment. It should also improve public training programs for the unemployed and for people with learning disabilities. The quality and relevance of such programs can be enhanced by encouraging stakeholder partnerships at the regional and local levels, thus facilitating private sector involvement and financing.

Bibliography

Anušić, Zoran, Zoran Barac, Dubravka Jurlina Alibegović, Ljiljana Marušić, Damir Ostović, Snježana Plevko, Blaženka Šimetić, and Ružica Terze. Mirovinska reforma – druga i treća razina mirovinskog osiguranja. Zagreb: Inženjerski Biro, 1999.

Babić Zdenko and Danijel Baturina, "Poverty in Croatia". In Poor Europe. The Problem of Poverty in Chosen European Countries, edited by Grzegorz Libor and Dorota Nowalska-Kapuścik. Katowice: University of Silesia, 2015.

Bađun, Marijana. "Pension Beneficiaries who have been Granted Pensions under More Favorable Conditions". Newsletter 44 (2009): 1–9. Accessed May 21, 2019. http://www .ijf.hr/eng/newsletter/44.pdf.

Barr, Nicholas. Economics of the Welfare State. Oxford and New York, Oxford University Press, 2012.

Bejaković, Predrag. "Povećati fleksibilnost zaposlenosti". In Zaposlimo Hrvatsku, edited by Davorko Vidović. Zagreb: Hrvatska gospodarska komora, 2015.

Bejaković, Predrag. "The Croatian Pension System and Challenges of Pension Policy". In Policy-Making at the European Periphery: the Case of Croatia, edited by Zdravko Petak and Kristijan Kotarski. Cham: Palgrave, 2018.

Bejaković, Predrag. "The Role of Economic and Political Measures in Alleviating Poverty in the Republic of Croatia". Financial Theory and Practice 29, no. 1 (2005): 97–118.

Bezeredi, Slavko, Marko Ledić, Ivica Rubil, and Ivica Urban. Making work pay in Croatia: an ex-ante evaluation of two in-work benefits using miCROmod. Zagreb: Institute of Public Finance 2018.

Broz, Tanja, and Sandra Švaljek. „Financiranje zdravstva u Hrvatskoj: od reforme do reforme". In O zdravstvu iz ekonomske perspektive, edited by Maja Vehovec. Zagreb: Ekonomski Institut, 2014.

Croatian Bureau of Statistics, Indicators of Poverty and Social Exclusion, 2017, First Release no. 14.1.1. Zagreb: Croatian Bureau of Statistics, 2018. Accessed May 4, 2019. https://www.dzs.hr/Hrv_Eng/publication/2018/14-01-01_01_2018.htm.

Croatian Bureau of Statistics. Yearbook of the Republic of Croatia, Various Years. Accessed June 10, 2019. https://www.dzs.hr.

Croatian Bureau of Statistics. Croatia in Figures. Zagreb: Croatian Bureau of Statistics, 2018. Accessed May 22, 2019. https://www.dzs.hr/Hrv_Eng/CroInFig/croinfig_2018.pdf.

Croatian Bureau of Statistics. Persons in Paid Employment, by Activities February 2019, First Release 9.2.1/2. Zagreb: Croatian Bureau of Statistics. 2019. Accessed June 2, 2019. https://www.dzs.hr/Hrv_Eng/publication/2019/09-02-01_02_2019.htm.

Croatian Bureau of Statistics. Poverty Indicators, 2001–2002, First Release 13.2.2. Zagreb: Croatian Bureau of Statistics, 2014. Accessed May 4, 2019. https://www.dzs.hr/Eng/publication/2004/13-2-2e2004.htm.

Croatian Employment Service and Ipsos. External Evaluation of Active Labor-Market Policy Measures 2010–2013. Summary Evaluation Report. The Croatian Employment Service and Ipsos, 2016.

Croatian Employment Service. Godišnjak 2017. Zagreb: Croatian Employment Service, 2018. Accessed April 4, 2019. http://www.hzz.hr/content/stats/0119/stat_bilten_01_2019.pdf.

Croatian Employment Service. Monthly Statistics Bulletin XXXII. Zagreb: Croatian Employment Service, 2019. Accessed June 2, 2019. http://www.hzz.hr/content/stats/0119/stat_bilten_01_2019.pdf.

Croatian National Institute for Public Health. Croatian Health Service Yearbook 2017. Zagreb: Croatian National Institute for Public Health, 2018. Accessed May 21, 2019. https://www.hzjz.hr/periodicne-publikacije/hrvatski-zdravstveno-statisticki-ljetopis-za-2017-tablicni-podaci/.

Croatiaweek. Croatia has 3rd. Highest Number of Smokers in EU. Zagreb: Croatiaweek, 2015. Accessed April 4, 2019. https://www.croatiaweek.com/croatia-has-3rd-highest-number-of-smokers-in-eu/.

Džakula, Aleksandar, Anna Sagan, Nika Pavić, Karmen Lončarek, and Katarina Sekelj-Kauzlarić. "Croatia Health System Review". Health Systems in Transition 16, no. 3 (2014): 1–162.

Esser, Ingrid, Tommy Ferrarini, Kenneth Nelson, Joakim Palme, and Olaf Sjöberg. Unemployment Benefits in EU Member States, European Commission, Employment, Social Affairs & Inclusion. Brussels, 2013.

Eurofound. Q18: Which of the Following Best Describes your Accommodation? Accessed April 10, 2019. https://www.eurofound.europa.eu/sites/default/files/ef_publication/field_ef_document/ef1438en.pdf.

Eurofound. Trends in Quality of Life – Croatia: 2007–2012. Dublin: Eurofound, 2014. April 10, 2019. https://www.eurofound.europa.eu/sites/default/files/ef_publication/field_ef_document/ef1438en.pdf.

European Commission. Do you Eat Fruit and Vegetables Daily? Brussels: European Commission, 2019. Accessed April 4, 2019. https://ec.europa.eu/eurostat/web/products-eurostat-news/-/DDN-20190401-1?inheritRedirect=true.

Eurostat. Adult Learning Statistics. Accessed June 10, 2019. https://bit.ly/3fMn3ww.

Eurostat. Life Expectancy by Age and Sex. Accessed May 19, 2019. https://ec.europa.eu/eurostat/web/products-datasets/-/sdg_03_10.

Eurostat. Mortality and Life Expectancy Statistics. Accessed May 19, 2019. https://ec.europa.eu/eurostat/statistics-explained/index.php/Mortality_and_life_expectancy_statistics.

Hrvatski zavod za mirovinsko osiguranje. Statističke informacije Hrvatskog zavoda za mirovinsko osiguranje 16, no. 6 (2019): 11. Zagreb: Hrvatski zavod za mirovinsko osiguranje. Accessed 21 May 2019. http://www.mirovinsko.hr/default.aspx?id=17932.

International Monetary Fund – IMF. Government Finance Statistics Yearbook. Washington: International Monetary Fund, 2014.

Jurlina-Alibegović, Dubravka, Miroslav Mastilica, Danijel Nestić, and Paul Stubbs. Social Protection and Social Inclusion in Croatia. Zagreb: The Institute of Economics, 2006. Accessed June 7, 2019. https://enil.eu/wp-content/uploads/2012/07/Social-Protection-Social-Inclusion-in-Croatia-Report-for-the-European-Commission.pdf.

Kulušić, Jasminka. Isplati li se fleksibilnost: hrvatsko tržište rada. Zagreb: TIM Press, 2009.

Leitner, Sebastian and Mario Holzner. Inequality in Croatia in Comparison. Research Reports |355. Vienna: The Vienna Institute for International Economic Studies, 2009.

Matković, Teo. Obrasci tranzicije iz obrazovno sustava u svije trada u Hrvatskoj [Patterns of Transition from Education System to the World of Work in Croatia]. Zagreb: Faculty of Law – School of Social Work, 2011.

Mihaljek Dubravko. „Kako financirati zdravstvo u doba financijske krize?". In O zdravstvu i zekonomske perspektive, edited by Maja Vehovec, 28–50. Zagreb: Ekonomski Institut, 2014.

Ministry of Health and Social Welfare, Report on the Implementation of the Joint Inclusion Memorandum of the Republic of Croatia in 2009. Zagreb: Ministry of Health and Social Welfare, 2010.

Ministry of Health and Social Welfare. Joint Memorandum on Social Inclusion of the Republic of Croatia. Zagreb: Ministry of Health and Social Welfare, 2007. Accessed May 17, 2019. https://mdomsp.gov.hr/print.aspx?id=130&url=print (accessed May 17, 2019).

Ministry of Social Policy and Youth of the Republic of Croatia. Structure of Social Benefits, Expenditures and Beneficiaries of Social Protection in the Republic of Croatia: The Report within the Project "Synergistic Social System". Zagreb: Ministry of Social Policy and Youth of the Republic of Croatia, 2016.

Nestić, Danijel, and Iva Tomić. "Primjerenost mirovina u Hrvatskoj: što mogu očekivati budući umirovljenici" (The adequacy of Pensions in Croatia: What Could Expect Furture Retirees). Privredna Kretanja i Ekonomska Politika 22, no. 130 (2012): 61–100.

Nestić, Danijel. "Economic Inequality in Croatia in 1998: Lower than Expected". Croatian Economic Survey 5, no. 1 (2003): 11–52.

Novi list. Ubojica broj jedan: Trećina ljudi u Hrvatskoj ima povišen tlak. Novi list, Rijeka, 2017. Accessed 4 April, 2019. http://www.novilist.hr/Zivot-i-stil/Zdravlje-ljepota/Zdravlje/Trecina-ljudi-u-Hrvatskoj-ima-povise n-tlak.

Plevko, Snježana, Blaženka Šimetić, and Ružica Terze. Mirovinska reforma – druga i treća razina mirovinskog osiguranja. Zagreb: Inženjerski Biro, 1999.

Poturica Gerić, Katarina, Nikolina Smajla, and Ksenija Klasić. "Analysis and Comparison of Health Insurance Systems in Croatia and Germany". American International Journal of Contemporary Research 6, no. 3 (2016): 32–46.

Report on the Implementation of the Joint Inclusion Memorandum of the Republic of Croatia in 2009. Accessed 10 June, 2019. https://mdomsp.gov.hr/UserDocsImages//arhiva/ files/42094//HR-JIM_REPORT_15_06_2009_ENG.pdf.

Šućur, Zoran. "Poverty and Social Transfers in Croatia". Financial Theory and Practice 29, no. 1 (2005): 17–38.

Šućur, Zoran. Siromaštvo: Teorije, koncepti i pokazatelji. Zagreb: Pravni Fakultet, 2001.

The Croatian Bureau of Statistics. Statistical Yearbook of the Republic of Croatia. Accessed May 22, 2019. www.dzs.hr.

The Institute for Social Research. Youth Study Croatia 2018/2019. The Institute for Social Research, Zagreb, 2019.

Tica, Josip. "The Macroeconomic Aspects of the Croatian Market". Ekonomski Pregled 55, no. 7–8 (2004): 641–659.

Urban, Ivica, and Slavko Bezeredi. EUROMOD Country Report Croatia. Colchester: University of Essex, 2016. Accessed 5 January, 2019. https://www.euromod.ac.uk/sites/default/files/country-reports/year10/Y10_CR_HR_Final.pdf.

Urban, Ivica, Slavko Bezeredi, and Martina Pezer. EUROMOD Country Report Croatia 2015 2018. Colchester: University of Essex, 2018.

Voncina, Luka, Nadia Jemiai, Sherry Merkur, Christina Golna, Akiko Maeda, Shiyan Chao, and Aleksandar Dzakula. "Croatia: Health System Review". Health Systems in Transition 8, no. 7 (2006): 1–108.

Vukorepa, Ivana. "Lost between Sustainability and Adequacy: Critical Analysis of the Croatian Pension System's Parametric Reform". Revija za socijalnu politiku 22, no. 3 (2015): 279–308. doi: 10.3935/rsp.v22i3.1307.

Žganec, Nino. "Social Welfare in the Republic of Croatia; on the Road Towards Reform". In Employment Policies and Welfare Reform, edited by Ljiljana Kaliterna Lipovčan and Svenn-Åge Dahl, 177–220. Zagreb: Institute of Social Sciences Ivo Pilar, 2002.

Žiljak, Tihomir, and Teodora Molnar. Croatian Education Policy in the EU Context. In EU Public Policies Seen from a National Perspective: Slovenia and Croatia in the

European Union, edited by Damjan Lajh and Zdravko Petak. Ljubljana: Faculty of
Social Sciences, 2015.

Zrinščak, Siniša. "Zdravstvena politika Hrvatske: u vrtlogu reformi i suvremenih društvenih izazova". Revija za Socijalnu Politiku 14, no. 2 (2007): 193–220.

Security Threats, Challenges and Risks in Bosnia and Herzegovina: Social Security Perspectives

Nevenko Vranješ, Velibor Lalić and Mile Šikman

1 Introduction

Bosnia and Herzegovina (BiH) was created following the dissolution of the former Socialist Federative Republic of Yugoslavia (SFRY). The 1992–1995 war in BiH was ended with the signing of the General Framework Agreement for Peace in Bosnia and Herzegovina[1] (the Dayton Peace Agreement) on 21 November 1995 in Dayton, Ohio, USA, which was again signed in Paris on December 14 of the same year.[2] Although more than two decades have passed since the end of the armed conflicts between the three major ethnic groups (Bosniaks, Serbs, Croats), BiH still remains an ethnically divided society faced with a number of problems. The tragic internal conflict between the three major ethnic groups (Bosniaks, Serbs, Croats) resulted in more than 100,000 human casualties.[3] The material damage done by the war has not yet been determined, and estimates suggest that it amounts to 90 billion USD by market value; this is equivalent to 25% to 30% of the total estimated economic potential of BiH at the beginning of the war.[4] Although it has been almost 24 years since the signing of the Dayton Peace Agreement and the end of the war, BiH still remains a deeply divided society which aside from the problems of post-socialist tension and neoliberalism, is also confronted with additional challenges such as unemployment, poverty, social exclusion, nationalism, ethnically and religiously motivated violence, hate speech, terrorism, religious radicalism, a migrant

---

1 Office of the High Representative, The General Framework Agreement for Peace in Bosnia and Herzegovina (Sarajevo: Office of the High Representative, 1995), http://www.ohr.int/?page_id=1252 (accessed May 10, 2018).
2 BiH is composed of two entities: Federation of Bosnia and Herzegovina and Republika Srpska, and the Brčko District, which has a special status and does not belong to any entity.
3 Ewa Tabeau and Jakub Bijak, "War-related Deaths in the 1992–1995 Armed Conflicts in Bosnia and Herzegovina: A Critique of Previous Estimates and Recent Results", European Journal of Population 21, no. 2–3 (2005): 187–215.
4 Meho Bašić, "Osnove ratne ekonomije, s osvrtom na rat u BiH 1992–1995. godine", Ekonomski Pregled 57, no. 1–2 (2006): 130–145.

crisis, and so on. Therefore, the planning, organization and implementation of any form of security, even social security, is a significant problem.

Article 22 of the United Nations' Universal Declaration of Human Rights (1948) stipulates that every member of society has the right to social security and the right to exercise the economic, social, and cultural rights that are necessary for their dignity and for the free development of their personality, with the help of the state and international cooperation in accordance with the organization and resources of each state.[5] In order to achieve social security, there is a need for social work that forms the basis of the social policy of a state. Social work is directed towards socially vulnerable groups and individuals to overcome social problems; in other words, social work means the preservation of the dignity of the individual, the development of his or her abilities, the promotion of interpersonal relations, and solutions for social problems.[6] Social security can be viewed from a narrower or broader perspective. From the former, social security includes protecting socially the whole population in the event of illness, disability, age, death or unemployment. From the latter, it is viewed as a complete, combined system of social measures guaranteeing an appropriate living standard and welfare of people.[7]

In line with this is the fact that the state, through its entities and social-work activities, has remained the key social security stakeholder. Therefore, the question arises as to how BiH can organize and implement the social security component at this stage of the socio-economic and political situation. BiH is faced with a number of security challenges, threats, and risks that to a certain extent are the result of social problems. The responses to them are significantly hampered by the fact that BiH has a highly complex social security system.[8]

Although a large number of measures for improving the situation in this area have been implemented since the end of the war (1992–1995), they have not resulted in significant improvements.

Previous research in the area of security in BiH has not sufficiently addressed the social security perspective. Bearing in mind the inadequate theoretical foundation of the concept of social security within security studies and the

5   UN General Assembly, Resolution 217 A (III), Universal Declaration of Human Rights, A/RES/217(III) A, http://www.un.org/en/universal-declaration-human-rights/ (accessed December 10, 2018).
6   Council of Europe, Pojmovnik socijalne sigurnosti (Skopje: Council of Europe, 2007), 58–59.
7   Ivana Ilić-Krstić, "Socijalno-ekološka bezbednost, održivi razvoj i kavlitet života", Doktorska disertacija (Niš: Univerzitet u Nišu, Fakultet Zaštitena Radu, 2016), 27.
8   Saša Mijalković and Dragomir Keserović, Osnovi bezbjednosti sa sistemom bezbjednosti Bosne i Hercegovine (Banja Luka: Fakultet za Bezbjednosti Zaštitu, 2010), 256.

lack of established methodologies in empirical research in BiH, our study is primarily exploratory in nature.

The aim of this paper is to examine the problems in the area of social security and their implications for the current security threats, challenges and risks faced by BiH. Our research focuses on two fundamental research questions:

–   what dominant problems, threats, challenges and risks exist in the area of social security in BiH?
–   what types of solutions have been implemented as part of the government system to resolve these problems?

The analytical basis of our research is a review of sociological and security-related literature, and a secondary data analysis of public policy documents and media reports addressing the issue of social security in BiH.

The next section of the paper addresses the social security system in BiH; this is followed by a special review of social security, population, migration and depopulation, poverty and social exclusion, unemployment, vulnerable social groups, and the issues of radicalization and terrorism in BiH.

2   The Social Security System in BiH

Although BiH is a signatory to international legal acts that grant numerous human rights and fundamental freedoms (including the European Social Charter), the main obstacle to developing a unified and coherent system of social policy and social protection lies in constitutional and legal-political arrangements. In other words, there is a constitutional division of competences between BiH and its entities, with the presumption of jurisdiction in favor of the latter, and the area of social protection falls within the competence of these entities. To further complicate the situation, the Federation of Bosnia and Herzegovina (FBiH) has largely transferred this competence to the ten cantons[9] that constitute this entity. Bearing in mind the existence of yet another territorial and constitutional entity in BiH (the Brčko District of BiH), we reach the conclusion that at least thirteen different levels of administrative authority are implemented in BiH. If we take into account the fact that the key institutional entities are the providers of the social protection system at the local level, then it may be said that there are at least 145 social service centers situated across the country. The extent to which the social protection system in

---

9   Cantons of the Federation of Bosnia and Herzegovina, https://www.worldstatesmen.org/ Bosnia_canton.html (accessed June 30, 2019).

BiH is complicated is illustrated by the fact that 27 ministries participate in its implementation in BiH at all lower levels of government, but, operatively, none of the ministries is operational at the state level of BiH.[10]

The BiH budget alone does not contain funds allocated to social categories; it is purely administrative in nature and is reduced to financing joint institutions and servicing the external debt of the state. In comparative legal models, there are a number of countries which have decentralized the social protection system and transferred it to territorial entities (e.g. Switzerland, Austria, Germany, and so on.). However, the fact that BiH is a state that formally and legally does not allow its citizens access to help regarding social welfare issues is very discouraging; in other words, BiH is unable to address its social needs in any segment of social protection.[11] The social protection system in BiH is particularly overwhelmed with obligations to veteran combatants from the BiH war at all levels of government. In other words, combatants (veterans) have significant rights to social welfare, but these rights are exercised exclusively through budgetary resources. Also, these categories of social welfare beneficiaries have a privileged position in the overall system of protection. For comparison purposes, the amount of money war invalids (military invalids) receive is several dozen times higher in relation to disabled civilians. The overall amount allocated to social welfare services in BiH amounts to 4% of GDP, which places BiH among the countries with a very high percentage of budget allocation (Croatia takes the first place in Southeast Europe, followed by BiH).[12] However, the World Bank and the International Monetary Fund (IMF) have repeatedly insisted on the reduction and redistribution of these allocations, noting that the category of combatants cannot have such a projected budgetary remuneration outside the system of contributions, especially not at the expense of other social categories because this favoring of one category of beneficiaries leads to inequality. More specifically, according to the World Bank's report, "funds allocated for social assistance to non-combatant categories amount to only 1/3 of the allowances that do not rely on contributions in the FBiH, and 1/4 of such allocations in Republika Srpska".[13]

An issue that has been worrying many countries, including BiH, over the last several years is how to include (in addition to numerous domestic categories) a

---

10   Aida Hunček-Pita, Socijalna zaštita na državnom nivou: pravni osnov i potreba dopune (BiH), in Sistem socjalne zaštite BiH i regija, Edin Šarčević ed. (Sarajevo: CJP, 2012), 9–10.

11   Ibid.

12   Organization for Security and Co-operation in Europe, Pravo na socijalnu zaštitu u Bosni i Hercegovini, pitanja primjerenosti i jednakosti (Sarajevo: OSCE Misija u BiH, 2012), 42.

13   Ibid.

new category in the social protection system that seems to be particularly vulnerable: migrants. Specifically, BiH is still not heavily affected by the migrant crisis, but the number of migrants suddenly increased in late 2017 and early 2018. Thus, it may be concluded that BiH has a very inefficient and dysfunctional social protection system.

3   Challenges, Threats and Risks to Social Security in BiH

Social security in BiH is determined by social, political, and economic factors that have a dominant influence on the situation in society. In the former Yugoslav state, Bosnia and Herzegovina was one of the least economically developed republics. The devastation of economic capacity and infrastructure during the war (1992–1995), the complete collapse of the economy,[14] non-transparent privatization, tycoonization and neoliberal policies in the post-war period have made the domestic market unprotected, resulting in general poverty and the social exclusion of the majority of inhabitants.[15]

The consequences of political and economic instability have had a considerable impact on the social sphere of society, primarily in terms of generating a number of social problems that implicitly affect social security and the safety of society in general. These are primarily issues that relate to the population, including migration and depopulation, poverty and social exclusion, unemployment, and the problems faced by vulnerable social groups (particularly Roma), victims of human trafficking, and migrants. There is also a problem of radicalization and terrorism in BiH. Although this is a complex phenomenon that has complex causes in the context of BiH, radicalization and terrorism should be viewed from the perspective of social security. Poverty, unemployment and insecurity represent fertile ground for radical ideologies and have an impact on identity politics in BiH.

In 2015 a document entitled "Reform Agenda for Bosnia and Herzegovina 2015–2018" (hereinafter referred to as RA) was drawn up as part of a British German project in BiH that was implemented through action plans at all levels of the BiH government (state level, entity levels and Brčko District). The main goals of this document are to stop negative economic trends, start the process

---

14   Mary Kaldor, New and Old Wars: Organized Violence in a Global Era (Beograd: Beogradski Krug, 2005), 81.
15   Borislav Brozek, Socijalna isključenost u Bosni i Hercegovini iz pogleda zaposlenih i sindikata: studija (Banja Luka: Friedrich-Ebert-Stiftung, 2009), 48, http://library.fes.de/pdf-files/bueros/sarajevo/06850.pdf (accessed July 8, 2016).

of rehabilitation and modernization of the economy, stimulate sustainable, efficient, socially equitable and equal economic growth, create new job opportunities, increase and properly direct social protection, create a favorable and equitable social environment, enforce the rule of law, and have zero tolerance for corruption. 73% of the measures in the RA were implemented by the joint institutions of BiH, 79% by the Republika Srpska, and 48% by the FBiH.[16]

4   Population, Migration and Depopulation

The last census in BiH was conducted in 2013 and showed the total population of BiH to be 3,531,159.[17] According to the 1991 census, BiH had a population of 4,377,033.[18] During the war (1992–1995), according to the estimates of the Ministry of Human Rights and Refugees of the Council of Ministers of BiH, about 2.2 million people, which accounts for more than half of the population, left their pre-war homes,[19] of which about 1.2 million sought refuge in over 100 countries around the world; at the same time, approximately one million people were displaced within BiH, and the return to BiH began immediately after the end of the conflict. Over one million returnees had been reported by 2010.[20] War casualties, large population migrations during the war, a decline in birth rates and migration of the population to developed countries have contributed to a significant decrease in the number of inhabitants. Depopulation is becoming one of the most important issues in BiH, particularly regarding young people. There are no official data on the current emigration of the

---

16   Ismet Hota and Tihomir Radić, Stanje nacije, Izvještaj broj 7 (Sarajevo: Centri civilnih inicijativa, 2018), 22, http://www.posaonarodu.ba/files/preview/104/1270 (accessed May 8, 2018).

17   Agency for Statistics of BiH, Census of Population, Households and Dwellings in Bosnia and Herzegovina, 2013 Final Results (Sarajevo: Agency for Statistics of BiH, 2016), 25, http://popis2013.ba/popis2013/doc/Popis2013prvoIzdanje.pdf (accessed July 8, 2016).

18   Agency for Statistics of BiH, Demography 2011 (Sarajevo: Agency for Statistics of BiH, 2012), 17, http://www.bhas.ba/tematskibilteni/demografija%20konacna%20bh.pdf (accessed July 8, 2016).

19   Ministarstvo za ljudska prava i izbjeglice BiH, Informacija o povratku izbjeglica i raseljenih osoba u bih za period 1995–2010. Godine (Sarajevo: Ministarstvo za Ljudska Prava i Izbjeglice, 2011), 1, http://www.mhrr.gov.ba/PDF/Izbjeglice/INFORMACIJA%20O%20 POVRATKU%20DO%202010.pdf (accessed May 5, 2018).

20   Ibid.

population, although BiH is among the countries with the highest number of citizens seeking asylum in the European Union for economic reasons.[21]

BiH also faces the acceleration of population aging. The share of children under the age of 15 among the total population is almost equal to the share of the population aged 65 and over.[22] Although the problem of depopulation is not adequately recognized by the policy makers, this phenomenon poses a significant security challenge that BiH will soon face unless a positive change occurs.

A low rate of natural increase, migration of youth[23] and aging have an impact on the economic potential of the country which indirectly distorts social security factors. There is no one to create new products, the costs of providing services are on the rise, while social health and pension funding is on the decline, and citizens' expectations of the government are becoming more and more challenging. Generally, all other policies and the population policies are not organized at the state level but fall within the competence of the two BiH entities and the Brčko District of BiH. In that sense, since 2018 Republika Srpska has intensified pro-natalist policies through the payment of unemployment benefits for a term not exceeding 12 months for a second child and 18 months for a third child. However, the fact that this and some other benefits can only be claimed by working families under very low-income conditions greatly reduces this measure's efficacy. Some of these measures include a one-time payment for a third and fourth child which amounts to 650 and 500 KM, financing two in-vitro fertilization attempts, a subsidy on home loan interest for young people and young married couples, financing the purchase of textbooks for the first and second grade of elementary school, and other measures. Bearing in mind that significant measures such as longer-term benefits for unemployed maternity and the financing of two in-vitro fertilization attempts were introduced only three years ago, we cannot speak of the significant effects of the pro-natalist policies of the Republika Srpska government. On the other hand, in response to emigration and the significant decline in the birth rate, the legislative and executive powers in the FBiH and the Brčko

21 Savjet ministara BiH, Izvještaj o razvoju 2015 (Sarajevo: Savjet ministara BiH, Direkcija za ekonomsko planiranje, 2016), 60, http://www.dep.gov.ba/razvojni_dokumenti/izvjestaji/?id=1783 (accessed May 5, 2018).

22 Miroslav Filipović, "Kodna i kobna riječ jest – egzodus", Aljazeera Balkans, http://balkans.aljazeera.net/vijesti/kodna-i-kobna-rijec-jest-egzodus (accessed May 7, 2019).

23 International Monetary Fund, IMF Country Report no. 18/39 (Washington: International Monetary Fund, 2018), https://www.imf.org/en/Publications/CR/Issues/2018/02/13/Bosnia-and-Herzegovina-2017-Article-IV-Consultation-First-Review-Under-the-Extended-45624 (accessed April 10, 2019).

District have not adopted any special measures other than a minimum maternity benefit allowed by the law, despite the fact that only two out of ten cantons in the FBiH report an increase in the birth rate (Sarajevo and the Zenica-Doboj Canton), while the population is falling rapidly in others (such as the Posavina Canton). In general, cantons prescribe social benefits for unemployed women for a term not exceeding 12 months. The amounts vary and range from a one-time payment below the average monthly salary and in the amount of the average monthly salary. The effect of additional measures cannot be seen because there are no such measures.

5   Poverty and Social Exclusion

The poverty and social exclusion of a large number of BiH citizens pose pivotal challenges regarding social security. Research on poverty in BiH is scarce, especially given the importance of this social problem. According to the 2007 poverty survey, 18.56% of BiH citizens lived in relative poverty,[24] and the situation has not changed significantly since then. According to the Development Report of the BiH Council of Ministers 2015,[25] one in six households in the country was poor. The average expenditure of poor households in BiH amounts to 25.2% below the poverty threshold. The report highlights substantial social differences not only between rich and poor citizens in the country, but also between urban areas and rural areas, in which the average monthly expenditure is 20% lower than in urban areas.[26]

In 2010, the BiH Council of Ministers developed a Draft Social Inclusion Strategy of BiH.[27] It has been eight years since the development of the draft, but it has not yet been adopted and therefore not implemented either.[28] However, in 2016 the Economic Planning Directorate within the BiH Council of Ministers published the Development Report for 2015,[29] which indicates

---

24   Savjet ministara BiH, Izvještaj o razvoju 2015, 13.
25   Ibid., 60.
26   The BiH Council of Ministers is the executive branch of the government of Bosnia and Herzegovina; it exercises its rights and duties as functions of government in accordance with the BiH Constitution, laws, and other regulations of Bosnia and Herzegovina.
27   Savjet ministara BiH, Strategija socijalnog uključivanja Bosne i Hercegovine (Sarajevo: Savjet Ministara, Direkcija za ekonomsko planiranje, 2010), http://www.mft. gov.ba/hrv/images/stories/medjunarodna_saradnja/9.%20Uz%20pitanje%2014.%20 Strategija%20socijalnog%20ukljucivanja%20BiH.pdf (accessed May 7, 2018).
28   Ibid.
29   Savjet ministara BiH, Izvještaj o razvoju 2015, 60.

that one of the strategic goals is to reduce poverty and social exclusion.[30] The report indicates that this objective is to be achieved in the next three years and will result in the improvement of the situation of vulnerable groups: persons with disabilities, Roma, returnees and internally displaced persons, families with two or more children, the elderly, the unemployed, low-skilled workers, women, young people and children. The existing social indicators indicate that the situation in the area of social security has not changed significantly, therefore the above statements were just words.[31]

According to the BiH Council of Ministers' data for 2018, over 170,000 households or over 500,000 inhabitants in BiH live below the relative poverty threshold. The relative poverty rate in BiH amounts to 16.9%. This means that over half a million citizens live below the relative poverty threshold.[32] In BiH, there are still 98,574 internally displaced people as a result of the war (1992–1995)[33] and the poverty level of this population category is higher in relation to the remainder of the population.[34]

Specifically, in 2006 the UK Government donated six million convertible marks to BiH to fight poverty. Between 2007 and 2013, BiH received €615 million through the IPA program from the European Union. The plan is to help BiH with an additional €165 million through the IPA II program for the period 2014–2020. These funds are used to strengthen the rule of law and enable economic reforms, sustainable development and poverty reduction.[35] In 2004, Bosnia and Herzegovina signed the European Social Charter and in 2008 it

---

30   There are different approaches to the notion of social exculpation, such as those that consider social exclusion and poverty as synonyms or subordinate social exclusion to the notion of poverty. However, the dominant view is that poverty is a form of social exclusion. Zoran Šućur, "Socijalna isključenost: pojam, pristupi i operacionalizacija", Revija za sociologiju 35, no. 1–2 (2004): 45–60.

31   Savjet ministara BiH, Izvještaj o razvoju 2015, 60.

32   Savjet ministara BiH, Saopštenje povodom 17. oktobra, Međunarodnog dana iskorjenjivanja siromaštva (Sarajevo: Savjet ministara BiH, 2018), 19, http://www.dep.gov.ba/naslovna/default.aspx?id=1985&langTag=bs-BA (accessed October 19, 2018).

33   United States Department of State, Country Reports on Human Rights Practices for 2017 (Washington: United States Department of State, Bureau of Democracy, Human Rights and Labor, 2017), https://www.state.gov/documents/organization/277391.pdf (accessed November 3, 2018).

34   Matthew Cline, Top 10 Facts About Poverty in Bosnia and Herzegovina, The Borgen Project (Seattle: The Borgen Project, 2018), https://borgenproject.org/facts-about-poverty-in-bosnia-and-herzegovina/ (accessed November 2, 2018).

35   Delegation of the European Union to Bosnia and Herzegovina & European Union Special Representative in Bosnia and Herzegovina, BiH i Evropska Unija (Sarajevo: Delegation of the European Union to Bosnia and Herzegovina & European Union Special Representative in Bosnia and Herzegovina, n.d.), http://europa.ba/?page_id=484 (accessed April 16, 2019).

was ratified. In 2015, BiH adopted the BiH Strategic Framework; among other objectives, this defines the objective of reducing poverty and social exclusion. The plan is to implement this objective through three priorities and 11 measures. The BiH Strategic Framework was developed on the basis of the Europe 2020 Strategy and the South-East Europe 2020 Strategy. According to the Development Report for 2016 and 2017 that was prepared by the BiH Economic Planning Directorate, which oversees the implementation of the aforementioned Development Strategy, it is not possible to conclude that poverty decreased in BiH over the observed period.[36]

6   Unemployment

The unemployment rate in BiH is very high. In February 2018, the number of registered unemployed people amounted to 472,957. The number of unemployed people amounted to 509,907 in 2017, while in 2016 the number of registered unemployed people amounted to 536,684. The share of women among the registered unemployed people amounts to 54.1%, or 256,064 women.[37]

According to the BiH Labor and Employment Agency, in April 2017 the unemployment rate amounted to 39.6%.[38] A particular problem is the high rate of youth unemployment. Such a situation in the young population creates a sense of hopelessness and a future without prospects. According to the 2013 census, young people (aged 15–24 years old) constituted 13.3% of the BiH population. According to the Report of the Directorate for Economic Planning of the BiH Council of Ministers,[39] youth unemployment in 2015 amounted to 59%, while the unemployment rate of young people up to 25 years of age in the European Union amounted to 20.6% in the same period. As the report also

---

36   Direkcija za evropsko planiranje BiH, Izvještaj o razvoju BiH, Godišnji izvještaj o raz-
         voju 2016 (Sarajevo: Direkcija za evropsko planiranje, 2017); Direkcija za evropsko plan-
         iranje BiH. Izvještaj o razvoju BiH, Godišnjii zvještaj o razvoju 2017 (Sarajevo: Direkcija
         za evropskoplaniranje BiH, 2018), http://www.dep.gov.ba/razvojni_dokumenti/izvjestaji/
         Archive.aspx?langTag=bs-BA&template id=140&pageIndex=1 (accessed April 16, 2019).

37   Agency for Statistics of BiH, Demography and Social Statistics, Registered Unemployment,
         Year: XII, no. 2 (Sarajevo: Agency for Statistics of BiH, 2018), http://www.bhas.ba/saop-
         stenja/2018/LAB_03_2018_02_ 0_BS.pdf (accessed May 8, 2018).

38   Alena Beširević, "Od ukupnog broja nezaposlenih u BiH 53,45 posto su žene", Oslobodjenje,
         30. juni 2017, https://www.oslobodjenje.ba/vijesti/bih/od-ukupnog-broja-nezaposlenih-
         u-bih-53-45-posto-su-zene, (accessed July 2, 2018).

39   Savjet ministara BiH, Izvještaj o razvoju 2015, 64.

states, young people in BiH are faced with a number of economic, social, and institutional problems. One in four young people work in a job that is unrelated to his or her qualification major. The greatest job prospects for young people are in the informal labor market, with poor working conditions, poor quality jobs, and without any security.

This situation encourages young people to leave the country; according to a UNDP study in BiH, two thirds of young people would leave the country to seek temporary work, marriage or permanent residence in another country.[40]

In order to overcome the current situation, the Council of Ministers annually adopts a Decision on the Adoption of the Plan on Guidelines for Labor Market Policies and Active Employment Measures for the current year. An integral part of this decision is the Plan on Guidelines for Labor Market Policies and Active Employment Measures in BiH for the current year. The plan contains an analysis of the current situation and concrete measures with indicators and financial implications at all levels of governance in BiH.[41] According to the latest statistics, the unemployment rate in BiH is on the decline. A large number of analysts attribute this to unrepresentative statistical methods and migration from BiH to other countries rather than to the effects of the employment policy measures. The statistical fact is that the unemployment rate in BiH has fallen by 4% over the last three years. In this regard, according to the RA,

> [e]xpressed in absolute numbers, from 2015 to date, the number of employed people has increased by about 93,678, while the number of unemployed people has decreased by 77,151. However, it should be noted that in January 2018 there was a change in the statistical agencies' methodology of representing the number of employed people which caused the number of employed people to rise from 753,302 to 790,943. Therefore, this growth is not a reflection of positive developments in the labor market, but it is merely a different way of processing statistical data related to the labor market.[42]

---

40   Ibid.
41   For further comparison: Odluka o usvajanju plana o smjernicama politika tržišta rada i aktivnim mjerama zapošljavanja za 2018 godinu, Službe niglasnik BiH, br. 58/18.
42   Ismet Hota and Tihomir Radić, Stanje nacije, Izvještaj broj, 7, 40.

7   Social Security and Vulnerable Groups

7.1   *Roma*

The Roma are the largest ethnic minority in BiH. According to the data provided by Roma associations in BiH, there are about 50,000 Roma.[43] It should be noted that the existing data on the number of Roma are contradictory. Thus, according to the 2013 population census in BiH, a total of 12,385 persons declared themselves Roma. Also, in 2009, when the Ministry of Human Rights and Refugees conducted the process of registering Roma and the needs of Roma, 16,771 Roma or 4,308 Roma households were found to need some form of assistance with housing, employment, healthcare, and education.[44]

In the context of social security, Roma are in a very vulnerable category of the population. Most Roma families live in poverty and face the problem of inadequate housing, high rates of unemployment, and discrimination in employment. Generally, Roma living in BiH have a low level of education and qualifications, which are the main causes of the low employment rate of Roma. Also, Roma face the problem of inadequate healthcare. Roma children are particularly vulnerable due to discrimination, family poverty, and social exclusion that repeats itself generation after generation.[45] BiH participated in the Decade of Roma Inclusion 2005–2015 project, which is an international initiative bringing together governments,[46] intergovernmental bodies, non-governmental organizations and civil society organizations in order to improve their socio-economic status. The priority areas included housing, education, employment and the regulation of health insurance; some progress has been made in these areas. BiH adopted the 2017–2020 Action Plan which provides for action to improve the integration of Roma into society in order to solve Roma problems in the areas of employment, housing, and healthcare.[47]

---

43   Institucija ombudsmena za ljudska prava BiH, Specijalni izvještajo položaju Roma u Bosni i Hercegovini (Sarajevo: Institucija ombudsmena za ljudska prava BiH, 2013), 21.

44   Ministarstvo za ljudska prava i izbjeglice BiH, Izvještaj o provođenju Akcionog plana Bosne i Hercegovine zarješavanje problema Roma u oblastima zapošljavanja, stambenog zbrinjavanja i zdravstvene zaštite 2017–2020 i o utrošku grant sredstava za 2017. godinu (Sarajevo: Ministarstvo za Ljudska Prava i Izbjeglice BiH, 2019), 2, https://www.ekon-sultacije.gov.ba/legislativeactivities/details/8663 (accessed July 2, 2018).

45   Ibid.

46   Member States of the 2005–2015 Decade of Roma Inclusion are Albania, Bosnia and Herzegovina, Bulgaria, Croatia, Czech Republic, Hungary, Macedonia, Montenegro, Romania, Serbia, Slovakia, and Spain.

47   Ministarstvo za ljudska prava izbjeglice BiH, Akcioni plan Bosne i Hercegovine za rješa-vanje problema Roma u oblastima zapošljavanja, stambenog zbrinjavanja i zdravstvene zaštite 2017–2020 (Sarajevo: Ministarstvo za ljudska prava i izbjeglice, 2017), http://www.mhrr.gov.ba/ljudska_prava/Akcioni%20plan%20BiH%20za%20rjesav-anje%20 problema%20Roma%202017-2020%20%20BOS.pdf (accessed July 4, 2018).

So far, over a period of nine years (2009–2018), BiH has ensured a total of 36,284,343.59 KM for the implementation of measures concerning employment, housing, and health care for Roma. On average, this amounts to four million KM annually. In 2009–2018, the construction of 992 residential units for Roma was financed by this fund. Regarding employment and self-employment, 800 Roma used the financial resources for these purposes over the observed period and 2,472,000 KM was allocated for the improvement of access to healthcare for Roma. These funds were used to finance health education of the Roma population, access to the health and social care systems, and preventive medical examinations. For example, 114 Roma people in BiH underwent preventive medical examinations in 2017. In total, 150 Roma undertook health mediator training courses.[48] Although a number of measures have been taken to improve the social position of Roma, they are still a marginalized and socially vulnerable category in BiH.

7.2 Victims of Human Trafficking

BiH is a country of destination and transit and in recent years it has become a country of origin of human trafficking victims. The problem of human trafficking in BiH escalated in the post-war period after the signing of the Dayton Peace Agreement (1995). Many factors influenced the expansion of human trafficking, primarily the geopolitical changes that occurred in the early 1990s in Eastern, Central and South-Eastern Europe due to a wave of migration. Further, there is social disintegration as a consequence of the civil war in BiH.

The presence of the international peacekeeping forces that were deployed after the conflict in BiH has also influenced the expansion of human trafficking due to the peace mission personnel's increased demand for sexual services. The economic circumstances or the impact of the economic situation on human trafficking may be viewed through the lens of the illicit economy, economic transition, and the high unemployment rate.[49] Following the war, the victims of human trafficking in BiH were mainly from the countries of Eastern Europe, but since then there has been a significant change in the origin of the victims, most of them being local victims – BiH citizens.

---

48 Ministarstvo za ljudska prava i izbjeglice BiH, Izvještaj o provođenju Akcionog plana Bosne i Hercegovine zarješavanje problema Roma u oblastima zapošljavanja, stambenog zbrinjavanja i zdravstvene zaštite 2017–2020 i o utrošku grant sredstava za 2017. godinu, 2.
49 Velibor Lalić, Trgovina ljudima u Bosni i Hercegovini (Banja Luka: Defendologija centar za bezbjednosna, sociološka i kriminološka istraživanja, 2007), 133.

According to the Human Trafficking Report of the USA State Department,[50] adult and juvenile women in BiH are trafficked for sexual exploitation within the country in private homes, motels, and gas stations. Economically marginalized, Roma children are subjected to forced begging and domestic service in forced marriage against their will. Women and girls from European countries are subject to sexual exploitation within BiH, which is a transit country for Ukrainians who are trafficked to Germany. In 2016, victims of trafficking from Cuba and Gambia were reported in BiH. Victims from BiH were trafficked for the purpose of sexual exploitation and forced labor in the construction sector and other sectors in countries across Europe, such as Croatia, France, Serbia, Slovenia, and Austria.[51]

In 2017, 82 potential victims of human trafficking were identified in Bosnia and Herzegovina. Most of them were victims of forced begging (52), sexual exploitation (15), forced labor (7), forced begging and sexual exploitation (7), and one victim for whom the type of exploitation was not reported. Of the total number of the victims, 47 were children.[52]

The 2008–2012 Action Plan for the Prevention of Human Trafficking in BiH contained a component entitled Social Support and Protection. This component included three objectives: (1) the improvement of the procedures for identifying the victims of human trafficking (for foreigners and citizens of BiH); (2) ensuring timely and appropriate assistance to the victims of human trafficking and witnesses of victims of human trafficking; (3) ensuring the appropriate rehabilitation and reintegration of the victims of human trafficking.[53] As a result the Handbook for Direct Assistance to the Victims of Human Trafficking was designed,[54] which, among other things, contains chapters with

---

50   U.S. Embassy in Bosnia and Herzegovina, Trafficking in Persons Report (Sarajevo: U.S. Embassy in Bosnia and Herzegovina, 2017), https://ba.usembassy.gov/wp-content/uploads/sites/270/2017/08/Bosnia-and-Herzegovina-2017-TIP-Report-Translation.pdf (accessed July 4, 2018).

51   Ibid.

52   U.S. Department of State, The Human Trafficking Report (Sarajevo: U.S. Embassy in Bosnia and Herzegovina, 2018), https://www.state.gov/j/tip/rls/tiprpt/countries/2018/282617.htm (accessed November 4, 2018).

53   Savjet ministara BiH, Akcioni plan za sprečavanje trgovine ljudima u BiH 2008–2012 (Sarajevo: Savjet Ministara BiH, 2008), 14, http://msb.gov.ba/anti_trafficking/dokumenti/planovi/Archive.aspx?langTag=bs-BA&template_id=104&pageIndex=1 (accessed May 7, 2019).

54   See more: Međunarodna organizacija za migracije, Misija u BiH, Priručnik za direktnu asistenciju žrtvama trgovine ljudima (Sarajevo: Međunarodna organizacija za migracije, Misija u BiH; Ministarstvo za ljudska prava i izbjeglice BiH; Državni koordinator za borbu protiv trgovine ljudima i ilegalne imigracije BiH, 2008).

specialized content intended for healthcare workers, social workers and persons working in shelters. Also, a series of seminars and training courses related to working with and treating victims and the prevention and treatment of human trafficking were held for judges, prosecutors, police officers, health and social workers. Subsequently, the 2013–2015 Strategy for Countering Human Trafficking in BiH[55] with the relevant Action Plans for Implementation (2013–2015[56] and 2016–2019)[57] was adopted. The measures continue to focus on education with the designing of an operational measure for providing the right to health and social protection for victims. Pursuant to the Report on the Current State of Human Trafficking in BiH for 2017, 83 victims of human trafficking were identified in BiH in 2017; this was 35 more than in 2016, when 48 victims were identified.[58] The Report had the following effects: administrative and legal support was provided for 106 children at risk of human trafficking; meals for children at risk of begging were provided (12,000 hot meals and 5,000 lunch packets; 246 children at risk of different forms of exploitation aged 4–17 years were educated; 28 children who were exposed to the risk of exploitation were placed in shelters; 617 victims of human trafficking underwent occupational therapy; 38 orders for conducting investigations into human trafficking by the prosecutor's offices were issued and 23 indictments were filed; the courts in BiH pronounced a total of 27 years in prison for human trafficking crimes).[59] It should be noted that support for this category of victims was mainly provided by NGO s with foreign donor funds.

7.3   *Migrants*

The migrant crisis that has arisen as a consequence of the war in Syria since 2011 has not bypassed the countries of the Western Balkans. The Western

---

55   Savjet ministara BiH, Strategija suprostavljanja trgovini ljudima u BiH 2013–2015 (Sarajevo: Savjet ministara BiH, 2013), http://msb.gov.ba/PDF/brosura%20bos%20final%20mail.pdf (accessed May 7, 2019).

56   Savjet ministara BiH, Akcioni plan implementacije Strategije suprotstavljanja trgovini ljudima u Bosni i Hercegovini 2013–2015 (Sarajevo: Savjet ministara BiH, 2013), http://msb.gov.ba/dokumenti/strateski/default.aspx?id=9085&langTag=bs-BA (accessed May 7, 2019).

57   Savjet ministara BiH, Akcioni plan suprostavljanja trgovini ljudima u Bosni i Hercegovini 2016–2019 (Sarajevo: Savjet Ministara, 2016), http://msb.gov.ba/PDF/AKCIONI_PLAN_2016-2019_30_12_2015.pdf, (accessed May 7, 2019).

58   Državni koordinator za borbu protiv trgovine ljudima, Izvještaj o stanju u oblasti trgovine ljudima u BiH za 2017. godinu (Sarajevo: Ministarstvo bezbjednosti BiH, Državni koordinator za borbu protiv trgovine ljudima, 2018), 3. http://msb.gov.ba/PDF/izvjestaj_trgovina_ljudima_2017.pdf (accessed May 7, 2019).

59   Ibid., 44–71.

Balkan route is used by migrants from Asian and African countries.[60] The migrant waves from Greece to the former Yugoslav Republic of Macedonia and Serbia peaked in the second half of 2015.

In 2016, as a result of the restrictions at the state borders of Western Balkan countries and the agreement between the EU and Turkey on the return to Turkey of migrants who arrive in Greece and do not meet the conditions for asylum,[61] there was a significant decline in the number of migrants on this route. BiH was not threatened by migrant waves and the number of migrants entering BiH was negligible until the end of 2017.

In 2018, there was a dramatic increase in the number of migrants in BiH compared to the previous period (91 refugees registered in BiH in 2016).[62] The sudden influx of migrants caught BiH authorities unprepared, and the crisis revealed the lack of institutional capacity to cope with the crisis. According to the data of the Ministry of Security of Bosnia and Herzegovina, from January 1 to June 21, 2018, 7,128 illegal migrants were reported to the Foreign Affairs Service.[63] 6,354 people expressed their intention to seek asylum in BiH, but only 611 applied for asylum; this suggests that migrants are not interested in staying in BiH but prefer to go to their final countries of destination, such as other European Union countries.[64]

The efforts of migrants to reach the border crossings between Bosnia and Herzegovina and the Republic of Croatia from Sarajevo in order to continue their journey to Western European countries resulted in a large concentration of migrants in the Una-Sana Canton of the BiH Federation, which borders with the Republic of Croatia. According to data from the European Commission, in September of 2018 there were 3,500 to 4,000 migrants in BiH, of which 3,350

---

60   Milan Lipovac i Slađana Đurić, "Migrantska kriza u EU i Zapadnobalkanska ruta", U Godišnjak Fakulteta bezbednosti, Ur. Božidar Banović (Beograd: Fakultet bezbednosti, 2015), 67–89.

61   The agreement implies that refugees arriving in Greece that are not eligible for asylum will be returned to Turkey.

62   Savjet ministara BiH, Održana 147. Sjednica Vijeća ministara Bosne i Hercegovine (Sarajevo: Savjet ministara BiH, 2018), http://www.vijeceministara.gov.ba/saopstenja/ sjednice/saopstenja_sa_sjednica/default.aspx?id=28621&langTag=hr-HR (accessed July 6, 2018).

63   It should be noted that there is considerable confusion regarding the exact number of migrants. In support of this, the statement by the Deputy Minister of Security of BiH indicates that at present there are over 10,000 registered entries of migrants. In Dnevnik. ba, "Krešić: Imamo preko 10.000 registriranih ulazaka migranata u BiH", Dnevnik.ba, 2. August 2018, https://www.dnevnik.ba/vijesti/kresic-imamo-preko-10000-registriranih-ulazaka-migranata-u-bih (accessed August 6, 2018).

64   Savjet ministara BiH, Održana 147. sjednica Vijeća ministara Bosne i Hercegovine.

were in this canton; this is a rather large concentration considering the size of this canton. Border crossings toward the Republic of Croatia were blocked for a while in 2018. This situation led to violent conflict between the migrants, the police and the local population. The data of the Cantonal Ministry of the Interior of the Una-Sana Canton for September and October 2018 indicate an increase in the number of serious crimes in which migrants were involved. Migrants caused more than 200 incidents involving more than 300 migrants and committed 20 criminal offenses involving more than twenty migrants. The crimes most often committed by migrants include theft, serious theft, attempted murder, violent behavior and burglaries. The local population is extremely intolerant of migrants, as demonstrated by the protests in larger cities of this canton. Local businessmen also joined these rallies and blamed the migrants for the blockade of the border crossings, which prevented them doing business. The capacities of the cantons in the domain of social protection, healthcare and security are considerably below those needed to provide a response to the migrant crisis.

Pursuant to the provisions of the Strategy and the Action Plan for the period 2016–2020[65] that pertain to migration and asylum, persons with refugee status or subsidiary protection status are granted access to the rights prescribed by law. Among other things, refugees and persons with subsidiary protection status in BiH exercise the rights to health and social protection, education and work.[66] With the aim of concretizing this right, a handbook on the manner of exercising the right to social protection by persons with granted international protection in Bosnia and Herzegovina[67] was adopted. However, there remains an unknown number of migrants who have exercised the right to health and social protection or sought access to the labor market or educational institutions. The Human Rights Ombudsman of BiH reported the improper care of unaccompanied children[68] and that a guardian had not been appointed for a number of children in Bosnia and Herzegovina in accordance with the law, and it is unclear who represented the interest of these children in proceedings.

---

65 Ministarstvo bezbjednosti BiH, Strategija u oblasti migracija i azila i Akcionog plana za period 2016–2020, http://sps.gov.ba/dokumenti/strateski/Strategija%20u%20oblasti%20 migracija%20i%20azila%202014-2020.pdf (accessed May 7, 2019).

66 Pravilnik o načinu ostvarivanja prava na socijalnu zaštitu osoba kojima je priznata međunarodna zaštita u Bosni i Hercegovini, Službeni glasnik BiH, br. 3/09 i 5/10.

67 Ministarstvo bezbjednosti BiH, Strategija u oblasti migracija i azila i Akcionog plana za period 2016–2020.

68 Ombudsman BiH, Specijalni izvještaj o stanju u oblasti migracija u BiH, 57, https://www. ombudsmen.gov.ba/documents/obmudsmen_doc2019010713545979bos.pdf (accessed May 7, 2019).

At the same time, 130 children were identified in the migrant categories, of whom five were unaccompanied children.

In 2018, BiH received two million euros from the European Commission on two occasions; this represented valuable humanitarian aid to address the growing needs of the refugees, asylum seekers, and migrants in BiH. The total value of the humanitarian aid provided by the European Commission for the purpose of addressing the needs in the Western Balkans has increased to €30.5 million since the beginning of the refugee crisis.

7.4   *Radicalization and Terrorism*

Over the last 30 years, we have witnessed the proliferation of extremism and religious fanaticism in many regions throughout the world. These negative phenomena are especially evident in relation to terrorism, especially those individuals whose ideology is profoundly rooted in religion or is guided by the ideas of extreme pan-Islamism, fundamentalism and jihad.[69] Radical Islamist attitudes and attempts to build an Islamic society based on these principles have been present in BiH since the 1970s, when a group arose with the aim of demolishing the existing order and establishing an Islamic state within BiH. For this purpose, the "Islamic Declaration"[70] text was written in the form of a call, i.e., a manifesto whose objective was to awaken the Islamic conscious-ness of individuals and to encourage the process of Islamic revival.[71] For these activities a criminal proceeding known as the "Sarajevo Process" was instituted in 1983, resulting in criminal convictions of those found guilty and long prison sentences.[72]

---

69   James Turner Johnson, "Just War Theory: Responding Morally to Global Terrorism", in The New Global Terrorism: Characteristics, Causes, Control, ed. Charles W. Kegley (Upper Saddle River, NJ: Prentice-Hall, 2003), 238, quoted in Mladen Bajagić, Osnovi bezbedno-sti, 219.

70   "Islamic Declension" is a document based on the foundations of Islamic fundamental-ism, aimed at the Islamization of the population within Muslim corps in predominantly Muslim countries or regions (and even BiH, although it is not a majority Muslim country). It is designed to achieve pan-Islamization through the unification of all Muslims across the globe and the creation of homogeneous Islamic religious–political units, with Sharia Law as the basis of a well-organized society; Zlatko Pinter, "Crtice uz biografiju rahmetli Alije Izetbegovića – 2. Dio", Kamernjar.com, 22. Septembar 2017, https://kamenjar.com/ crtice-uz-biografiju-rahmetli-alije-izetbegovica-2-dio/ (accessed May 10, 2018).

71   Zlatko Pinter, "Crtice uz biografiju rahmetli Alije Izetbegovića – 2. Dio".

72   A total of 11 persons were charged and all were found guilty and sentenced to five months to 15 years in prison in Judgement of the District Court in Sarajevo, no. K: 212/83 of 20.08.1983.

As a result, the process of radicalization continued in the 1990s. Specifically, as early as the beginning of the civil war in Bosnia in 1992, foreign fighters and mujahideen engaged in armed conflicts and the spreading of radical fundamentalist ideology among the local population. In fact, the war in BiH provided a great opportunity for Al Qaeda because many mujahideen supported it (primarily fighters from Afghanistan), but it contributed to the radicalization of the local population, which represented the first cases of radicalization using this ideology in Europe. Following the war, many mujahideen left the territory of BiH, while others stayed mainly in isolated places. The local population gradually began to join them, and the traditional Islamic teachings and practices were replaced by the Wahhabi/Selafi teachings. As the Wahhabi/Selafi movement was spreading fast, some radicalized members became involved in violent clashes with traditional Muslims and sought to impose their public behavior standards. For this reason, the official bodies of BiH regard extremism and radicalism in BiH as a very important security issue.[73]

Subsequently, all the terrorist-related events and specific terrorist acts were linked to the activities of these communities.[74] There were occurrences of terrorist attacks in BiH.[75] Also, since 2012, BiH citizens have travelled to the Syrian

---

73   Ministarstvo bezbjednosti BiH, Informacija o stanjusigurnosti u Bosni i Hercegovini u 2016. godini (Sarajevo: Ministarstvo bezbjednosti BiH, 2017), 30, http://www.msb.gov.ba/ PDF/info2017.pdf (accessed May 5, 2018).

74   Edina Bećirević, Salafism vs. Moderate Islam: a Rhetorical Fight for the Hearts and Minds of Bosnian Muslims (Sarajevo: Atlantska inicijativa, 2016), 18, http://atlantskainicijativa. org/bos/wp-content/uploads/2015/dokumenti_i_publikacije/Salafism_vs_moderate_ islam-web.pdf (accessed May 5, 2018).

75   One of the first terrorist acts occurred in Mostar in mid-September 1997, when a car bomb was activated, with 29 people being severely or lightly injured, including three police officers, while about 120 cars and as many apartments were destroyed. In 2002, in Kostajnica village near Konjic, a terrorist who was motivated by "ideological-religious fanaticism" killed three members of a Croatian family on Christmas Eve, for which he was sentenced to 35 years in prison. An attempt was made in 2005 to commit a terrorist attack and four persons were convicted of planning a terrorist attack on an unidentified target in Europe. In late 2008, an explosive device was detonated at the FIS shopping center in Vitez, killing one person. In March of the same year, in Sarajevo and Bugojno a terrorist group was prosecuted for the planning of terrorist attacks on facilities of the RS Government, the Catholic Church, the EUFOR unit, and the BiH Armed Forces. In June 2010 in Bugojno, a group of radical extremists placed an explosive device at a police station, killing a policeman and injuring six people. In October 2011 in Sarajevo, a member of the Wahhabi movement shot at the US Embassy, wounding a policeman. In 2015 three terrorist attacks were carried out: one occurred in Republika Srpska when a radicalized individual entered a police station, killing one and wounding two police officers. The second attack was carried out in November, when a person close to the Wahhabi movement in Rajlovac killed two members of the Armed Forces of Bosnia and Herzegovina; the third attack occurred

and Iraqi fronts to join ISIL and the Al-Nusra Front. Clearly, this is the same ideology that emerged in BiH in the early 1990s, leading to the fact that BiH citizens started traveling to war-torn countries as foreign terrorist fighters. In this regard, when the State Department introduced the 2014 Terrorism Report on BiH, it stated that BiH,[76] along with Albania and Kosovo, is seen as a significant source of foreign fighters for the Islamic State terrorist organization.[77]

In addition to contributing to the achievement of terrorist ideology goals, such persons pose a security threat to the countries of their origin once they return to them. Criminal proceedings were brought before the Court of BiH against several returnees from Syria and Iraq, and although the defendants participated in the war in Syria and Iraq on the side of ISIL as foreign terrorist fighters, many of them were sentenced to minimum sentences or imprisonment below the envisaged minimum by the law (one year); some entered into a plea agreement, while others were acquitted by the court of first instance.[78]

Radicalization and terrorism pose significant security threats to BiH. Particularly worrying is the fact that no serious measures encompassing the process of deradicalization and the reintegration of individuals into the community have been taken so far in BiH. In this regard, Beslin and Ignjatijevic stated that "criminalizing foreign fighters and introducing repressive measures without any prevention and de-radicalization strategies in place could prove to be counterproductive and perilous".[79] In fact, the process of deradicalization is not exclusively related to law enforcement agencies, whereby the leading role should be played by actors of informal social control, including

in Zavidovići, where an explosive device was thrown at the police station in Zavidovići. Some of the accused individuals were tried for these crimes and prison sentences were imposed on some of them. In Mile Šikmani Predrag Ćeranić, "Ugrožavanje bezbjednosti Republike Srpske, sa posebnim osvrtom na terorizam", Politika nacionalne bezbednosti 8, no. 1 (2017): 84–87.

76   According to Amil Dučić, "BiH ostaje značajan izvor stranih boraca!", Dnevni Avaz, 21. Jun 2015, http://www.avaz.ba/clanak/183608/bih-ostaje-znacajan-izvor-stranih-boraca?url=-clanak/183608/bih-ostaje-znacajan-izvor-stranih-boraca (accessed June 10, 2018).

77   Specifically, it was noted that a significant number of BiH citizens traveled to Syria and Iraq during the same year, emphasizing that "the ideology of Islamic extremists and the regional extremist group represented potential sources of violent extremism in BiH". Amil Dučić, "BiH ostaje značajan izvor stranih boraca!"

78   Mile Šikman, "Strani teroristički borci i krivični postupci u Bosni i Hercegovini", 208.

79   Jelena Beslin, Marija Ignjatijević, "Balkan Foreign Fighters: From: Syria to Ukraine". BRIEF 20/2017 (Paris: European Union Institute for Security Studies – EUISS, 2017), 4, https://www.iss.europa.eu/sites/default/files/EUISSFiles/Brief%2020%20Balkan%20foreign%20fighters.pdf (accessed April 24, 2019).

educational institutions and religious communities.[80] This is best illustrated with the example of certain religious authorities that demanded the closure of pseudo jamaats,[81] which was not well-received by the radicalized groups.[82] This is why this question is perhaps the most important one but also the biggest challenge in BiH.[83]

8 Conclusion

BiH is as a post-conflict country which has failed to build a stable society even two decades after the end of the war. Ethnic divisions and long-term political and economic instability have manifested themselves in the social sphere of society and have revealed numerous problems in the security sector. In the context of social security, major challenges are present for BiH in relation to national identity and the political, economic and social problems in society. In such an unstable environment, BiH has failed to build an effective social protection system that would enable efficient responses to numerous problems in the social sphere of society.

The legacy of war represents a significant burden on the social protection system in the form of obligations to Bosnian war combatants who exercise significant rights in the existing system. BiH is faced with the problem of depopulation, particularly youth migration, poverty and social exclusion of large

---

80 Mile Šikman, "Return of the Foreign Terrorist Fighters – Criminal Persecution and Deradicalization", in Violent Extremism and Radicalization Processes as Driving Factors to Terrorism Threats, ed. Denis Čaleta and Corinna A. Robinson (Ljubljana: Ministry of Defense of Slovenia, Joint Special Operations University from Tampa, USA and Institute for Corporative Security Studies, 2018), 132.

81 The Islamic community in BiH has demanded the closure of facilities at which illegal religious rituals (pseudo Jamaat) were held as they are not performed by legal and legitimate religious authorities chosen by the Islamic Community. For more details, see: Islamska zajednica u Bosni i Hercegovini, "Saopćenje Ureda za odnose s javnošću Rijaseta o paradžematima" (Sarajevo: Islamska Zajednica u Bosni i Hercegovini, January 13, 2016).

82 For more details, see: Jutarnji. hr. "Jeziva prijetnja Islamske Države Bosni i Hercegovini Zaklat ćemo vašeg vjerskog vođu. Trovat ćemo vas i dizati u zrak i u BiH i u Sandžaku", Jutarnji.hr 23.03.2016, https://www.jutarnji.hr/globus/jeziva-prijetnja-islamske-drzave-bosni-i-hercegovini-zaklat-cemo-vaseg-vjerskog-vodu.-trovat-cemo-vas-i-di zati-u-zrak-i-u-bih-i-u-sandzaku/35527/ (accessed April 24, 2019); Aida Hadžimusić, "N1 saznaje: Tzv. Islamska država prijeti imamima u BiH". N1 BiH, 17.05.2017, http://ba.ninfo.com/Vijesti/a154457/N1-saznaje-Tzv-Islamska-drzava-prijeti-imamima-u-BiH.html (accessed April 24, 2019).

83 Mile Šikman, "Return of the Foreign Terrorist Fighters – Criminal Persecution and Deradicalization", 132.

numbers of residents, as well as a high unemployment rate. Regarding the issue of depopulation, the existing trends will pose a serious security problem in the long term.

Social exclusion and poverty are also an important issue in the context of social security. Unemployment, social stratification, huge differences between rich and poor citizens, and economic differences between urban and rural areas at the expense of the latter have negative implications for social stability. In the context of social security, we have identified certain vulnerable social groups that are, in a way, more predisposed to risks than other categories of the population. These are primarily Roma, who despite the measures taken to improve their position, continue to be a marginalized and socially vulnerable category of the population.

Regarding the victims of human trafficking, BiH is increasingly becoming a country of origin of human trafficking victims. Such trends are a consequence of the unemployment and poverty of especially young people in BiH. Regarding migrants, BiH was not affected until the end of 2017, when an influx of a large number of migrants began. However, the migrant crisis further burdens the limited capacity of state institutions, which are already unable to deal with internal problems.

There is also the problem of radicalization and terrorism in BiH. Poverty, unemployment, and insecurity represent fertile ground for radical ideologies. Functioning institutions that are capable of providing adequate solutions to numerous problems in society need to be built in BiH.

Due to the constitutional structure of BiH, the entities (Federation of BiH and Republika Srpska) and cantons have broad competences and organizational capacities in the field of social security. At the state level, there is no single institution responsible for dealing with social security issues. The implementation of strategies and action plans adopted by the BiH authorities at the state level depends solely on the entities (Federation of BiH and Republika Srpska) and cantonal authorities. If the ruling elites originate from different political entities, the process of adopting and implementing public policies often falls into crisis. Such a case regarding policies in the area of migration and asylum occurred recently when the BiH Council of Ministers obliged the BiH entities (Federation of BiH and Republika Srpska), cantons and the Brčko District to implement education, social welfare, healthcare, and other forms of protection for migrants; however, this almost does not happen at all because a significant number of these policies were not harmonized when they were designed. The percentage of implemented policies in the area of social security is extremely low due to the lack of financial resources and the lack of political will and ongoing internal political tensions. Also, it should be borne in mind that in every respect BiH depends on financial support and donations from the international community, even in the domain of social security provision. In BiH, there is no codified research in the area of social security, and the data presented originates from a large number of different but rather reliable sources. Therefore, in the future meticulous attention should be paid to analyzing the adoption and implementation of political and legal documents in the area of social security and the encouragement of scientific and professional public to deal with this socially important area more energetically.

Bibliography

Agency for Statistics of BiH. Census of Population, Households and Dwellings in Bosnia and Herzegovina, 2013 Final Results. Sarajevo: Agency for Statistics of BiH, 2016. Accessed July 8, 2016. http://popis2013.ba/popis2013/doc/Popis2013prvoIzdanje.pdf.

Agency for Statistics of BiH. Demography 2011. Sarajevo: Agency for Statistics of BiH, 2012. Accessed 8 July 2016. http://www.bhas.ba/tematskibilteni/demografija%20 konacna%20bh.pdf.

Agency for Statistics of BiH. Demography and Social Statistics, Registered Unemployment. Year: XII, No. 2. Sarajevo: Agency for Statistics of BiH, 2018. Accessed May 8, 2018. http://www.bhas.ba/saopstenja/2018/LAB03_2018_02_0 _BS.pdf.

Bašić, Meho. "Osnove ratne ekonomije, s osvrtom na rat u BiH 1992–1995. godine". Ekonomski Pregled 57, no. 1–2 (2006): 130–145.

Bećirević, Edina. Salafism vs. Moderate Islam: a Rhetorical Fight for the Hearts and Minds of Bosnian Muslims. Sarajevo: Atlantska Inicijativa, 2016. Accessed May 5, 2018. http://atlantskainicijativa.org/bos/wp-content/uploads/2015/dokumenti _publikacije/Salafism_vs_moderate_islam-web.pdf.

Beširević, Alena. Od ukupnog broja nezaposlenih u BiH 53,45 posto su žene. Oslobođenje, 30. juni 2017. Accessed July 2, 2018. https://www.oslobodjenje.ba/ vijesti/bih/od-ukupnog-broja-nezaposlenih-u-bih-53-45-posto-su-zene.

Beslin, Jelena, and Marija Ignjatijević. Balkan Foreign Fighters: From Syria to Ukraine. BRIEF 20/2017. Paris: European Union Institute for Security Studies – EUISS, 2017, 4. Accessed April 24, 2019. https://www.iss.europa.eu/sites/default/files/EUISSFiles/ Brief%2020%20Balkan%20foreign%20fighters.pdf.

Brozek, Borislav. Socijalna isključenost u Bosni i Hercegovini iz pogleda zaposlenih i sindikata. Sarajevo: Fridrih Ebert Stiftung, 2009. Accessed July 8, 2016. http:// library.fes.de/pdf-files/bueros/sarajevo/06850.pdf.

Cline, Matthew. Top 10 Facts About Poverty in Bosnia and Herzegovina, The Borgen Project. Seattle: The Borgen Project, 2018. Accessed November 2, 2018.

Council of Europe. Pojmovnik socijalne sigurnosti. Skopje: Council of Europe, 2007. Accessed July 15, 2018. https://www.coe.int/t/dg3/sscssr/Source/GlossCRO.pdf.

Delegation of the European Union to Bosnia and Herzegovina & European Union Special Representative in Bosnia and Herzegovina. BiH i Evropska Unija. Sarajevo. Accessed April 16, 2019. http://europa.ba/?page_id=484.

Direkcija za evropsko planiranje BiH. Izvještaj o razvoju BiH, Godišnji izvještaj o razvoju 2017. Sarajevo: Direkcija za evropsko planiranje, 2018.

Direkcija za evropsko planiranje BiH. Izvještaj o razvoju BiH, Godišnji izvještaj o razvoju 2016. Sarajevo: Direkcija za evropsko planiranje, 2017. Accessed April 16, 2019. http://www.dep.gov.ba/razvojni_dokumenti/izvjestaji/Archive.aspx?langTag=bsBA&template_id=140&pageIndex=1.

Dnevnik.ba. Krešić: Imamo preko 10.000 registriranih ulazaka migranata u BiH. Dnevnik.ba, 2 Avgust 2018. Accessed August 6, 2018. https://www.dnevnik.ba/vijesti/kresic-imamo-preko-10000-registriranih-ulazaka-migranata-u-bih.

Državni koordinator za borbu protiv trgovine ljudima. Izvještaj o stanju u oblasti trgovine ljudima u BiH za 2017. godinu. Sarajevo: Ministarstvo bezbjednosti BiH, Državnikoordinator za borbu protiv trgovine ljudima, 2018. Accessed May 7, 2019. http://msb.gov.ba/PDF/izvjestaj_trgovina_ljudima_2017.pdf.

Dučić, Amil. "BiH ostaje značajan izvor stranih boraca!". Dnevni Avaz, 21. Jun 2015, Accessed June 10, 2018. http://www.avaz.ba/clanak/183608/bih-ostaje-zna-cajan-izvor-stranih-boraca?rl=clanak/183608/bih-ostaje-znacajan-izvor-stranih-boraca.

Filipović, Miroslav. "Kodna i kobna riječ jest – egzodus". Aljazeera Balkans, 15. mart 2017. Accessed May 7, 2018. http://balkans.aljazeera.net/vijesti/kodna-i-kobna-rijec-jest-egzodus.

Hadžimusić, Aida. „N1 saznaje: Tzv. Islamska država prijeti imamima u BiH". Accessed April 24, 2019. http://ba.n1info.com/Vijesti/a154457/N1-saznaje-Tzv-Islamska-drzava-prijeti-imamima-u-BiH.html.

Hota, Ismet, and Tihomir Radić. Stanje nacije, Izvještaj broj 7. Sarajevo: Centri civilnih inicijativa, 2018. Accessed May 8, 2018. http://www.posaonarodu.ba/files/preview/104/1270.

Hunček-Pita, Aida. "Socijalna zaštita na državnom nivou: pravni osnov i potreba dopune (BiH)". In Sistem socijalne zaštite BiH i regija, edited by Edin Šarčević, 7–26. Sarajevo: CJP, 2012.

Ilić–Krstić, Ivana. "Socijalno-ekološka bezbednost, održivi razvoj i kavlitet života". Doktorska disertacija. Niš: Univerzitet u Nišu, Fakultet Zaštite na Radu, 2016.

Institucija ombudsmena za ljudska prava BiH. Specijalni izvještajo položaju Roma u Bosni i Hercegovini. Sarajevo: Institucija ombudsmena za ljudska prava BiH. Accessed July 3, 2018. https://www.osce.org/bs/bih/110497?download=true.

International Monetary Fund. IMF Country Report No.18/39. Washington: International Monetary Fund, 2018. Accessed April 10, 2019.

Islamska zajednica u Bosni i Hercegovini. Saopćenje Ureda za odnose s javnošću Rijaseta o paradžematima. Sarajevo: Islamska zajednica u Bosni i Hercegovini, January 13, 2016. Accessed April 24, 2019. http://www.islamskazajednica.ba/vijesti/ mina-vijesti/23393-saopcenje-za-javnost-uredaza-odnose-s-javnoscu-rijaseta.

Johnson, James Turner. "Just War Theory: Responding Morally to Global Terrorism". In The New Global Terrorism: Characteristics, Causes, Control, edited by Charles W. Kegley, 222–240. Upper Saddle River: Prentice-Hall, 2003.

Judgement of the District Court in Sarajevo, No. K: 212/83 of 20.08.1983.

Jutarnji. hr. Jeziva prijetnja Islamske Države Bosni Hercegovini 'Zaklat ćemo vašeg vjerskog vođu. Trovatćemovas i dizati u zrak i u BiH i u Sandžaku. Jutarnji.hr 23.03.2016. Accessed April 24, 2019. https://www.jutarnji.hr/globus/jeziva-prijetnja-islamske -drzave-bosni-i-hercegovini-zaklat-cemo-vaseg-vjerskog-vodu-trovat-cemo-vas-i -dizati-u-zrak-i-u-bih-i-u-sandzaku/35527/.

Kaldor, Mary. New and Old Wars – Organized Violence in a Global Era. Beograd: Beogradski Krug, 2005.

Lalić, Velibor. Trgovina ljudima u Bosnii Hercegovini. Banja Luka: Defendologija centar za bezbjednosna, sociološka i kriminološka istraživanja, 2007.

Lipovac, Milan, and Đurić Slađana. "Migrantska kriza u EU i Zapadnobalkanska ruta". In Godišnjak Fakulteta bezbednosti, edited by Božidar Banović. Beograd: Fakultet Bezbednosti, 2015.

Međunarodna organizacija za migracije, Misija u BiH. Priručnik za direktnuasistenciju žrtvama trgovine ljudima. Sarajevo: Međunarodna organizacija za migracije, Misija u BiH; Ministarstvo za ljudskaprava i izbjeglice BiH; Državni koordinator za borbu protiv trgovine ljudima i ilegalne imigracije BiH, 2008. Accessed May 7, 2019. http:// msb.gov.ba/anti_trafficking/dokumenti/prirucnici/?id=5315.

Mijalković, Saša, and Dragomir Keserović. Osnovi bezbjednosti sasistemom bezbjednosti Bosne i Hercegovine. Banja Luka: Fakultet za bezbjednost i zaštitu, 2010.

Ministarstvo bezbjednost i BiH. Informacija o stanju sigurnosti u Bosni i Hercegovini u 2016. godini. Sarajevo: Ministarstvo bezbjednosti, 2017. Accessed May 5, 2018.

Ministarstvo bezbjednosti BiH. Strategija u oblasti migracija i azila i Akcionog plana za period 2016–2020. Sarajevo: Ministarstvo bezbjednosti BiH, 2016, Accessed May 7, 2019, http://sps.gov.ba/dokumenti/strateski/Strategija%20u%20oblasti%20 migracija%20i%20azila%202014-2020.pdf.

Ministarstvounutrašnjih poslova Unsko-Sanskog kantona Federacije BiH. „Bilteni i saopštenja Ministarstva unutrašnjih poslova Unsko-Sanskog kantona za dane: 03.09. do 25.09.2018. godine i od 04.10. do 15. 10.2018. godine". Bihać: Ministarstvo unutrašnjih poslova Unsko-Sanskog kantona Federacije BiH, 2018.

Ministarstvo za ljudska prava i izbjeglice BiH. Akcioni plan Bosne i Hercegovine za rješavanje problema Roma u oblastima zapošljavanja, stambenog zbrinjavanja i zdravstvene zaštite 2017–2020. Sarajevo: Ministarstvo za ljudska prava i izbjeglice,

2017. Accessed July 4, 2018. http://www.mhrr.gov.ba/ljudska_prava/Akcioni%20 plan%20BiH%20za%20rjesavbanje%20problema%20Roma%202017-2020%20 %20BOS.pdf.

Ministarstvo za ljudska prava i izbjeglice BiH. Informacija o povratku izbjeglica i raseljenih osoba u bih za period 1995–2010. godine. Sarajevo: Ministarstvo za Ljudska Prava i Izbjeglice, 2011. Accessed May 5, 2018. http://www.mhrr.gov.ba/PDF/ Izbjeglice/INFORMACIJA%20O%20POVRATKU%20DO%202010.pdf.

Ministarstvo za ljudska prava i izbjeglice BiH. Izvještaj o provođenju Akcionog plana Bosne i Hercegovine za rješavanje problema Roma u oblastima zapošljavanja, stambenog zbrinjavanja i zdravstvene zaštite 2017–2020 i o utrošku grant sredstava za 2017. godinu. Sarajevo: Ministarstvo za ljudska prava i izbjeglice BiH, 2019. Accessed July 2, 2018. http://www.mhrr.gov.ba/Javne_konsultacije/Arhivski/Izvjestaj%20 o%20provedbi%20Akcionog%20plana%20i%20utroska%20grant%20sredstava %20.pdf.

Odluka o usvajanju plana o smjernicama politika tržišta rada i aktivnim mjerama zapošljavanja za 2018 godinu. Službeni glasnik BiH, br. 58/18.

Office of the High Representative. The General Framework Agreement for Peace in Bosnia and Herzegovina. Sarajevo: Office of the High Representative, 1995.

Organization for Security and Co-operation in Europe. Pravo na socijalnu zaštitu u Bosni i Hercegovini, pitanja primjerenosti i jednakosti. Sarajevo: OSCE Misija u BiH, 2012.   ·

Pinter, Zlatkko. "Crtice uz biografiju rahmetli Alije Izetbegovića – 2. Dio". Kamernjar. com, 22. Septembar 2017. Accessed May 10, 2018. https://kamenjar.com/crtice-uz -biografiju-rahmetli-alije-izetbegovica-2-dio/.

Pravilnik o načinu ostvarivanja prava na socijalnu zaštitu osoba kojima je priznata međunarodna zaštita u Bosni i Hercegovini. Službe niglasnik BiH, br. 3/09 i 5/10.

Rmandić, Boban. „Vehabizam i njegov prodor na Balkan". Vojno delo 69, no. 3 (2017): 392– 401. DOI: 10.5937/vojdelo1703392R.

Savjet ministara BiH. Akcioni plan implementacje Strategije suprotstavljanja trgovini ljudima u Bosni i Hercegovini 2013 – 2015. Sarajevo: Savjet ministara BiH, 2013. Accessed May 7, 2019. http://msb.gov.ba/dokumenti/strateski/default. aspx?id=9085&langTag=bs-BA.

Savjet ministara BiH. Akcioni plan suprostavljanja trgovini ljudima u Bosni i Hercegovini 2016–2019. Sarajevo: Savjet ministara BiH, 2016. Accessed May 7, 2019. http://msb.gov.ba/PDF/AKCIONI_PLAN_2016-2019_30_12_2015.pdf.

Savjet ministara BiH. Akcioni plan za sprečavanje trgovine ljudima u BiH 2008–2012. Sarajevo: Savjet ministara BiH, 2008. Accessed May 7, 2019. http://msb.gov .ba/anti_trafficking/dokumenti/planovi/Archive.aspx?langTag=bs-BA&template _id=104&pageIndex=1.

Savjet ministara BiH. Izvještaj o razvoju 2015. Sarajevo: Savjet ministara, Direkcija za ekonomsko planiranje, 2016. Accessed May 5, 2018. http://www.dep.gov.ba/razvojni _dokumenti/ izvjestaji/?id=1783.

Savjet ministara BiH. Održana 147. sjednica Vijeća ministara Bosne i Hercegovine. Sarajevo: Savjet ministara BiH, 2018.

Savjet ministara BiH. Saopštenje povodom 17. oktobra, Međunarodnog dana iskorjenjivanja siromaštva. Sarajevo: Savjet ministara BiH, 2018.

Savjet ministara BiH. Strategija socijalnog uključivanja Bosne i Hercegovine. Sarajevo: Savjet ministara. Direkcija za ekonomsko planiranje, 2010. Accessed May 7, 2018. http://www.mft.gov.ba/hrv/images/stories/medjunarodna_saradnja/ 9.%20Uz%20pitanje%2014.%20Strategija%20socijalnog%20ukljucivanja%20 BiH.pdf.

Savjet ministara BiH. Strategija suprostavljanja trgovini ljudima u BiH 2013–2015. Sarajevo: Savjet ministara BiH, 2013. Accessed May 7, 2019. http://msb.gov.ba/PDF/ brosura%20bos%20final%20mail.pdf.

Šikman, Mile, and Predrag Ćeranić. "Ugrožavanje bezbjednosti Republike Srpske, sa posebnim osvrtom na terorizam". Politika nacionalne bezbednosti 8, no. 1 (2017): 75–96.

Šikman, Mile. "Return of the Foreign Terrorist Fighters – Criminal Persecution and Deradicalization". In Violent Extremism and Radicalization Processes as Driving Factors to Terrorism Threats, edited by Denis Čaleta and Corinna A. Robinson, 109– 136. Ljubljana: Ministry of Defense of Slovenia, Joint Special Operations University from Tampa, USA and Institute for Corporative Security Studies, 2018.

Šikman, Mile. "Strani teroristički borci i krivični postupci u Bosni i Hercegovini". In Krivično zakonodavstvo i fukncionisanje pravne države, uredio Stanko Bejatović, 208–230. Trebinje: Srpsko udruženje za krivičnopravnu teoriju i praksu, 2018.

Šućur, Zoran. "Socijalnaisključenost: pojam, pristupi i operacionalizacija". Revija za sociologiju 35, no. 1–2 (2004): 45–60.

Tabeau, Ewa, and Jakub Bijak. "War-related Deaths in the 1992–1995 Armed Conflicts in Bosnia and Herzegovina: A Critique of Previous Estimates and Recent Results". European Journal of Population 21, no. 2–3 (2005): 187–215.

U.S. Department of State. "The Human Trafficking Report". Washington: United States Department of State, 2018. Accessed November 4, 2018. https://www.state.gov/j/tip/ rls/tiprpt/countries/2018/282617.htm.

U.S. Embassy in Bosnia and Herzegovina. Trafficking in Persons Report. Sarajevo: U.S. Embassy in Bosnia and Herzegovina, 2018. Accessed July 4, 2018. https://ba.usembassy .gov/wp-content/uploads/sites/270/2017/08/Bosnia-and-Herzegovina -2017-TIP-Report-Translation.pdf.

UN General Assembly. Resolution 217 A (III), Universal Declaration of Human Rights, A/RES/217(III)A, December 10, 1948.

United States Department of State. Country Reports on Human Rights Practices for 2017. Washington: United States Department of State, 2017. Accessed November 3, 2018. https://www.state.gov/documents/organization/277391.pdf.

The Functionality of the Social Security Scheme in Albania: Challenges and Perspectives

Teuta Nunaj Kortoci and Shkëlzen Macukulli

1   Introduction

Following the fall of the Iron Curtain at the end of the 1990s, the era of democracy began to spread in Albania by overthrowing the fierce Communist dictatorship that had been operating for half a century. As in other Balkan countries, apart from changing the form of the regime from socialism to democracy, changes also took place in the economic and social life of the country. The closure of many state-owned enterprises; the increase of two-figure informality; job cuts; many active and working-age workers turned to assistance, receiving 60% of their previous salary or early retirement; as well as the collapse of cooperatives and state-owned enterprises, led to an alarming growth in unemployment, as a result of which the number of contributors and the value of social security contributions decreased considerably. Thus, social security was one of the areas most affected by the change of the political and economic system in Albania.

A pension system was first introduced in Albania in 1923 and pension annuity was first regulated by the law and then a law on civil pensions was adopted in 1927. With the change of the regime's form, in 1947 Parliament passed the pension law as a unique social security system built on the Soviet model. In 1966, the pension scheme for state employees in urban areas was remodeled, and only in 1972 was the scheme extended to provide cover for employees in cooperatives and agricultural enterprises.

The long and still incomplete transition over three decades has left a deep mark on the pension system of Albania. Slow economic development, political and economic crises and political instability; lack of proper development strategies; corruption at high levels of government, the justice system and public administration; high emigration among the labor force, mainly among those of younger ages; and the informality of the economy resulted in sluggish economic growth, which also led to a low-level of employment. All of these factors directly contributed to the reduction of the number of contributors, the reduction of direct contributions and the continued failure of the pension scheme.

The Albanian Law on Social Security which is in operation stipulates that the general insurance system is accompanied by:
– compulsory social security,
– voluntary social insurance,
– supplementary social insurance,
– special state pensions,
– social pensions,
– professional funds and voluntary pension funds.[1]
In this chapter compulsory social insurance will be analyzed, which is also the largest component of the social insurance scheme in Albania. This is also because what is first perceived of as social security in Albania is the mandatory social insurance. As we will see, although private pensions are paid in Albania, they are at a low level compared to state pensions. Given their very low percentage share of the financial market, private pensions have not provided solutions to mitigate and reduce the deficit gap between income and social security spending in Albania.

Throughout this chapter, it is intended to describe the beginnings, performance and developments of social insurance in Albania, mainly in the old age pension sector. We analyze the function of the current social security scheme and the causes of the problems in this scheme. Next, we outline the positive changes brought by the 2014 pension reform in Albania as well as the issues that emerged and possible implementation recommendations for the future. The main purpose of this study is to present a historical overview of social security in Albania, to provide a comprehensive and expanded analysis of the functioning of the pension scheme as well as to show the factors and indicators that have brought the success and failure in the implementation of the pension system reform in Albania. The schematic model of variables and indicators is reflected in Figure 3.1.

The authors argue that the stability of the pension scheme in Albania is directly influenced by the number of contributors to the scheme, the value of the direct contributions and the number of pensioners. Therefore, this study of social security in Albania is aimed at contributing to one of the areas of the greatest importance for the low-income population, but at the same time with the greatest needs. The study will answer the following questions: *What is the effect of changing the number of contributors to the stability of the pension scheme? What is the effect of changing the value of direct contributions to the stability of the pension scheme? What is the effect of changing the number of pensioners on the stability of the pension scheme?*

---

1   Law No. 104 on Some Changes and Supplements in Law No. 7703, November 5, 1993, on Social
    Security in the Republic of Albania, Article 1 (Tirana: Albanian Parliament, 2014).

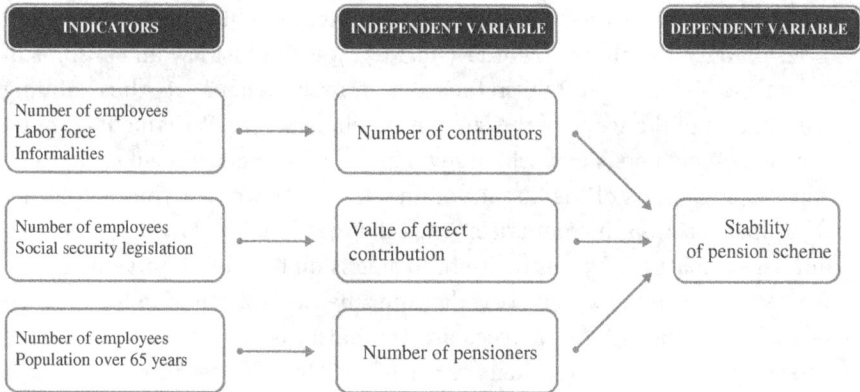

FIGURE 3.1   Schematic model of variables and indicators
SOURCE: OWN ELABORATION.

The research is based on secondary data and has been conducted using three methods: qualitative, quantitative, and comparative. A narrative approach is used to present the history and development of social and pension insurance of Albania in this chapter.

The analysis presents a study of the pension system reform conducted in Albania in 2014 and its effects on the pension scheme. Comparative analyses are presented of the variables taken under consideration in the paper during the period 2009 – 2018.

2   Historical Development of Social Security in Albania

The proclamation of Albania's independence in 1912, the creation of the Albanian government and the administrative institutions brought the need to regulate the new labor relations in Albania, since Ottoman legislation had operated until then. The approval of the "Unknown Civilian Canyon of Albania" on November 22, 1913 was "the stone that laid the foundations for the establishment and functioning of the [public]"[2] administration and the first legal basis of work in Albania. At this time, we had civil servants who worked in the public administration, but employees in the private sector were not

---

2   Departmenti i Administratës Publike, 100 vjet Administratë, no. 12–14, (Tirana: Departmenti i Administratës Publike, 2012), 100. http://dap.gov.al/images/revistat/revista12.pdf (accessed November 25, 2019).

identified. The Law on the Resignation and Retirement from the Army and Constabulary, adopted on February 15, 1923, was the first law on pensions in Albania, which would establish the rules for military pensions, thus defining a limitation of the scope of the law. On October 28, 1927, Parliament adopted the Law on civil pensions, which regulated the pensions of civil servants in Albania, regardless of the institution in which they worked, thus increasing its scope of action in comparison with the 1923 law. The law made important determinations such as the right to a pension for all civil servants beginning after November 29, 1912 (the day after the Declaration of Independence of Albania)[3] and "[...] employees are compulsorily retired when they have served 35 years or have reached the age of 60",[4] but the law also provided for early retirement if the employee had served 25 years in the administration. For the administration of pension funds, the establishment of the General Pension Fund for Civil Servants was foreseen, which "establishes a special institute and functions in the Ministry of Finance".[5] On June 20, 1934, the unified law on Civil and Military Pensions – On the civil and army pensions was adopted.

After the Second World War, Albania changed its form of government from a Monarchy to a Parliamentary Republic, which was accompanied by a change of the pension scheme. On August 26, 1947, Parliament adopted Law No. 528 on pensions in Albania, creating a unique social security system, based on the Soviet model, which included sickness insurance, old age and disability pensions.[6] Law No. 2803, dated December 4, 1958, reduced the retirement age and seniority at work for women giving birth to six or more children.. Likewise, it was decided that the calculation of pensions was to be made on the salary of three consecutive years during the last ten years of work, in addition to the calculation based on the salary of the last year at work. Over the next 20 years the legislation was revised several times. On September 13, 1966, Law No. 417 on city pensions – On state social insurance brought the re-modeling of the pension scheme. The basic shortcoming of this law was that it did not include workers in rural areas in the pension scheme, who for the first time could retire

---

3 Law No. 129 on Civil Pensions, no. 129, Article 7, par. 9 (Tirana: Albanian Parliament, 1927); Mirela Selita, Një vështrim mbi historikun e Sigurimeve Shoqërore në Shqipëri (Tirana: Albanian Institute of Statistics, 2001), http://www.issh.gov.al/?p=10013 (accessed November 27, 2019).
4 Ibid., Article 4, par. 9.
5 Ibid, Article 31, par. 9.
6 Low No. 528 on Social Security of Servants and Functionaries (Tirana: Albanian Parliament, 1947).

only in 1972, through Law No. 4976, dated March 26, 1972 On pensions of agricultural cooperatives – For pensions of agriculture co-operative members. This law granted an old-age pension to employees of agricultural cooperatives, disability pensions, family pensions and allowances for pregnant women and the birth of a baby. Although agricultural cooperative employees were included in the pension scheme, they faced significant differences from employees in the cities. The two main differences were (i) the retirement age for employees in the cooperatives was five years higher, for men and women, compared to other employees in Albania; and (ii) the minimum pension in the village was 100 and the maximum was ALL 350, while the minimum pension in the cities was ALL 350 and the maximum was ALL 700.[7]

Throughout the Monism period, the pension scheme was centrally operated and funded entirely by the state budget. The social security system was state-owned, which means that the sums collected by contributors to social security were transferred to the state budget. Further, the state budget allocated pensioners the amount for planned pensions. It was the state that organized, conducted and controlled the financing of the entire social insurance scheme. The characteristic of the scheme was low retirement age and the occupational categorization of the supplement for the retirement age.

Political, economic and social changes after the collapse of the communist dictatorship in Albania in late 1990 were accompanied by the reform of the social security system. On May 11, 1993, Parliament adopted Law No. 7703 On Social Security in the Republic of Albania, which has changed 20 times in the 23 years of its operation. These changes indicate the instability and weak foundation of the system. This law preserved the pension rights set forth in Law No. 4171, dated April 13, 1966 and Law No. 4976, dated June 29, 1972, calling it "well-being and will not be subject to any change except indexation and compensation".[8]

The basic legal elements that characterize social security in Albania today are:

– constitutionality of social security, since Article 51, point 1 of the Constitution of Albania states: "everyone has the right to social security in old age or when he is unable to work, according to a system set by law"[9];

---

7 Dokumenti i Politikave të Pensioneve, 11 prill 2014 (Tirana: Ministria e Mirëqënies Sociale dhe Rinisë, 2014), 6.

8 Law No. 7703, Amended (Tirana: Albanian Parliament, 1993), 28.

9 The Constitution of the Republic of Albania, approved by referendum on November 22 (Tirana: Albanian Parliament, 1998), 10.

–   legal obligation, since Law 7703/1993 in Article 13, point 1 states: "the con-
    tributions [to social and health insurance] shall be paid by the insured
    persons"[10];
–   payment of contributions when one is in employment and the same law
    in Article 13, point 2 provides "contributions of persons employed under a
    contract of employment shall be shared between the insured person and
    his employer in accordance with the provisions of this Law and shall be
    discharged by the employer";[11]
–   payment of voluntary social insurance, where Article 3, point 1 of the
    law states: "a person who is compulsorily insured, where for a reasonable
    time and reason cannot be compulsorily provided, has the right to con-
    tinue insurance, according to voluntary system".[12]

3   Construction of a Social Insurance Scheme in Albania

The social security scheme in itself simplifies the pension development plan
in Albania, which is used to help the individual financially at retirement age.
The scheme has three basic elements in its function: an individual's retirement
age; the number of years of work that the individual has to complete to receive
partial or full pension; the income he/she receives from the pension. Table 3.1.
shows changes in retirement age and years at work for men and women throughout the period that the pension scheme has been in effect in Albania.

The data indicate important information:
–   until World War II, the law did not provide for pensions for women,
    which shows that women were not involved in work in the Albanian pub-
    lic administration;
–   in 1966, the retirement age was divided into three categories, which con-
    tinues to apply today;
–   from 1927 to 2011, the retirement age for men hardly changed, but the
    number of years at work increased by seven years (for category III);
–   from 1966 to 2001, the retirement age for women in the third category
    remained the same, but the number of years at work increased by
    ten years;
–   only in 1972, for the first time, was it decided to establish pensions for
    citizens residing in the village and working in agricultural cooperatives.

---

10   Law No. 7703, Amended (Tirana: Albanian Parliament, 1993), 5.
11   Ibid.
12   Ibid., 2.

TABLE 3.1   The changes of retirement ages over time in Albania

Years	Retirement ages		Years of contribution for full pension	
	Men	Women	Men	Women
1927	60 years	–	25 years	–
1947	65 years	60 years	–	–
1949	60 years	55 years		
1966 (Category I – city)	50 years	45 years	20 years	15 years
1966 (Category II – city)	55 years	50 years	25 years	20 years
1966 (Category III – city)	60 years	55 years	25 years	20 years
1972 (Cooperatives)	65 years	60 years	25 years	20 years
1993 (Category I)	50 years	45 years	20 years	15 years
1993 (Category II)	55 years	50 years	25 years	20 years
1993 (Category III)	60 years	55 years	25 years	20 years
2001 (Category I)	54 years	49 years	24 years	22 years
2001 (Category II)	59 years	54 years	32 years	30 years
2001 (Category III)	60 years	55 years	32 years	30 years

SOURCE: OWN ELABORATION BASED ON DATA FROM NATIONAL SOCIAL INSURANCE INSTI-
TUTE, HTTP://WWW.ISSH.GOV.AL/ (ACCESSED NOVEMBER 27, 2019).

The social security system in the monist period was modeled on the development of a centralized economy. Since 1972 it has highlighted the scheme for public sector employees residing in cities and for the public sector employees, who lived in the village and worked in agricultural cooperatives. In the 1976 Constitution, the economic order in Albania was defined as "a socialist economy based on socialist property and on means of

production".[13] Socialist property itself consisted of state property and cooperative property in agriculture while at the same time eradicating private ownership,[14] which automatically brought with it the absence of private enterprises, which is why the only employees were state employees. The differences
between these two schemes were substantial, and the most significant ones
were the retirement age, seniority at work and retirement income. Employee
pensions in cities were twice as high as those in villages, while the retirement
age of the retirees in the town was lower than the retirees in the village, a
scheme that discriminated openly against workers in villages.

     In the early 1990s, with the start of the functioning of the market economy,
the legal basis and the social security scheme underwent significant changes.
Basic elements in the law that are in force in Albania and that have brought
innovation to the social security system are:

–   social pensions – is a benefit granted to any Albanian citizen who has
     reached the age of 70, has been permanently resident in Albania for at
     least the last five years, does not meet the conditions for any pension from
     the compulsory social insurance scheme and has no income, or income
     that benefits from any other source, that is lower than the income of the
     social pension benefits;[15]
–   the voluntary social security system where every individual, although not
     in an employment relationship, has the legal right to voluntary insurance
     in accordance with legal provisions;
–   acquisition of the right to old age pension for persons insured with not
     less than 15 years of social security;[16]
–   gradual retirement age.

According to Law No. 8889, dated April 25, 2002 and Law No. 104, dated July
31, 2014, the retirement age increases gradually every six months and then year
after year. This increase began on July 1, 2002 and is foreseen to increase until
December 31, 2056. So, the retirement age in the third category will increase
from 60 years and 6 months to 67 for men and the number of years worked
from 33 to 40. The retirement age for women will rise from 55 years and

13   The Constitution of People's Socialist Republic of Albania Law No. 5506 (Tirana: Albanian
      Parliament, 1976), 4.
14   Ibid.
15   Law No. 104 on Some Changes and Supplements in Law, no. 7703, November 5, 1993,
      on Social Security in the Republic of Albania, Amended, Article 4 (Tirana: Albanian
      Parliament, 2014).
16   Ibid., Article 16.

6 months to 67 and the number of years worked from 32 to 40.[17] So, over the 54 years from 2002 to 2056 the retirement gender gap will be closed and both men and women will retire at 67 and have to work for 40 years.

4   The Impact of Demographic Change on the Pension Scheme during Pluralism

The change of the political and economic regime in Albania in the early 1990s brought many social consequences. The pension system was one of the most affected areas as a result of (i) the significant increase in unemployment; (ii) the high-level of informality in the economy; (iii) the increasing number of individuals receiving social assistance at a rate of 60% of their last salary; (iv) and early retirement of many of these active employees and working age, due to the closure of a large number of state-owned enterprises and the collapse of agricultural cooperatives.

These social and economic consequences will be felt in the insurance scheme years later, when these unemployed people would start to retire, while not having reached the number of years at work provided by the law. From INSTAT[18] and ISSH[19] as two public and independent institutions, in 1990 there was a population of more than 3.2 million people in Albania, of which more than 1,451,212 individuals were contributors to the social insurance scheme and 319,107 pensioners. The contributor/pensioner ratio was 4.5 contributors per one pensioner.[20] Based on the data from INSTAT and SII, in Albania we had:

– on January 1, 2019, a population of 2,862,427 (7,897 fewer inhabitants than a year before);
– at the end of 2018 we had a labor force of (15–64 years old) 1,965,783 individuals (8,424 individuals less than a year before) of which only 721,160 or 36.7% of the workforce were contributors or individuals covered by the social security system;
– 512,507 pension or 17.90% of the population of Albania;

---

17   Law No. 7703, Amended, Articles 92.
18   INSTAT – Institutii Statistikës, Albanian Institute of Statistics.
19   ISSH – Instituti i Sigurimeve Shoqërore, National Social Insurance Institut.
20   Dokumenti i Politikave të Pensioneve, 11 prill 2014 (Tirana: Ministria e Mirëqënies Sociale dhe Rinisë, 2014), 5.

- the average pension in the city was ALL 15,875 /month or EUR 126.88 / month;[21]
- in the village is ALL 8,792 per month or EUR 70.27 per month;
- contributor / pensioner at the end of 2018 was 1.24 contributors per one pensioner.[22]

Thus, compared with the beginning of the transition period, we noticed a few changes in the reduction of contributors to the pension scheme by 49.69%, an increase in the number of pensioners by 193,400 individuals or 37.7%; and a very critical reduction of the contributor / pensioner ratio of 3.6 less per pensioner.

Some of the underlying reasons for this change are:
- high-level emigration, mainly at younger ages, or working age;
- reduction of the size of active population in work as a result of closure of a large number of manufacturing enterprises; the collapse of the agricultural cooperatives of state farms, making the rural population contribute to the social security scheme at a much lower rate; relocating a large number of people from rural to urban areas where they were left without work and sought social assistance;
- informality of the economy; by non-declaration of employees, who did not become part of the social security scheme; by declaring employees with a minimum wage, concealing in this way the real wage, which resulted in the reduction of social security income into the scheme and distortion of the social security fund;
- aging of the Albanian population, which is currently moving rapidly and worryingly, which results in fewer people contributing to the scheme and more people benefiting from the pension scheme;
- reduction of the natural increase of the population in Albania, which resulted from the decline in the number of births and the increase in the number of deaths with a significant difference in birth defects. According to INSTAT data, for the period 2014–2018, natural growth has decreased by

---

21   Official exchange rate of Bank of Albania, on April 05, 2019, 1 Euro = 125.11 Albanian Lek. Banka e Shqipërisë. Kursi zyrtar i këmbimit. (Tirana: Bank of Albania, 2019), https://www. bankofalbania.org/Tregjet/Kursi_zyrtar_i_kembimit/ (accessed December 12, 2019).

22   Statistika të Sigurimeve Shoqërore viti 2018, January 2019 (Tirana: Instituti i Sigurimeve Shoqërore, 2014), 1, http://www.issh.gov.al/wp-content/uploads/2019/04/Statistika_ISSH_2018.pdf (accessed April 5, 2019).

more than 50% or by 7,974 individuals. In 2014, the natural increase was 15,104 individuals, in 2018; the natural increase was 7,130 individuals.[23]
To design social insurance policies should take into account the following factors: demographic – aging population; migration – departure of the active working population from Albania; economic – high growth unemployment; politics – the implementation of public and fiscal policies.

5   Functioning of the Current Pension Scheme

The insurance scheme in Albania includes Social Insurance and Health Insurance. Currently the contribution paid for social insurance in sickness, maternity and pension insurance funds is for employers 13.8% of the gross amount of payroll and for the employed person 9.5% of their total payment (gross). Contribution is calculated and paid on gross wage, within the minimum wage limits at national level and the maximum wage. In consequence the contribution effect is indexed at the same time and to the extent that the minimum wage is indexed at national level.[24]

In 1991, the contribution rate was 15%[25] and is currently 23.3%.[26] The increase of the contribution rate, in addition to increasing direct contributions, has also brought the opposite effect for social security, concealing real wages, and increasing the number of wage statements with the minimum wage. Until 2014, with the beginning of pension reform, this form of declaration (minimum wage and minimum insurance) was a 'norm' declaration for private businesses, with a view to reducing their spending and increasing their profits. Since the job supply is lower than demand, the employees would not risk being left out of work, accepted the compromise of not declaring their real wages and then taking the salary difference in cash, which still happens today. At present, with the Council of Ministers Decision, the minimum monthly

23   Albanian Institute of Statistics, Popullsia, 2019, http://www.instat.gov.al/al/temat/ treguesit-demografik%C3%AB-dhe-social%C3%AB/popullsia/#tab2 (accessed April 7, 2019).

24   Law No. 104 on Some Changes and Supplements in Law, no. 7703, November 5, 1993, on Social Security in the Republic of Albania, Amended (Tirana: Albanian Parliament, 2014), 4, Article 10.

25   Dokumenti i Politikave të Pensioneve, 11 prill 2014 (Tirana: Ministria e Mirëqënies Sociale dhe Rinisë, 2014), 5.

26   Law No. 104 on Some Changes and Supplements in Law, no. 7703, November 5, 1993, on Social Security in the Republic of Albania, Amended (Tirana: Albanian Parliament, 2014), 4, Article 10.

basic salary of ALL 22,000 was set "to be ALL 24,000",[27] an increase of 9.1%
and is likely to grow again. However, as from January 1, 2015, the minimum
wage and maximum pay for social and health contributions are indexed at the
same time and to the same extent, the maximum salary increased by 9.1% and
from ALL 97,030[28] (or EUR 556)[29] became to ALL 105,850 (or EUR 846).[30] The
pay ceiling after the 2002 reforms has brought two positive effects, which was
increased direct incomes and reduced tax evasion. Even though it did not stop
the concealment of the real wage, again the definition of the wage bill remains
an important factor in the stability of the pension scheme.

The general system of social security consists of a few elements: compulsory social security; voluntary social security; supplementary social security;
special state pensions; social pensions; professional funds and voluntary pension funds.[31] Social security provides financial protection for individuals who
have contributed during the years they have been in employment and have
contributed to the pension scheme and have reached the legal retirement age.
According to the law, they receive either a retirement pension or a reduced
retirement pension.

According to the representatives of ISS, in Albania, the current social insurance scheme is a charitable system using the 'pay-as-you-go' (PAYG) standard,
employing the rule of individuals being responsible for the future social hazards and generational solidarity.[32] The preset scheme system in Albania is
illustrated in Figure 3.2. This means that the sums paid in by today's contributors toward their retirement are used for the payments that current pensioners
receive. The Albanian pension scheme is administered by ISI.

The three categories of contributions that are included in the pension
scheme are not taxed. Since the Social Insurance Fund is smaller than the
Pension Fund, the balancing of the financial deficit would be realized with

---

27   Decision No. 399 on The Definition of Minimal Wage Nationwide, May 3 (Tirana: Këshillii
     Ministrave, 2017), 1.
28   Statistika të Sigurimeve Shoqërore (Tirana: Albanian Institute of Statistics, 2015), 2. http://
     www.issh.gov.al/wp-content/uploads/2014/02/Perb_12_15.pdf (accessed December 2, 2019).
29   Official exchange rate of Bank of Albania, on April 05, 2019, 1 Euro = 125.11 Albanian Lek.
     Banka e Shqipërisë, Kursi zyrtar i këmbimit (Tirana: Bank of Albania, 2019), https://www
     .bankofalbania.org/Tregjet/Kursi_zyrtar_i_kembimit/ (accessed December 12, 2019).
30   Official exchange rate of Bank of Albania, on April 05, 2019, 1 Euro = 125.11 Albanian Lek.
     Banka e Shqipërisë. Kursi zyrtar i këmbimit (Tirana: Bank of Albania, 2019), https://www
     .bankofalbania.org/Tregjet/Kursi_zyrtar_i_kembimit/ (accessed December 12, 2019).
31   Albanian Parliament, Law No. 104 on Some Changes and Supplements in Law No. 7703,
     November 5, 1993, Amended (Tirana: Albanian Parliament, 2014), 1.
32   Mirela Selita, Një vështrim mbi historikun e Sigurimeve Shoqërore në Shqipëri.

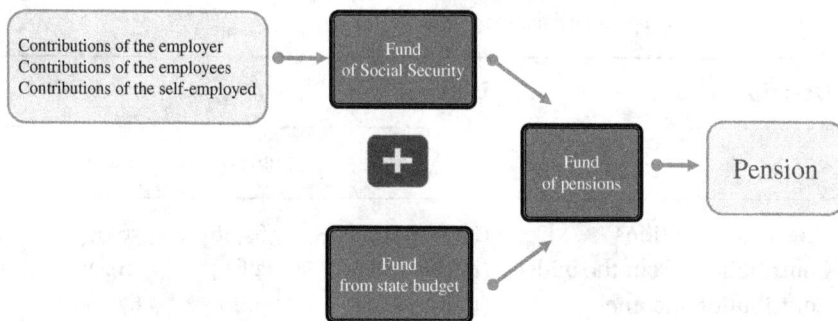

FIGURE 3.2   Pension scheme in Albania
SOURCE: OWN ELABORATION.

subsidy from the Government, through the state budget fund. Therefore, the pension scheme is co-funded by the government.

As may be seen in Table 3.2, direct contributions have increased year by year in the analyzed 2009–2018 period. 2018 has the highest value of over ALL 76.6 billion (over EUR 612 million) and 2012 has the lowest contribution value of around ALL 50 billion (approximately EUR 394 million).

From the data in Table 3.2, we can see that contributions from the state budget rise and fall. For 2015, the state budget contribution was as much as 42% of the pension fund, which is also the largest amount allocated by the state budget for the period under analysis, which indicates the volatility of the scheme. While the direct contributions for the period under analysis, although increasing, are insufficient to provide for the coverage of old age pensions, when, as explained above, old age pensions are only one item in the social security scheme. Thus, having a deficit in the pension scheme, the state budget finances the social security scheme permanently and annually. The inadequacy of direct contributions and co-financing by the state brings:

–   Low monetary pensions. In 2009 the average pension amount in urban areas was ALL 12,032 per month and in 2018 it became ALL 15,875 per month (Table 3.2). While the pension in rural areas is lower than in urban areas, in 2009 the average pension amount was ALL 6,665 per month and in 2018 it became ALL 8,792 per month (or EUR 70).

–   Low pension growth realized through price indexing and not as a public policy of the government for their growth, also because of high public spending, including on high public debt. From the processed data of the Social Insurance Institute displayed in Table 3.2 it may be observed that in the analyzed period the average pension measure in urban areas has

TABLE 3.2   Selected pension data, 2009–2018

Description	Units	Years		
		2009	**2010**	**2011**
Direct contributions	(in mln ALL)	56,486	56,073	58,532
Contributions from the budget	(in mln ALL)	12,624	11,235	10,773
Contribution income	(in mln ALL)	69,110	67,308	69,305
Retirement income	(in mln ALL)	59,240	63,785	67,471
Urban contributors	In No.	384,214	399,566	431,013
Rural contributors	In No.	294,783	252,604	261,097
Total contributor	In No.	678,997	652,170	692,110
Old-age retired urban areas	In No.	285,630	285,875	288,533
Old-age retired rural areas	In No.	142,742	142,015	140,776
Total old-age retirees	In No.	428,372	427,890	429,309
Mean pension in urban areas	(in ALL)	12,032	12,711	13,278
Mean pension in rural areas	(in ALL)	6,656	7,499	7,859
Older retirement pensions urban areas	In No.	8,066	10,725	10,216
New rural retirement pensions rural areas	In No.	3,521	4,060	2,514
Total new pensions (in no.)	In No.	11,587	14,785	12,730

SOURCE: OWN ELABORATION BASED ON DATA FROM NATIONAL SOCIAL INSURANCE
INSTITUTE, HTTP://WWW.ISSH.GOV.AL/ (ACCESSED DECEMBER 14, 2019).

2012	2013	2014	2015	2016	2017	2018
49,330	51,390	61,720	60,068	65,173	72,237	76,655
7,988	40,132	35,709	43,439	15,104	14,721	14,950
57,318	91,522	97,429	103,507	80,277	86,958	93,626
71,632	76,877	82,357	86,071	90,529	96,771	101,571
434,891	446,473	480,791	579,087	608,487	635,885	662,220
168,513	64,274	127,728	89,527	53,168	58,526	58,940
603,404	510,747	608,519	668,614	661,655	694,411	721,160
296,076	311,382	327,604	345,314	363,664	379,349	398,744
137,771	135,904	133,132	129,161	124,378	118,794	113,763
603,404	447,286	460,736	474,475	488,042	498,143	512,507
14,104	14,076	14,518	14,585	14,873	15,527	15,875
8,048	7,465	7,825	8,330	8,556	8,808	8,792
17,500	23,702	27,206	28,987	Na	Na	Na
12,719	2,449	2,760	1,003	Na	Na	Na
30,219	26,151	29,966	29,990	23,240	21,864	24,259

increased by ALL 3,843 (or EUR 30.7) over 10 years and in rural areas it has increased by ALL 2,136 (or EUR 17) over 10 years.

– Inability to accumulate a reserve fund for pensions, which at a later stage could somewhat ease the scheme, stabilize it, and could bring about a reduction in state budget funding. The law in Article 35 requires the Social Insurance Institute to create a reserve fund that covers at least one-month of pension expenditures,[33] which imposes a limitation but also the inability to accumulate value.

– Serious burden on the state budget. Since the number of contributors in Albania over the decade has fallen to an average increase of 4,216 contributors per year, which is lower than the increase in the number of new pensioners, who are growing steadily with an average of 8,414 pensioners per year, this obliges the Albanian government to finance annually the distribution of income and expenses for the coverage of the pension scheme. Taking a closer look at the data provided, one may observe that the subsidy of the state budget in relation to GDP has increased on a yearly basis. Supplementary pensions[34] and special pensions[35] are disbursed directly from the state budget, in addition to the deficit between contributions and spending on old-age pensions.

– The instability of the scheme is also due to the instability that the Albanian economy is experiencing, both in development and fiscal policy.

Increasing youth emigration, unemployment, informality, constant changes in the number of contributors to the scheme, decreasing birth rates and increasing life expectancy are the main factors that affect the failure of the pension scheme and the increase of the direct dependency that this scheme has on the state budget.

From 2009 to 2018 the average time of pension enjoyment, both for men in urban and rural areas, and for women in urban and rural areas has increased (Table 3.3). For men, the average time of pension enjoyment has increased by 2.3 years over 10 years, and for women the average time of pension enjoyment has increased by 3.7 years over 10 years. Additionally, the increase in the number of new pensions by an average of 1,267 new pensions each year in the period under analysis and the indexation of pensions consistently, where only in 2018 were these indexed to 2.8%.[36]

---

33   Law No. 104 on Some Changes and Supplements in Law No. 7703, November 5, 1993, on Social Security in Republic of Albania, Amended (Tirana: Albanian Parliament, 2014), 22.

34   For more see Article 4, Law No. 7703, Amended, May 11, 1993.

35   For more see Article 5, Law No. 7703, Amended, May 11, 1993.

36   Decision No. 348 on The Indexing of Pension, June 12 (Tirana: Council of Ministers, 2018).

TABLE 3.3   Other important pension data, 2009–2018

Description	Units	Year									
		2009	2010	2011	2012	2013	2014	2015	2016	2017	2018
No. of contributors / No. of pensions	In No.	1.32:1	1.26:1	1.30:1	1.20:1	0.98:1	1.12:1	1.2:1	1.19:1	1.22:1	1.24:1
The average urban retirement length (male)	Years	18.1	19.1	18.9	19.1	19.3	19.4	19.7	19.7	19.7	19.4
The average rural retirement length (male)	Years	17.1	18.0	18.0	18.4	19.0	19.7	20.3	20.6	21.1	21.7
Average male retirement length (total)	Years	17.6	18.8	18.8	18.9	19.2	19.5	19.8	20.0	20.0	19.9
The average urban retirement (women)	Years	22.6	23.4	23.5	23.4	24.3	24.9	25.0	25.3	25.4	25.5
Average leisure time of rural retirement (women)	Years	22.4	23.0	23.9	22.5	24.2	25.1	25.9	26.2	26.9	27.1
Average time of female pension enjoyment (total)	Years	22.4	22.5	23.2	23.0	24.2	25.0	25.3	25.6	26.0	26.1
Income SII/ GDP	In % of GDP	4.91	4.53	4.45	4.70	5.62	5.81	5.77	6.07	6.59	7.07
Expenses/PPB	In % of GDP	5.38	5.41	5.41	6.10	7.08	7.18	7.59	8.08	8.42	8.87
Subsidy/PPB	In % of GDP	0.47	0.88	0.96	1.40	1.5	1.37	1.82	2.01	1,83	1.8

SOURCE: OWN ELABORATION BASED ON DATA FROM NATIONAL SOCIAL INSURANCE INSTITUTE, HTTP:// WWW.ISSH.GOV.AL/ (ACCESSED DECEMBER 15, 2019).

There is a general understanding of the existential and functional needs of the pension scheme for continuous funding, because funding from the social security fund is insufficient. All this creates the dependence of the pension fund on other financing, where the solution is found in the form of funding from the state budget.

6   Private Pensions in Albania

The passage of Law No. 7943 dated 01.06.1995. on Supplementary Pensions and Private Pensions Institutions, amended, marked the first legal step toward the implementation of private voluntary pensions in Albania. The purpose of this law was "to provide supplementary benefits to insured persons in old-age, invalidity and (or) family pensions by means of supplementary pension arrangements, in addition to those provided by the law on compulsory social security".[37] The law would change three times by 2006 and be repealed in 2009.

The new private pension law adopted on December 10, 2009 would completely transform the private pension market in Albania. It would be aimed at the most effective management of voluntary pension funds, through diversification of investments, with the aim of increasing the contributions made to the pension fund, and supervision of the voluntary pension fund business with defined contributions, in order to ensure the protection of the member of the pension fund.[38] This law regulates the functioning, management and supervision of pension funds, the management companies of these funds, the investment, and fundraising policies of funds, etc. An important and facilitating element of the law as well as state pensions is that the contribution made by each member of a pension fund is deducted from its personal income tax effect.[39] In classification of this law, besides being a participant of the voluntary pension fund, it still requires these individuals to have an insurance determined by the standing legislation.[40] The old age pension in Albania is not a substitute for the state pension, but is an additional pension on top of the state pension that a retiring individual receives.

---

37   Law No. 7943 on Supplements Pensions and Private Institute of Pensions (Tirana: Albanian Parliament, 1995), 3.
38   Law No. 10197 on Voluntary Pension Funds, December 10 (Tirana: Albanian Parliament, 2009), 1.
39   Ibid, 6.
40   Ibid.

Only in 2004, approximately ten years after the drafting of the legal basis in Albania, was the company "SIGAL Life" joint-stock company authorized as the first life insurance company.[41] Further development of the private pension market came as a consequence of the liberalization of the banking market in Albania, where banks were introduced to this strategic sector by bringing in new experience, as there was a significant lack of experience in the area of private pensions in Albania. Until 2014, Private Pension Funds taxed profit and contribution twice, while only profits should be taxed,[42] which has served as a fundamental factor in curbing the development of the voluntary pension fund market. The private pension scheme, considered as a third pillar, "functions as a supplementary scheme to the state pension scheme. This scheme is completely optional and addresses individuals wishing to have an additional pension in support of the pension distributed by the public entity."[43]

The Albanian Financial Supervisory Authority is the only authority to issue private sector funding in Albania. To date, licenses to operate in the private pension fund market in Albania are held by:

- Raiffeisen Voluntary Pension Funds, under the administration of "Raiffeisen Invest-Management Company of voluntary pension funds and collective investment undertaking assets", joint-stock company, company with foreign capital, with depositary for assets: First Investment Bank joint-stock company;
- SIGAL Voluntary Pension Funds, under the administration of "Sigal-Life Uniqa Group Austria Pension Funds Management Company", joint-stock company, company with domestic capital, with depositary for assets: American Investment Bank joint-stock company;
- Credins Voluntary Pension Funds, on administration "Credins-Invest – Management Company of Voluntary Pension Funds and collective investment undertaking", joint-stock company, company with domestic and foreign capital, with depositary for assets: Tirana Bank joint-stock company.[44]

41   Sigal Uniqa Group Austria, "Rreth Sigal Uniqa" (Tirana: Sigal Uniqa Group Austria, 2018), http://sigal.com.al/rreth-kompanise/# (accessed November 14, 2018).

42   Dokumenti i Politikave të Pensioneve, 11 prill 2014 (Tirana: Ministria e Mirëqënies Socialedhe Rinisë, 2014), 22.

43   Ina Petraj, "Private Pensions in Albania (The Need of a Reform According to the European Standards)", Academic Journal of Interdisciplinary Studies 2, no. 2 (Italy: MCSER-CEMAS-Sapiena University of Roma, 2013), 239, http://www.mcser.org/journal/index.php/ajis/article/viewFile/384/400 (accessed August 10, 2018).

44   Albanian Financial Supervisory Authority, Register of Licensed Persons/Entities: Voluntary Pension Fund Market (Tirana: Albanian Financial Supervisory Authority, 2011), http://amf.gov.al/tfp_shoqeri.asp and http://amf.gov.al/tfp_fond.asp (accessed September 13, 2018).

The private pension is realized through the monthly contributions of the contributors and the monthly benefit is made on the basis of the number of years of contributions. The overall performance of the members and assets of the three private pension funds operating in Albania are reflected in Table 3.4.

On December 31, 2018 there were 25,298 Pension Fund Members and these are divided as follows: Credins Pensions 60.56%, Sigal 27.94%, Raiffeisen 11.51%. The net assets of Pension Funds are ALL 2,289,089,112 (or over EUR 18 million) and these are divided as follows: Credins Pensions 25.36%, Sigal 47.43%, Raiffeisen 27.21%.[45] Over a period of three years the number of members and the assets of private pension funds in Albania has doubled (Table 3.4). However, despite the continued growth and the tendency to continue growth, we see that in the financial markets overseen by the Albanian Financial Supervisory Authority the pension market is small and at the end of 2017 it was only 1.7% of this market.[46]

TABLE 3.4   Indicators of private pension funds

Description	Units	Date						
		2015	2016		2017		2018	
		Dec-31	Jun-30	Dec-31	Jun-30	Dec-31	Jun-30	Dec-31
Pension fund members	In No.	12,559	14,840	17,317	19,514	20,947	23,511	25,298
Net assets by pension fund	In mln ALL	928	1,112	1,318	1,496	1,728	2,007	2,289

SOURCE: OWN ELABORATION BASED ON DATA FROM ALBANIAN FINANCIAL SUPERVISORY AUTHORITY, HTTPS://AMF.GOV.AL/ARKIVARV.ASP (ACCESSED DECEMBER 15, 2019).

---

45   Statistics, Voluntary Private Pension Market, December 31 (Tirana: Albanian Financial Supervisory Authority, 2018), http://amf.gov.al/statistika.asp?id=3&s=2 (accessed April 6, 2019).

46   Annual Report (Tirana: Albanian Financial Supervisory Authory, 2018), 22, http://amf.gov.al/pdf/publikime2/raport/RaportiVjetor2017_2.pdf (accessed October 12, 2018).

The comparison of the two categories of pensions presented in the tables above, showed at the end of 2017 that there were (i) 694,411 contributors to state pensions and 20,947 members of private pension funds; and (ii) ALL 72,237 million in contributions to state pensions and ALL 1,728 million in assets in pension funds, which shows the low level of private pensions in the Albanian pension market. Different companies in Albania, mainly foreign-owned companies, have begun in recent years to offer their employees the opportunity to be part of a private pension scheme by providing a contribution to this scheme as an element of their remuneration. One example is Vodafone Albania, which on the basis of a plan contributes as a partner with the employee to his or her private pension fund.

The fast-paced development of the private pension market in Albania is occurring for several reasons, but the main ones are:
–   low wages and low incomes in the majority of the population;
–   the Albanian tradition that obliges children to care for parents, mainly in their old age, does not stimulate the payment of contributions for private pensions, which is also reflected in the high levels of remittances, as Albanians working abroad send income to parents and family members in Albania;
–   the lack of a culture for long-term and prospective investment, both by employees and by companies, does not stimulate this form of compensation;
–   the lack of confidence in capital and financial markets in Albania, which is also due to the instability and lack of security and stability in the country's economic development, as well as the frequent changes in the laws in Albania;
–   the long and still unfinished transition, slow development and unstable Albanian economy limit the opportunities for the development of the private pension market.

The main challenges faced by the private pension market are:
–   Awareness – retirement savings is not on everybody's financial agenda.
–   Stimulus – the truth is that many Albanians do not have enough income. Therefore, the need for convenience and fiscal incentives is welcome.
–   Financial opportunities.
–   Rapid growth of population age – as a problem affecting the private market.[47]

---

47   Drita Luzo, Drejt qëndrueshmërisë së sistemit të pensioneve në Shqipëri (Tirana: University of Tirana, 2017), 34, http://www.doktoratura.unitir.edu.al/wp-content/uploads/2017/05/Drita-LUZOKLLAPI-Ph.D-.pdf (accessed November 20, 2018).

7   Pension Reform in Albania

The three basic factors that have affected the social security scheme in Albania in the transition years are economic, demographic, and political factors. A stable, formalized, developed economy that produces new jobs and at the same time increases the income of its workers increases direct contributions. Higher monthly income means the highest contributions to the pension scheme and at the same time increasing the number of contributors. But the economic factor is closely linked and directly affects the demographic factor. Economic sustainability reduces the migration of younger people, thereby avoiding the decline in the number of contributors to the scheme. It also increases the number of contributors, which translates into higher income in the pension scheme. At the same time, it also keeps potential emigrants in place, as having a job at home, individuals or families will not be forced to migrate to other areas, which would increase the amount of cheap migrant labor and wage cuts (because job demands will be greater than job offers). This in turn results in lowering contributions and reducing the number of contributors. Public government policies that promote employment, formalize the economy, and create fiscal stability help to increase direct contribution income and increase the number of contributors to the pension scheme.

There are a few problems which were found in the pension scheme over the years:

–   The low number of contributors in the first years of implementation of the scheme has come to stabilize in subsequent years. But compared to the number of retirees, this creates a big problem, putting the scheme in jeopardy. Thus, the rate of dependency expressed as the ratio between the number of contributors and the number of pensions continued to fall steadily, reaching a negative value in 2013, namely 0.98 contributors per one pensioner. Some of the factors leading to the deterioration of the dependency rate are still low number of employees, high employment rate in the black market, inclusion of certain specific categories of pensions in the scheme.[48]

–   The high number of pension beneficiaries compared to the number of contributors in the first years of transition. After the closure of

48   Dokumenti i Politikave të Pensioneve, 11 prill 2014 (Tirana: Ministria e Mirëqënies Sociale dhe Rinisë, 2014), 13.

agricultural enterprises and farms, the number of pensioners came to normalize and "after 2002, as a result of the pension age increase reform, there has been a decrease in the pace of new pension rises".[49] From 2009 to 2013 (over five years) there were 95,472 new pensions. At the same time, the number of contributors in rural areas has fallen considerably and in 2013 there were only 64,274 contributors in rural areas, down from 294,783 in 2009 (Table 3.2). This has led the contribution of the state budget to the pension scheme to remain high, which managed to fund 44% of the pension fund for 2013.

– The rate of coverage of retirement contributors compared to the labor force "has gradually decreased from 33.76% to 32.41% in the period 1994–1999. This indicator rose thereafter, reaching 58.4% in 2012".[50] From 2005 to 2013, "only one-third of the working age population is covered by the social security system, which means that almost two-thirds of the working-age Albanians are at risk of retiring in the future".[51]

– Increasing contributions and reducing expenses are the main challenges for any social security scheme. Until 2013, there were fluctuations in revenues with decreases and increases, while expenditures have increased, which has led to the steady growth of subsidies from the state budget.

– Urban pension ahead of the rural pension. After the transition to 2012, the continued growth of pensions has favored rural pensions versus urban ones. Thus, in 2012 the ratio between average pension size and average wage in the city reached 46.3% (decreasing) and in the village it reached 41.6% (increasing).[52] This has happened as a result of the continued increase in the minimum pension and the existence of the maximum pension, while the amount of the contributions of an employee in rural areas is lower than in urban areas.

– Determining the pension ceiling. Along with the minimal and maximum pensions, one more reason for tax evasion was not declaring the real wage. Highly paid workers, who contributed more, were the most discriminated against. Even if they made higher contributions relative to the salary they received, it would not influence their retirement pension, as no overpayment was possible.

---

49   Ibid., 12.
50   Ibid., 13.
51   Ibid.
52   Ibid., 16.

– The prevalence of the public social security market, as the private pension market, although it has been growing over the last decade, still remained weak compared to the public social insurance market.

– Low pension level. As discussed above, the growth of pensions by governments is carried out only in the context of price indexing and not as a pension growth policy.

This situation and issues left unresolved by previous reforms in the social security system led to the necessity of further reforms to the pension scheme in Albania. There is no specific stipulation in the Constitution of Albania for the protection of pensioners, as it has for the protection of other sections of the population (for more, see Article 54 of the Constitution). Meanwhile Article 59 on Social Objectives the Constitution states: "[...] the state, within its constitutional powers and the means at its disposal, and to supplement private initiative and responsibility, aims at: [...] care and help for the aged, orphans and persons with disabilities".[53] This constitutional definition is translated into an obligation for the government and public institutions to structure and protect pensioners. But according to the 2013 Progress Report of the European Commission, one of the most important public policies for pensioners, pension reform, "[...] is not moving ahead due to a lack of political will".[54]

Meanwhile, 2013 was accompanied by the change of political power, and the new socialist government set pension reform as one of its priorities. Initially, a draft for reform was drawn up and presented to interest groups for discussion through the "Pension Policy Document", which was drafted by the Ministry of Social Welfare and Youth with the assistance of the World Bank. The aim is to provide the pension system with stability, efficiency, sustainability and functionality. A year later, the European Commission reached the opinion that "[...] preparations for pension reform have advanced, with basic legislation amended accordingly in July".[55]

Long-term reform of the pension scheme which marked its beginning with Parliament's approval of the Law on Amendments and Amendments to Law No. 7703, dated May 11, 1993 determined that retirement is earned by "insured persons, who have completed no fewer than 15 years of social insurance, are

---

53   The Constitution of the Republic of Albania, approved by referendum on November 22 (Tirana: Albanian Parliament, 1998), 12, https://www.osce.org/albania/41888?download=true (accessed October 23, 2018).

54   Albania 2013 Progress Report, October 16 (Brussels: European Commission, 2013), 34.

55   Ibid.

entitled to retirement when they reach the specified age".[56] Individuals who have less than 15 years of work experience and who do not meet the eligibility criteria for retirement are provided with economic support, called social retirement. The social pension, as a novelty of the reform, does not completely solve the problem of the lost transition generation who, due to the lack of contributions to social security or partial contributions, cannot benefit from a state pension. Three issues were omitted and remain unresolved as far as social retirement is concerned. Firstly, the social benefit is extremely low, only ALL 6,650 per month (or EUR 53). This amount is the legal definition; since then, based on a decision of the Council of Ministers, the social pension has increased as part of price indexation. Thus, in 2018, the Council of Ministers decided "[...] the indexation, at 2.8%, of social pensions, designated in accordance with Law No. 7703, dated May 11, 1993, on Social Insurance in the Republic of Albania, as amended."[57] Secondly, in the circumstance when there is still no definition of a minimum living in Albania, determining the amount of social pension is ungrounded in any scientific or factual indicators. Thirdly, it is obtained at the very high age of 70, while the scheme foresees that in the future, the retirement age for men and women will be 65 years old, so it is does not provide benefits at the age that the law provides as the beginning of pension eligibility. After the implementation of the reform of the pension scheme, the number of social pension beneficiaries has been increasing, which is accompanied by an increase of subsidies from the state budget (Table 3.5). This is because this item is funded entirely by the state budget, so this needs to be kept under control. At the same time, we can see from the data that the number of social pension beneficiaries relative to the population over 70 is fairly small. Thus, in 2018, only about 1% of the population over 70 years received this pension.

If we analyze the effectiveness of the reform today in solving the problems cited at the beginning, we can conclude that dependency rate in the period of implementation of the reform and beyond, in the years 2014–2018 the number of contributors and pensioners has fluctuations, bringing about a decrease in the dependency rate, which expressed as a ratio between the number of contributors and the number of pensions continued to be in critical condition and by the end of 2018 we have 1.24 contributors per one pensioner from 0.98 contributors per one pensioner, which was in 2013 (Table 3.3). Moreover,

---

56   Law No. 104, on Some Changes and Supplements in Law No. 7703, November 5, 1993, on Social Security in the Republic of Albania, Amended (Tirana: Albanian Parliament, 2014), 3, Article 31.

57   Decision No. 348 on The indexing of Pension, Article 1/b, June 12 (Tirana: Council of Ministers, 2018).

TABLE 3.5   Indicators of social pensions

Description	Units	Years			
		2015	2016	2017	2018
Population over 70 years old*[a]	in No.	245,234	250,477	258,141	267,172
Beneficiaries of social pension**	in No.	n/a	2,412[b]	2,589[c]	2,632[d]
Social pension expense**	(in mln ALL)	99[e]	140[f]	155[g]	172[h]

* Population is on January 1.** Selected data are on December 31 of the previous year.

[a] Popullsia, Albanian Institute of Statistics, 2019, http://www.instat.gov.al/al/temat/treguesit
-demografik%C3%AB-dhe-social%C3%AB/popullsia/#tab2 (accessed April 7, 2019).

[b] "Raport vjetor 2016" (Tirana:[National] Social Insurance Institute, 2016), 40, http://www.issh
.gov.al/wp-content/uploads/2017/10/raporti_vjetor_2016.pdf (accessed April 7, 2019).

[c] "Raport vjetor 2018"(Tirana: [National] Social Insurance Institute, 2018), 56, http://www.issh.gov
.al/wp-content/uploads/2019/09/raport2018.pdf (accessed April 7, 2019).

[d] Ibid.

[e] Raport vjetor 2015 (Tirana: [National] Social Insurance Institute, 2015), 54, http://www.issh.gov
.al/wp-content/uploads/2014/02/raportit-vjetor-shqip.pdf (accessed April 7, 2019).

[f] Raport vjetor 2016 (Tirana: 2016: [National] Social Insurance Institute), 50, http://www.issh.gov
.al/wp-content/uploads/2017/10/raporti_vjetor_2016.pdf (accessed April 7, 2019).

[g] Raport vjetor 2018 (Tirana: [National] Social Insurance Institute, 2018), 38, http://www.issh.gov
.al/wp-content/uploads/2019/09/raport2018.pdf (accessed April 7, 2019).

[h] Raport vjetor 2018 (Tirana: [National] Social Insurance Institute, 2018), 37, http://www.issh.gov
.al/wp-content/uploads/2019/09/raport2018.pdf (accessed April 7, 2019).

SOURCE: OWN ELABORATION BASED ON DATA FROM NATIONAL SOCIAL INSURANCE INSTI-
TUTE AND ALBANIAN INSTITUTE OF STATISTICS.

the high number of pension beneficiaries is intended to be kept under control
by increasing the retirement age for both women and men, which by 2056 is
predicted to be 67 years for both sexes. One of the reasons for this increase in
the retirement age is the increase in life expectancy. In 2018, the average time
of pension enjoyment was 19.9 years for men and 26.1 years for women, rising
from 19.2 years for men and 24.2 years for women in 2013 (Table 3.3).

The rate of coverage of contributors to retirement compared to the labor
force in 2018, only 36.68% of K-Albanians are included in the social insurance scheme, from 25.8% in 2013 (Table 3.6). Thus, in the five years of pension reform, there has been an increase in the rate of coverage of contributors

TABLE 3.6   Population vs. contributors in Albania, 2014–2018

Description	Units	Years					
		2013	2014	2015	2016	2017	2018
Population*[a]	In No.	2,892,394	2,885,796	2,875,592	2,876,591	2,870,324	2,862,427
Labor force*[b]	In No.	1,979,307	1,977,828	1,976,078	1,976,530	1,974,207	1,965,783
Contributors[c]	In No.	510,747	608,519	668,614	661,655	694,411	721,160
Coverage rates	In %	25.80	30.76	33.83	33.47	35.17	36.68

* On December 31.

[a] Popullsia, Albanian Institute of Statistics, 2019, http://www.instat.gov.al/al/temat/treguesit-demografik%C3%AB-dhe-social%C3%AB/popullsia/#tab2 (accessed April 7, 2019).

[b] Punësimi dhe papunësia, Albanian Institute of Statistics, 2019, http://www.instat.gov.al/al/temat/tregu-i-pun%C3%ABs-dhe-arsimi/pun%C3%ABsimi-dhe-papun%C3%ABsia/#tab2 (accessed April 10, 2019).

[c] Raport vjetor 2018 (Tirana: [National] Social Insurance Institute, 2018), 41.

SOURCE: OWN ELABORATION BASED ON DATA FROM NATIONAL SOCIAL INSURANCE INSTITUTE AND ALBANIAN INSTITUTE OF STATISTICS.

versus the labor force from 1/4 to 1/3. This indicates that the reform has yielded a positive effect, but it is also indicative of the continuity of the problem in the social security scheme.

The remaining 63.32% of Albanians who are not included in the scheme risk being left without pension when they reach retirement age unless they are addressed and offered employment policies. This means that they could return to the contingent to benefit from a social pension in the future, which would make it even more difficult to operate the pension scheme. This situation may continue to be problematic if we consider that demographic studies, including those of the United Nations, anticipate a rapid aging of the Albanian population, which increases the number of people who will want a full pension, partial or social. Thus, according to a study conducted by the United Nations, in 2015 the population aged 60 or over was 515,000 or 17.8% of the population, in 2030, the population aged 60 or over is projected to be 752,000 or 25.5%, and in 2050, the population aged 60 or over will be 838,000 or 30.9% of the population.[58]

58   World Population Ageing (New York: United Nations, 2015), 124, http://www.un.org/en/development/desa/population/publications/pdf/ageing/WPA2015_Report.pdf (accessed November 2, 2018).

According to the same report, the causes of "population aging accelerated as a result of international migration".[59] Growth in the third-generation population automatically leads to an increase in the retirement age and the decline of the labor force, which results in reduced contributions, increased spending, and a greater gap between them.

Regarding income and expenditure, although direct incomes have been rising and retirement spending has been decreasing, again the state subsidy to the pension scheme remains high, which means that the scheme continues to be unbalanced and directly dependent on the state budget. The other observation is urban pension ahead of the rural pension. In 2018 the number of rural contributors was 8.17% of total contributors, while the number of rural retirees is 22.19% of total pensioners; the average time of pension enjoyment by both males and females in rural areas is greater compared to urban ones, which makes rural retirees the greatest beneficiaries of the pension scheme. Meanwhile, the average pension rate in rural areas continues to be less than half of the pension in urban areas, the average rural retirement rate is 55% of the urban average. Beside this the change in the pension measure was estimated. The reform of the pension scheme brought a fundamental change in the assessment of the pension provision in Albania. Since 1958, the pension was calculated as 75% of the average net salary of three consecutive years in the last 10 years of work (chosen were the three years with the highest salary). While with the new law, the old-age pension measure consists of a base amount and a supplement through contributions.[60] Specifically, the old-age pension will never be lower than the social pension. This new calculation made it impossible for us to have a maximum pension. There is a need to emphasize the low level of pensions. Even after the reform, pension growth has continued to be only through price indexing. But what is to be noted as a concern is the fact that excluding the first year of implementation of the reform, 2015, the average new pension provision overall dropped from ALL 16,538 in 2014 to ALL 14,449 in 2018. One of the underlying reasons is the significant reduction of the average pension for women (Table 3.7). Meanwhile, the retirement age for men (category I) by the end of 2014 was 60 years and 6 months, with 35 years of working, while for women it was 55 years and 6 months and 35 years of working. At the end of 2018, the age for men to retire (category I) was 62 years and 6 months, with a number of work

---

59   Ibid.
60   Law No. 104 on Some changes and supplements in Law, No. 7703, November 5, 1993, on Social Security in the Republic of Albania, Amended, July 31 (Tirana: Albanian Parliament, 2014), Article 18.

TABLE 3.7   The average new pension rate, 2012–2018

Description	Units	Years						
		2012	2013	2014	2015	2016	2017	2018
Average new pensions (men)	In ALL	14,810	15,367	16,804	18,862	15,958	15,961	15,838
Average new pensions (women)	In ALL	15,314	15,851	16,721	18,044	13,083	12,982	12,808
Average new pension provision (total)	In ALL	15,014	15,580	16,538	18,549	14,497	14,443	14,449

SOURCE: OWN ELABORATION BASED ON DATA FROM NATIONAL SOCIAL INSURANCE INSTI-TUTE, HTTP://WWW.ISSH.GOV.AL/ (ACCESSED APRIL 10, 2019) AND ALBANIAN FINANCIAL SUPERVISORY AUTHORITY, HTTP://WWW.ISSH.GOV.AL/?PAGE_ID=75 (ACCESSED APRIL 10, 2019)

years of 36 years and 4 months; and for women it was 57 years and 6 months and 35 years of working.[61] So the age to retire and number of years at work has increased, while new pensions have come down, which indicates a negative effect of the reform in this regard.

As a solution to the aging population, declining labor force and declining employment by the World Bank could be: "Making better use of available human capital could also help mitigate the fiscal burden of higher pensions and increased health spending on an aging population".[62] The comprehensive analysis of the pension scheme reform allows to point out the following advantages and disadvantages presented in Table 3.8.

During the period following the implementation of the pension reform 2014–2018, the working-age population of 15–64 years of age has undergone

61   Ibid., 29–31.
62   Western Balkan Labour Market Trends 2018, March (Word Bank Group and the Vienna Institute for International Studies Economic, 2018), 2, https://www.worldbank.org/en/region/eca/publication/labor-trends-in-wb (accessed November 2, 2018).

TABLE 3.8   Advantages and disadvantages of the pension scheme reform

Advantages	Disadvantages
– increase in direct contributions through increasing contributions to urban areas and increasing the number of urban contributors, which has led to lower funding from the state budget. – abolition of the maximum pension limitation, which was previously set at double the minimum pension. This innovation can stimulate the declaration of real wages to be able to benefit even more from the pension, which can also lead to a reduction in the scheme's deficit. – reducing the difference between the urban and rural pension by increasing the retirement contributions in rural areas. – the calculation of pensions on the basis of a number of years at work and contributions paid over the years. – increase in the retirement age for both men and women, which leads to a reduction in the number of new pensioners.	– increase in retirement expenditures. – the number of contributors in rural areas has increased very rapidly and since 2014 has decreased more than two times, while the number of retirees from urban areas has been increasing. – at the end of 2018, there were 0.52 rural contributors to one rural pensioner or one rural contributor to 1.93 rural pensioners (there are 58,940 rural contributors and 113,763 rural retirees). This situation has not only exacerbated the problems of the pension scheme, but has created a significant disparity with urban contributors, as we have 1.66 urban contributors to one urban retiree, or one urban contributor to 0.60 urban retirees (we have 662,220 urban contributors and 398,744 urban retirees).

SOURCE: OWN ELABORATION.

significant changes. The number of this population has fallen year by year by an average of 2,409 individuals per year.[63] Significant working-age population

63   Popullsia, Albanian Institute of Statistics, 2019, http://www.instat.gov.al/al/temat/ treguesit-demografik%C3%AB-dhe-social%C3%AB/popullsia/#tab2 (accessed April 7, 2019).

decline is visible in the following groups: 15–24 years by 61,528 individuals and 40–54 years by 39,032 individuals. Meanwhile for the 60–64 age group there has been an increase of the population by 30,174 individuals.[64] These major changes in the working age groups pose difficulties to the current pension scheme because it creates opportunities for reducing the number of contributors. This has led to a significant increase in the number of pensioners in a few years, while the number of contributors is also significantly reduced.

In the same period, we conclude that the number of people over 65 who are of retirement age has increased, by an average of 8,792 individuals per year.[65] This makes the revision of the pension scheme a necessity, as the constant increase of the deficit exacerbates the state budget. Moreover, in a low-growth economy, the continued financing of the pension scheme from the budget is likely to produce subsidizing difficulties. These may occur as producing the government's "obligation" from public revenues to consistently spend significantly on the social security scheme, as well as reducing expenditures on other budget items. Additionally, preventing and slowing down the strengthening of the independence of the public social security market and affecting the maintenance of direct dependence on the government budget. Finally, maintaining low-value pensions and increasing their growth only through price indexation.

To stabilize the pension scheme, it is necessary to deepen pension reform in two key directions:

- encouraging real wage declaration by employees, in order to increase the volume of direct contributions;
- including a higher number of rural contributors in the pension scheme because there is a very low number of contributors from rural areas. Thus, by the end of 2018, there are 58,940 contributors in rural areas, compared to 662,220 contributors in urban areas, or only 8.4% of the total contributors are from rural areas.

At the same time, it is essential to review the criteria for obtaining a social pension, which if it is not kept under constant control, may pose a risk to the solution for the pension-free population, as it may return to boomerang back to the pension scheme. This is because the law foresees as beneficiaries any Albanian citizen over 70 years of age who has no income or whose income is smaller than the social security measure. But the law does not foresee, for example state provision for Albanian citizens over 70 years of age who have no income or income is smaller than the social security measure, but

---

64   Ibid.
65   Ibid.

who also own more assets than a residential house, for example agricultural land.[66]

8   Conclusion

The key word for a sustainable pension scheme is its management. The functioning and stabilization of the pension scheme in Albania requires significant changes. First of all, an increase in direct contributions from urban and rural workers, which can be achieved through increasing the number of contributors through the reduction of informality, reduction of evasion, reduction of emigration mainly to young people, or opening up new jobs, the addition of new items to income, which would serve as a new flow into the scheme, and cost reduction, which is achieved through good financial management.

The pension scheme in Albania is not sustainable due to the low number of contributors compared to the labor force and the number of pensioners in Albania, resulting in a low contributor/pensioner ratio. Other reasons are the failure of pension reform in rural areas, because of a low number of contributors and consequently, very low contributions to the scheme from this population group, as well as the non-inclusion of private pensions in the state pension scheme. Finally, the avoidance of real wage declaration by employers and the employees. Therefore, this study allowed to conclude that the stability of the pension scheme in Albania is directly influenced by the number of contributors in the scheme, the value of the direct contributions that flow into the pension scheme and the number of pensioners who benefit from the pension.

The government's public policies for pensions in Albania cannot be seen in isolation from economic development, fiscal policies, and social policies in the country. Their harmonization today will help to avoid profound financial and social problems tomorrow. As a country with high and sustainable growth rates, fiscal policy in favor of business development, professional public administration, social policies that support vulnerable groups, and formalization of the economy will bring more new jobs, more income for the individual and society will result in an increase in the number of contributors, direct contributions, to private pension funds. This would not only reduce the necessity for funding from the state budget, but may even boost savings for the voluntary private pension fund.

---

66   Law No. 104 on Some Changes and Supplements in Law No. 7703, November 5, 1993, on Social Security in the Republic of Albania, Amended, Article 4, dated July 31 (Tirana: Albanian Parliament, 2014).

As one of the weaknesses of 2014 pension reform was to reduce the number of contributors in rural areas, which also led to a reduction in direct contributions from this part of the population, it is recommended that the reform be deepened by strengthening the agricultural sector, self-declarations and contribution payments, as in 2016, on average 40.2% of the employed in the country are in the agricultural sector[67] and in 2017 employed in agriculture private sector are 453,383 or 39.95% of those employed in Albania.[68] If this decline does not stop, a worsening of the pension scheme is at risk, as all individuals who do not receive a pension today and tomorrow, but who have reached the age of 70, under the law will receive a social pension even if they have not paid contributions. In order to avoid this potential economic and social problem, it is recommended that individuals residing in villages be required to pay a fixed monthly fee.

For the benefit of pensions, two categories of contributions are applied, namely compulsory public contributions and voluntary private contributions. These pension contributions are totally different from one another, both in their collection and management. Compulsory pension contributions are paid by the employee, the employer and the self-employed on the basis of a fixed percentage set by law and administered by the Social Insurance Institute, which is an independent public institution[69] but does not generate income from the collected contributions because contributions that are collected today are used to pay pensions today.

The opposite is the case with private contributions, which are voluntary and are managed by private companies, whose income is collected as a contribution to private retirement, investing today by generating income through which insurance companies are willing to pay tomorrow to their members a higher pension than the state pension. Awareness of the payment of a voluntary pension by high salaried employees, which would help them enjoy a better pension in the future, would capitalize more income that would serve as a source of investment in capital markets, therefore they should be classified by the individuals themselves as long-term investments for a better life in

---

67   INSTAT, "Labor Market" (Tirana, 2017), 19, http://www.instat.gov.al/media/1695/labour-market-2016.pdf (accessed November 5, 2019).

68   INSTAT, "Employed by Administrative Source and Agriculture Sector, Q.4.2015–Q.4.2018" (Tirana, 2019), 1, http://www.instat.gov.al/al/temat/tregu-i-pun%C3%ABs-dhe-arsimi/ t%C3%AB-dh%C3%ABna-administrative-t%C3%AB-tregut-t%C3%AB-pun%C3%ABs/ #tab2 (accessed November 8, 2019).

69   Law No. 9377 on Some Changes and Supplements in Law No. 7703, November 5, 1993, on Social Security in the Republic of Albania, Amended, April 21, Article 26 (Tirana: Albanian Parliament, 20015).

old age. Therefore, it is recommended that the pension scheme be included as a compulsory contribution to the private pension, so that we can have a more stable and stronger scheme.

Two pillars currently operate in Albania, the first through contributions to the state pension fund and the third pillar through voluntary contributions to private pension funds. In order to strengthen the pension scheme, to increase the value of the pension and at the same time to reduce the financing from the state budget in the scheme, it is recommended that a second pillar be applied through the inclusion in the pension system of compulsory insurance payments in private pension funds and the creation of a forced private system, contributions that are mandatory. This payment would help the contributor from retirement age to receive a higher pension than the state pension, but at the same time would directly affect the consolidation of the pension scheme in Albania. Strengthening the third pillar would also increase the credibility of the private pension system.

Bibliography

Albania 2013 Progress Report, October 16, 2013. Brussels: European Commission, 2013.

Albanian Financial Supervisory Authority, Registry of Licensed Persons/ Entities: Voluntary Pension Fund Market. Tirana: Albanian Financial Supervisory Authority, 2011. Accessed September 13, 2018. http://amf.gov.al/tfp_shoqeri.asp.

Annual Report. Tirana: Albanian Financial Supervisory Authority, 2018. Accessed October 12, 2018. http://amf.gov.al/pdf/publikime2/raport/RaportiVjetor2017_2.pdf.

Banka e Shqipërisë. Kursi zyrtar i këmbimit. Tirana, 2019. Accessed April 6, 2019. https://www.bankofalbania.org/Tregjet/Kursi_zyrtar_i_kembimit/.

Decision No. 348 on The Indexing of Pension. Tirana: Këshilli i Ministrave – Council of Ministers, 2018.

Decision No. 399 on The Definition of Minimal Wage Nationwide. Tirana: Këshilli i Ministrave – Council of Ministers, 2017.

Departmenti i Administratës Publike, 100 vjet Administratë, no. 12–14. Tirana: Departmenti i Administratës Publike, 2012. Accessed November 25, 2019. http://dap.gov.al/images/revistat/revista12.pdf.

Dokumenti i Politikave të Pensioneve, 11 prill 2014. Tirana: Ministria e Mirëqënies Sociale dhe Rinisë, 2014.

INSTAT. "Employed by Administrative Source and Agriculture Sector, Q.4.2015–Q.4.2018". Tirana, 2019. Accessed November 8, 2019. http://www.instat.gov.al/al/temat/tregu-i-pun%C3%ABs-dhe-arsimi/t%C3%AB-dh%C3%ABna-administrative-t%C3%AB-tregut-t%C3%AB-pun%C3%ABs/#tab2.

INSTAT. "Labor Market". Tirana, 2017. Accessed November 5, 2019. http://www.instat .gov.al/media/1695/labour-market-2016.pdf.

Law No. 10197 on Voluntary Pension Funds. Tirana: Albanian Parliament, 2009.

Law No. 104 on Some Changes and Supplements in Law No. 7703, November 5, 1993, on Social Security in the Republic of Albania, Amended. Tirana: Albanian Parliament, 2014.

Law No. 129 on Civil Pensions. Tirana: Albanian Parliament, 1927.

Law No. 4171 on Pensions of the City. Tirana: Albanian Parliament, 1966.

Law No. 528 on Social Security of Servants and Functionaries. Tirana: Albanian Parliament, 1947.

Law No. 7703 on Social Security in Albanian Republic, Amended. Tirana: Albanian Parliament, 1993.

Law No. 7943 on Supplements Pensions and Private Institute of Pensions, Amended. Tirana: Albanian Parliament, 1995.

Law No. 9377 on Some Changes and Supplements in Law No. 7703, November 5, 1993, on Social Security in the Republic of Albania, Amended, dated April 21. Tirana: Albanian Parliament, 2015.

Luzo, Drita. Drejt qëndrueshmërisë së sistemit të pensioneve në Shqipëri. Tirana: University of Tirana, 2017.

National Social Insurance Institute. Accessed April 10, 2019. http://www.issh.gov.al/.

Petraj, Ina. "Private Pensions in Albania: The Need of a Reform According to the European Standards". Academic Journal of Interdisciplinary Studies 2, no. 2 (2013): 237–242. Accessed August 10, 2018. http://www.mcser.org/journal/index .php/ajis/article/viewFile/384/400.

"Popullsia". Albanian Institute of Statistics, 2019. Accessed April 7, 2019. http://www .instat.gov.al/al/temat/treguesit-demografik%C3%AB-dhe-social%C3%AB/ popullsia/#tab2.

"Punësimi dhe papunësia". Albanian Institute of Statistics, 2019. Accessed April 10, 2019. http://www.instat.gov.al/al/temat/tregu-i-pun%C3%ABs-dhe-arsimi/ pun%C3%ABsimi-dhe-papun%C3%ABsia/#tab2.

"Raport vjetor 2015". Tirana: [National] Social Insurance Institute. Accessed April 7, 2019. http://www.issh.gov.al/wp-content/uploads/2014/02/raportit-vjetor-shqip. pdf.

"Raport vjetor 2016". Tirana: [National] Social Insurance Institute. Accessed April 7, 2019. http://www.issh.gov.al/wp-content/uploads/2017/10/raporti_vjetor_2016. pdf.

"Raport vjetor 2018". Tirana: [National] Social Insurance Institute. Accessed April 7, 2019. http://www.issh.gov.al/wp-content/uploads/2019/09/raport2018.pdf.

Rreth Sigal Uniqa. Tirana: Sigal Uniqa Group Austria, 2018. Accessed November 14, 2018. http://sigal.com.al/rreth-kompanise/#.

Selita, Mirela. Një vështrimmbi historikun e Sigurimeve Shoqërore në Shqipëri. Tirana: Albanian Institute of Statistics, 2001, Accessed November 25, 2019. http://www.issh.gov.al/?p=10013.

Statistics. Voluntary Private Pension Market, December 31, 2019. Tirana: Albanian Financial Supervisory Authority, 2018. Accessed April 6, 2019. http://amf.gov.al/statistika.asp?id=3&s=2.

Statistika të Sigurimeve Shoqërore. Tirana: Albanian Institute of Statistics, 2015. Accessed December 2, 2019. http://www.issh.gov.al/wp-content/uploads/2014/02/Perb_12_15.pdf.

Statistika të Sigurimeve Shoqërore viti 2018. Tirana: Instituti i Sigurimeve Shoqërore, 2019. Accessed April 5, 2019. http://www.issh.gov.al/wp-content/uploads/2019/04/Statistika_ISSH_2018.pdf.

The Constitution of the Republic of Albania approved by referendum on 22 November 1998. Tirana: Albanian Parliament, 1998.

The Constitution of People's Socialist Republic of Albania Law No. 5506. Tirana: Albanian Parliament, 1976.

Western Balkan Labour Market Trends 2018, March. USA: Word Bank Group and the Vienna Institute for International Studies Economic, 2018. Accessed November 2, 2018. https://www.worldbank.org/en/region/eca/publication/labor-trends-in-wb.

World Population Ageing. New York: United Nations, 2015. Accessed November 2, 2018. http://www.un.org/en/development/desa/population/publications/pdf/ageing/WPA2015_Report.pdf.

PART 2

Pension System: Scheme and Development

∵

CHAPTER 4

The Pension System in Greece

Effrosyni E. Kouskouna and Aspasia Strantzalou

1   Introduction

The pension system (in Greece, but also in most European and other industrialized countries) has proven to be a preferred policy tool for containing state budget spending and for correcting for any economic effects due to the weight of pension spending in governmental budgets, especially in view of population ageing. A series of interventions (from 1992 onwards) improved some aspects of the functioning of the Greek pension system; however, the majority of the exceptional retirement conditions remained as did the high level of pension expenditures. Both were exacerbated by the problems that had already begun to emerge at that time, which became more severe during the period of the economic crisis. During the period of the Memorandums, within the context of fiscal consolidation, a series of reforms were adopted (in Greece, as in most European countries), the majority of which concerned the reduction of pensions paid and the increase in the retirement age. Pension cuts are once again becoming the main tool for cutting public expenditures, since pensions occupy a large part of the state Budget (in 2012, as shown in Greece's bail-out-Memorandum). Evaluation studies of these reforms show that forecasts for the financial viability of the Greek pension system are improving, but further improvements are still needed.[1] This is also evident from the statements by the new government of the country (elected in May 2019) on the creation of a "new insurance framework", which is expected in 2020.

    With these in mind, we are trying to understand and analyze the Greek pension system in terms of its structural development and the many changes it has undergone, in order to exploit the statistical and qualitative data to see

---

1 Pension expenditure as a share of GDP is on the rise from 2003 (11.1% of GDP) to 2012 (17.7% of GDP). Following the 2012 reform pension expenditure is again on the rise from 2013 (16.7% of GDP) to 2017 (just below 18% of GDP). As discussed in section 2, increases in pension expenditure are not only a structural outcome of the system, but also depend on exogenous factors (e.g., GDP growth and the number of new pensioners each year). See Nektarios, Milton and Platon Tinios, "The Greek pension reforms: crises and NDC attempts awaiting completion", World Bank Group Discussion Paper 1906/2019, World Bank Group, April 2019.

whether the public pension system in Greece can remain viable and able to pay adequate pensions in the long run without further major reforms.

In the second section, we briefly critically review the main elements of pension reforms in Greece from the 1990s to today, and we then present (in the third section) key features of its operation (at the end of the 'memoranda era') and, based on statistical data, we make (in the fourth section) an assessment of whether drastic interventions will be required in the future to ensure its viability and its ability to pay adequate pensions in the long run. Finally, before concluding (section 6), we present (in section 5) a brief review of recent reports and studies related to the Greek pension system and its long-term viability.

2   Reforms and Developments of the Greek Pension System in the Most Recent Years

Until the late 2000s, being employed was the prerequisite for being directly covered by social security in Greece, while the affiliation with a scheme mainly depended on the nature and the type of work performed. Social security covered the entire population in the country through self-governed social insurance organizations that operated along three pillars providing main and supplementary/auxiliary insurance and providing lump sum[2] benefits (1st pillar), the occupational-supplementary systems (2nd pillar)[3] and private insurance policies (3rd pillar).[4] The affiliation to a social insurance fund of the 1st pillar remains compulsory for all those employed and those affiliated with them, while, provided that certain prerequisites are met, individuals who become unemployed may also continue their coverage. Social security coverage is

---

2 Lump sum benefits are provided to specific professions (such as civil servants, military staff, engineers, lawyers etc.). The benefit consists of two parts: the first concerns accrued rights up to 31/12/2013 and is calculated based on defined benefit rules for all those affiliated with the relevant funds, while the second part corresponds to accrued rights from 1/1/2014 onwards and is calculated on the basis of notional defined contribution rules.

3 The 2nd pillar is a funded scheme covering all insurance risks. Affiliation with it depends on the nature and the type of work performed. The pension benefits provided by occupational funds are supplementary to the main pension of the 1st pillar. Occupational insurance schemes are not particularly widespread in the country (as reported in PAR 2018, the coverage rate of occupational pension funds is estimated at about 1.3% of the working-age population); in 2018, only 18 occupational pension funds operate providing benefits in kind and in cash (paid as a lump-sum or, in some cases in monthly annuities).

4 Personal or group pension plans of the 3rd pillar are the least developed ones. They operate through individual pension accounts providing an insignificant percentage of the total benefits (about 1%, as reported in PAR 2018).

extended from old age (main and auxiliary pensions, lump sum benefits), survivors and disability (invalidity pensions and other allowances), to family (child benefits and maternity allowances) and sickness protection.

The Greek pension system had been operating as a multi-fund, multi-tier one with numerous rules determining pension benefits and eligibility for them across sectors of employment and occupational categories (consisting of 133 social insurance funds, each with its own legal framework determining eligibility and requirements for receiving a pension as well as the determination of the pension benefit and eligibility for various allowances and additional benefits).

In 1992, the first attempt to unify rules on contributions and benefits was made (law 2084).[5] That harmonization only affected the insured from 1/1/1993 onwards. In 2008, in an attempt to harmonize the regulation governing the take up and calculation of pension benefits and in order to improve administrative efficiency, law 3655[6] reduced the number of social insurance funds (down to thirteen funds) and provisioned a road map towards the harmonization of provisions and entitlements. Nevertheless, the planned harmonization was not actually achieved in practice, since regulations regarding contributions, pension entitlement and pension calculation remained diversified as did the financial administration of the merged funds.

Following the economic crisis of 2008 and in view of the country's high and increasing public debt, coupled with ominous expectations regarding the financial sustainability of the pension system itself, a new reform was introduced in 2010. That reform was justified as[7] "a measure that would contribute to restoring the country's fiscal sustainability and as the only solution for a country in a state of emergency and with no time available".[8] The crucial element in this reform was the change in the structure of the pension system (affecting the prerequisites for pension entitlements planned to be effective from 2013 onwards and the structure and the calculation of pension benefits to be effective from 2015 onwards), together with remarkable pension cuts in an attempt to restrain pension expenditures. It was the first time that a

---

5   Law 2084 of 1992, Amended, https://www.e-nomothesia.gr/kat-ergasia-koinonike-asphalise/
    n-2084-1992.html (accessed September 6, 2019).
6   Law 3655 of 2008, Amended, https://www.e-nomothesia.gr/suntaksiodotika/n-3655-2008.
    html?q=3655 (accessed September 6, 2019).
7   The reform is evaluated in Marina Angelaki and Leonardo N. Carrera, "Greece and Argentina
    Show why Pension Reforms Should Not Be Used as a Quick Fix for a Financial Crisis", https://
    blogs.lse.ac.uk/europpblog/2019/03/01/greece-and-argentina-show-why-pension-reforms-
    should-not-be-used-as-a-quick-fix-for-a-financial-crisis/ (accessed January 14, 2020).
8   Ibid.

non-contributory flat rate pension benefit (the then so-called basic pension) was provisioned for all pensioners, topped up by the contributory part which introduces a closer link between contributions paid during the individual's working life and the pension benefit. The time foreseen for the completion of the transitional period for the implementation of the reforms was long, casting doubt on the financial effectiveness of the measures.

These changes, in conjunction with the unstable economic climate and the increased unemployment rates observed in the country, led many individuals to take advantage of the old (under repeal) retirement options and retire (sometimes early, entitled to reduced pension benefits). Specifically, in one year (from 2009 to 2010) the number of new pensioners increased[9] up to 150%, endangering the pension system's financial stability and introducing unfavorable prospects for future pension adequacy because of the increased number of reduced pension benefits resulting from early retirement.

The effects of the crisis on the financial sustainability of the pension system have been considerable, stemming not only from the increased number of new pensioners (implying increased pension payments at the time and in the future), but also from high unemployment rates and lower wages and salaries (both implying lower social security contributions paid into the system). In addition to these, the implementation in 2012 of the debt restructuring deal via the Private Sector Involvement (PSI) has had a crucial negative impact[10] on social insurance funds (because of the legal obligation to invest their assets in state bonds).

Following an assessment of the economic impact of the legislated reforms in 2012, further attempts to consolidate the system were made in the following years in accordance with the Memorandum of Understanding the country had made with its lenders (the so-called TROIKA)[11] and with the aid of the Organization of Economic Co-operation and Development (OECD), in an attempt to put the country's fiscal and economic performance back on track. Consequently, further reductions in pension benefits were imposed (by means of a new lower and upper ceiling for benefits paid, and by newly applied pension cuts, among other measures). An extension of working lives was attempted by linking the statutory retirement age to demographic and

9   As reported in "Pension Adequacy Report 2018. Current and Future Income Adequacy in Old Age in the EU", Social Protection Committee (1), (Brussels: European Commission, 2018).

10   As stated in the INE-GSEE. Greek Economy and Employment. Annual Reports 2012–2019, https://www.inegsee.gr/ekdoseis/meletes/ekthesi/ (accessed July 30, 2019).

11   i.e., the European Union (EU), the European Central Bank (ECB) and the International Monetary Fund (IMF).

economic developments. A new structure for auxiliary pensions was legislated, which turned the system from a defined benefit (DB) to a self-financed
notional defined contribution (NDC) one, on the basis of individualized pension accounts, ceasing any transfers from the state budget to the system. This
introduced a sustainability factor which would revise existing and future auxiliary pensions on the basis of the amount of revenues from contributions paid
as well as demographic developments.

Successive laws from 2010 to 2016 increased retirement ages significantly by
unifying age thresholds for males and females, by imposing longer career prerequisites and closing paths to early retirement gradually by 2021. Nevertheless, the
situation at the time did not leave much room for labor market activation policies to activate the unemployed and keep the senior workforce active,[12] while the
incentives for the senior workforce not to retire had not been adequate to prevent
retirement/exit from the labor market.

In addition to the above, the framework of arduous and unhealthy occupations, which allowed favorable retirement conditions for those employed in the
related occupations, was amended in 2011 after a long period during which nei-
ther changes nor updates were made. Amendments were made in relation to
which occupations are considered as such,[13] as well as to the retirement conditions. The framework for determining degrees of disability and the conditions
for being eligible for favorable treatment in retirement was also reconsidered in
2011. A major step in this regard was the establishment of KEPA,[14] the Invalidity
Certification Center legislated already in 2010, as the single body to verify degrees
of disability for any individual who might require a certification of disability (with
the exception of similar bodies that retain their competence of verifying disability
for people within the armed forces, and police).

In terms of administrative efficiency and clarity, a computerized system of
databases (HDIKA) was set up in 2013. The ILIOS system records all pensioners
and their characteristics (pension amount, sex, nationality, age etc.), publicly

---

12   As explained in Celine Colin and Bert Brys, "Population Ageing and Sub-Central
Governments: Long-Term Fiscal Challenges and Tax Policy Reform Options," OECD Working
Papers on Fiscal Federalism no 30. November 2019, labor market, health and education policies are crucial in ensuring that the members of workforce have the right skills (no matter
their age), are healthy and do have incentives to actively participate in the labor market.

13   A Committee of experts had determined the arduousness and the list of occupations (61
places of work) included within this scheme, formally set by a Ministerial Decision in
2011, https://bit.ly/3ihMrLY (accessed September 9, 2019).

14   More on KEPA can be found (in Greek), https://www.efka.gov.gr/el/menoy/kentro-
pistopoieses-anaperias-kepa (accessed September 6, 2019).

available at the competent Ministry's web page.[15] ESTIA records the social insurance funds' real estate assets, allowing assessment of the funds' financial situation. In addition, the use of the Social Security Number allocated to each individual who is legally registered in the country for all transactions related to social security and social solidarity issues via the ATLAS system was established in 2014, allowing for cross-checks among social insurance funds and making transactions with public services easier. Measures to combat contribution evasion and undeclared work were enhanced, with the computerization of the registries facilitating the efficiency of the measures taken.

The Social Insurance Debt Collector Center (KEAO) was established in 2013 in order to deal with contribution arrears in the major social insurance funds. Later, in an attempt to increase the collectability of arears, KEAO allowed (in 2015) for a debt repayment agreement in a maximum of 100 installments (for debts exceeding 5,000 euro), progressively reducing the penalties for delays. Subsequent decisions increased the maximum installments for payment of arrears.

Overall, the reforms introduced during the "period of the crisis" aimed at safeguarding and strengthening the financial sustainability of the pension system. Indeed, the result was that pension expenditures were reduced in real terms in the period 2011–2014 (from 27.14 billion euro in 2011 to 24.03 billion in 2014) despite the significant increase of the number of pensioners (by about 130,000 new pensioners per year).[16] Even though the austerity measures have had a remarkable effect on pensions, it is, nevertheless, the case that pensions have played a significant role in cushioning the negative effects of the crisis on pensioners; in 2013 the at-risk-of-poverty rate for pensioners in Greece was 25.4 percentage points lower compared to the rate for the total population. Yet the challenge for the system to achieve adequate pensions still remains.[17]

---

15   Ministry of Employment, Social Security and Welfare, Single Pension Control and Payment System "ILIOS" (Ενιαίο Σύστημα Ελέγχου & Πληρωμών Συντάξεων «ΗΛΙΟΣ»), 2013–2018 Editions, http://www.idika.gr/eseps-mhniaies-ek8eseis (accessed July 30, 2019).

16   The fact that (as reported in the Pensions Adequacy Report of 2015) pension expenditure increased as a percentage of GDP (from 13.02% of GDP in 2011 to 13.21% in 2014, excluding pensions to public servants, which at that time are estimated to 2.9% of GDP) is attributed to the shrinking of GDP during this period.

17   For a more detailed assessment of strengths and weaknesses of the Greek pension system after the reforms introduced, see Maria Petmesidou, "Country Document. Update 2014 Pensions, Health and Long-Term Care, Greece", Analytical Support of the Socio-Economic Impact of Social Protection Reforms, 2013, https://ec.europa.eu/social/BlobServlet?docId=12961&langId=en (accessed June 29, 2019).

A new reform law in 2016 redefines the pension structure and introduces amendments to strengthen the long-term financial sustainability of the pension system and to preserve pension adequacy despite the decreasing replacement rates and the risks due to population ageing, which is projected to increase well above the average increase in the EU.

3   Main Pension Provision

The main pension system currently in place is determined by law 4387 of 2016 as amended in later years, which introduced a comprehensive pension reform regarding the administrative structure of the system as well as the contribution and pension take-up prerequisites. The main pension system provides old-age, invalidity and survivor pensions.[18]

The new law (applied immediately as of May 2016) integrates all social insurance main pension funds, including the former social insurance funds for agricultural workers and for seafarers (which were not affected by previous reforms), into one single social insurance pension fund (the so called EFKA) with a common governance, administration and accounting framework for all. Public servants (whose insurance was previously provided by the state) are also affiliated in EFKA.

This law harmonizes contribution rates and pension benefit rules for all the insured, also affecting the previously accrued rights of both pensioners (except agricultural workers) and active insured (for insured agricultural workers, a fifteen-year transition period is provided) by applying the common pension benefit rules on those as well. It also includes a sustainability clause, which stipulates that if the long-term projections (up to 2060) show a rise in public pension expenditures that exceeds 2.5 percentage points of GDP in reference to the 2009 pension expenditures, then the parameters of the pension system shall adjust in order to bring the increase below the target threshold.

3.1   *Pension Calculation*
The key element for main pension provision is the introduction of a flat-rate pension (financed by the state), which together with the (defined benefit) contributory part (earnings related) form the pension benefit.

---

18   Law 4387 of 2016, Amended, https://www.ilo.org/dyn/natlex/docs/ELECTRONIC/104502/127509/F-285913200/GRC104502%20Grk.pdf (accessed September 6, 2019).

The flat-rate element (called the national pension) is set at 384 euros per month for those who have made at least twenty years of contributions. This amount is decreased by 2.5% for each year of residence below 40 years during their adult life and by 0.5% for each month of age below the statutory retirement age. It is also reduced by 2% for each year the contributory period is below twenty years and up to fifteen years (it reduces to 345.60 euros for fifteen years). Pensioners with two or more pension entitlements by their own right may only receive one national pension.

For pensioners entitled to a disability pension, the national pension is also granted, at a share that depends on their degree of disability (as this is certified by KEPA). Pensioners with a degree of disability above 80% are entitled to 100% of the national pension, for a degree of disability of 67% to 79.9% pensioners receive 75% of the national pension, while lower disability rates (50% to 66.9%) lead to the payment of 50% of the national pension.

For the calculation of the contributory pension part, the system introduces marginally applied accrual rates, with the same profile for all, that depend only on the length of their working/contribution paying career.[19] The new accrual rates are in broad terms lower than those in previous systems. The following Table 4.1 shows the accrual rates, which are applied marginally and not over the entire contributory career.[20]

Pensions are paid monthly (i.e., in 12 monthly payments). Recent legislation of 2019 (Law 4611)[21] provided for a pension-type 13th payment for old-age, invalidity and survivors pensioners (the so-called 13th pension),[22] which was ceased from 2020 under new legislation. For calculating the contributory

---

19 This replaces the previous calculation system which was based on the earnings during the last five years of one's career, making it easier for older workers to accept lower-paid jobs at the end of their career (having no substantial negative effects on their pension benefit). This accrual rate system has been criticized for not providing sufficient incentives for staying active for longer in the labor market (due to the progressivity of the accrual rate at longer career records, but also due to the pension cuts applied to pensioners who take up paid employment).

20 Law 4387 of 2016, Amended, https://www.ilo.org/dyn/natlex/docs/ELECTRONIC/104502/127509/F-285913200/GRC104502%20Grk.pdf (accessed September 6, 2019).

21 Law 4611 of 2019, Amended, https://www.e-nomothesia.gr/kat-oikonomia/nomos-4611-2019-phek-73a-17-5-2019.html (accessed September 6, 2019).

22 The amount of this payment is determined by the amount of the gross monthly main pension (flat rate plus the contributory pension part) or the sum of main pensions on May, 1st of the year in which it is granted, as follows: 100% is paid for main pensions of up to 500.00 euro, for main pensions from 500.01 up to 600 euro 70% is paid, 50% is paid for main pensions of 600.01 up to 1,000 euro and 30% of the main pension is paid when the latter exceeds 1,000 euro.

TABLE 4.1   Statutory accrual rates for the contributory pension component

Years of insurance		Annual accrual rate
From	To	
0	15	0.77%
15.01	18	0.84%
18.01	21	0.90%
21.01	24	0.96%
24.01	27	1.03%
27.01	30	1.21%
30.01	33	1.42%
33.01	36	1.59%
36.01	39	1.80%
39.01+		2.00%

SOURCE: LAW 4387 OF 2016[a].

[a] Law 4387 of 2016, as Amended, https://www.ilo.org/dyn/natlex/docs/ELECTRONIC/104502/127509/F-285913200/GRC104502%20Grk.pdf (accessed September 6, 2019).

component of a pension, the pensionable earnings are derived taking into account the average monthly earnings of the insured for the whole of their insurance life. This average is calculated as the quotient of the remuneration of total earnings divided by the total insurance period. Total earnings are the sum of the monthly earnings subject to contributions throughout the individual's insurance life. For the self-employed, the monthly earnings are the actual income on which contributions have been paid throughout their insurance life; for the period up to the entry into force of law 4387 (of 2016), monthly earnings are the result of dividing the monthly contribution paid (based mainly on insurance classes) by the rate of the contribution. Any payments from social sources in favor of the corresponding funds and any contributions paid by the employer are taken into account on an individual basis. For those who retired by the end of 2016, the pensionable earnings were derived taking into account the monthly earnings of the insured from 2002 until the end of their insurance life. From 2017 onwards this reference period has been increased annually by one year. For those with less than fifteen years of contributions (and who are thus not eligible for a main pension) a flat rate means-tested benefit (360 euro) is provided which constitutes an important social safety net.

A three-year transition period for new retirees (with the exception of farmers) is foreseen, during which a pro-rata pension is granted. Two amounts are calculated, one amount on the basis of the old system and one based on the new system. If the amount resulting from the provisions of the new system is lower than the amount resulting from the old calculation method by more than 20%, then a proportion of the difference is paid as a personal difference to the new retiree. From 2019 onwards, new pensions are calculated based on the new rules for the whole working life of the insured (including also accrued rights up to the adoption of the reform). For farmers, there is a fifteen-year transition period for new retirees, in which a pro-rata pension is granted, as the sum of a decreasing proportion of the old system pension and an increasing proportion of the new system pension.

All main pensions granted up to the entry into force of law 4387 are recalibrated according to the new system's rules, in such a way that each pension benefit consists of three components: the national pension, the contributory pension according to the new rules and the personal difference, which is the difference between the total pension amount according to the old and the new rules. Personal differences that correspond to pensions with a higher pension amount according to the new rules are granted in five installments starting from 2019. Total personal differences corresponding to pensions with a lower pension amount according to the new rules are compensated with a future pension indexation starting from 2023.[23]

The minimum pensionable earnings that may be taken into account equal the minimum wage of an unmarried employee aged over 25 years and the maximum pensionable earnings are ten times the minimum.[24] Hence, until January 31, 2019 the minimum pensionable earnings were 586.08 euro and the maximum 5,860.80 euro, while since February 1, 2019 (after the increase of minimum wages),[25] the minimum pensionable earnings have been 650.00 euro and the maximum 6,500.00 euro. Farmers are exempted from this rule; the minimum pensionable earnings for them are set at 70% of the minimums for other occupations. For the period up to 2020, pensionable earnings are

---

23   Law 4583/2018, Article 1, https://www.e-nomothesia.gr/suntaksiodotika/nomos-4583 -2018-phek-212a-18-12-2018.html (accessed September 6, 2019).

24   These limits indirectly determine the minimum and the maximum pension amounts payable. In 2019, Law 4623 legislated a maximum monthly pension amount of 4,608 euro, Newspaper of the Government of the Hellenic Republic, https://bit.ly/3gi8lMT (accessed September 6, 2019).

25   Ministerial Decision no. 4241/127/30-1-2019, https://bit.ly/34IDeof (accessed September 6, 2019).

valorized by the change in the average annual general consumer price index (CPI), while from 2021 onwards the increase in pensionable earnings is carried out on the basis of the salary change index (which will be formally calculated by the Hellenic Statistical Authority, ELSTAT).

Pension indexation is frozen until 2022; from then onwards it is foreseen that the indexation (for both the national pension and the contributory part) shall equal the minimum of CPI and the sum of 50% CPI and 50% GDP growth.[26]

3.2   *Contributions*

The contribution rate for the main pension (as set by law 4387 of 2016) is 20% for all insured persons (6.67% paid by employees and 13.33% by employers) and all main pension social contribution rates had to gradually be harmonized to this rate.[27] But from January 1, 2019, in order to alleviate the burden for the self-employed and farmers, their contribution rate has been reduced[28]; however, pensionable earnings are still calculated on the basis of the 20% rate.[29]

A provision is made for those who have paid social insurance contributions towards a main pension at a rate higher than 20% of their pensionable salary; the contributory part of their pension benefit will be increased by an additional amount, which is calculated with an annual replacement rate of 0.075% of the pensionable salary (which has been used for the determination of the contributions paid) for each percentage point (1%) of additional contribution.

3.3   *Conditions for Drawing a Main Pension*

The full contributory period is set at 40 years and the minimum at 15 years. The legal unified statutory retirement age is set for all at 67 years, while a minimum age for retirement, at 62, is foreseen for certain cases,[30] including a 40 year insurance payment record, retiring under the scheme of arduous and unhealthy professions or for early retirement (in which case the pension benefit is decreased, depending on the number of years the pensioner is younger than 67; this decrease is permanent). It is possible, under certain conditions and period limitations, to buy-back certain non–contributory periods (including periods of military service, educational leave and child raising leaves)

---

26   Indexation = min{CPI, 50% GDP growth +50% CPI}.
27   EFKA is also financed annually by the state.
28   Law 4578 of 2018, Article 1 and 3, https://bit.ly/3wVDmwN (accessed September 6, 2019).
29   Law 4578 of 2018, Article 7.
30   Details on the prerequisites for all cases may be found at the MISSOC database (www .missoc.org).

or regularized time based on the number of children[31] both for building the required insurance time to draw a pension as well as for calculating the pension benefit.

According to recent legislation, the age thresholds have been re-determined in line with the change in life expectancy of the country's population at the age of 65 years. This comes into effect as of January 1, 2021 and upon its first implementation the change within the 2010–2020 ten-year period will be taken into account. After the first implementation the change in life expectancy will be re-examined every three years.

A pension is awarded to the surviving spouse. Pensions due to the death of a pensioner or an insured individual are paid to surviving spouses, irrespective of their age. The transfer rate of the pension is 70%. After a period of three years, if the survivor is employed or self-employed or receives a pension from any source, fifty percent (50%) of the survivor pension is paid, depending on the length of work or self-employment.[32] A pension, at a rate of 25%, is also awarded to orphans under the condition that they are not married and have not reached the age of 24 (with the exemption of children with severe disabilities). The total amount of the monthly survivor's pension may not be less than the amount of the national pension corresponding to twenty years of insurance i.e., as is currently the case, 384 euros per month. If the deceased's insurance period was less than twenty years, the amount is reduced by 1.25% for each year of insurance below twenty years and up to fifteen years of insurance, i.e., for fifteen years or less, the pension amount is 360 euro per month.[33]

The total amount of the survivor spouse's pension and the orphans' pension may not exceed the amount of the deceased's pension. If the sum of the beneficiaries' percentages exceeds the amount of the pension of the deceased, the proportion of the children is equally reduced.

Current legislation also provides unified eligibility rules for disability pensions based on the degree of disability, provided that an official confirmation of disability has been issued by KEPA. Based on the degree of disability,

---

31   This provision smooths the gender impact on pension up-taking, which would otherwise result to women being entitled to lower pensions having shorter employment careers due to childbirth and caring responsibilities. See Estelle James, Alejandra Cox Edwards and Rebeca Wong, "The Gender Impact of Pension Reform", Journal of Pension Economics and Finance 2, no. 2 (2003): 181–219.

32   Law 4611/2019, Article 19, https://www.e-nomothesia.gr/kat-oikonomia/nomos-4611-2019 -phek-73a-17-5-2019.html (accessed September 6, 2019).

33   Law 4499/2017, Article 1, https://www.e-nomothesia.gr/suntaksiodotika/nomos-4499 -2017-fek-176a-21-11-2017.html (accessed September 6, 2019).

employees who have the minimum required contribution period may[34] be entitled to a full pension (when they have severe disability of at least 80%) or to a lower pension (75% of full pension) in the case of an ordinary disability (with a degree of disability between 67% and 79.9%).

A pension type social allowance is granted to the uninsured elderly (aged at least 67) who do not receive nor are entitled to any pension benefit. This is a means-tested, non-contributory flat rate allowance, currently at 360 euro per month. The uninsured elderly persons are also entitled to a 13th pension (of 360 euro).

4   Auxiliary Pension Provision

The provision of auxiliary pensions began in the 30's on the basis of the legislation governing main pension provision which had already been implemented. Since then, several auxiliary funds were founded in which employees from many different companies and professions have been insured. The majority of the working population was affiliated with an auxiliary pension fund in the 1980s. This resulted in a highly fragmented auxiliary pension system and brought with it, on the one hand, the need to harmonize contribution rates and pension benefit rules (at least for the newly insured) and, on the other hand, the need to drastically reduce the number of auxiliary pension funds in order to improve their organization, their management and financial monitoring of them. Law 2084 of 1992 unified the contribution rates and the pension formulae of the auxiliary pension system for all employees who were first insured from January 1, 1993 onwards. With the pension reform law of 2008, many of the auxiliary funds merged and were incorporated into newly founded ones. As a result, the number of funds was reduced.

The auxiliary pension provision is mandatory for most of the employed and provides old-age, disability and survivor pensions. It operates independently of the main pension provision, though it works parallel to it and is awarded under the prerequisite of receiving a main pension. It is financed separately from the main pension from both the employer and the employee, without any state contribution.

---

34   Law 4387 of 2016, Articles 6 and 27, https://bit.ly/3wOvIEf (accessed September 9, 2019).

4.1 Pension Calculation

Following a reform of the auxiliary pension system, a unified auxiliary pension fund (called ETEAEP) was established recently, incorporating all employees' funds, and introducing[35] a pay-as-you-go (PAYG) notional defined contribution (NDC) system for those insured after 2013. The pension calculation method is the same for all new affiliates.[36]

Auxiliary pensions granted from January 1, 2015 onwards to pensioners who have insurance time before 2014 entail a pro-rata pension calculation method. Pensions in these cases have two components: the first, applied for as many years as the pensioner was insured prior to 2015, is the outcome of the application of the previous defined benefit system with an annual replacement rate of 0.45% and pensionable earnings determined according to the main pension method. The second component is the outcome of the new NDC system applied for the years of insurance after 2014.

All auxiliary pensions already granted before the new reform-law had come into force are recalibrated on the basis of a unified annual replacement rate of 0.45% and – for those cases where the newly calculated pension is lower than the formerly granted pension – it is topped up with a "personal difference" that equals the difference between the resulted pension amount when applying the old and the new rules. Personal differences were completely eliminated starting from the second half of 2016, in cases when the sum of main and auxiliary pension amounts exceeded 1,300 euro.

4.2 Contributions

Contributions to ETEAEP are paid at a gradually decreasing rate, from 7% for the period from June 1, 2016 – May 31, 2019, to 6.5% from June 1, 2019 – May 31, 2022 and 6% from June 1, 2022 onwards. This rate is applied to employee wages and salaries following the same rules applied for the main pension, while for the self-employed the contribution rate is applied to the national minimum wage.

The financial sustainability of the auxiliary pension system is based mainly on the following factors: (i) Contributions paid by affiliates are kept in individual accounts and grow over time depending on the endogenous notional rate of return. This rate of return depends on the year-on-year rate of change

---

35   Law 4052 of 2012, Chapter IA (Articles 35–48), https://www.e-nomothesia.gr/kat-ergasia-koinonike-asphalise/n-4052-2012.html (accessed September 9, 2019).

36   Law 4387 of 2016, Article 85, https://bit.ly/3wOvlEf (accessed September 6, 2019).

(positive or negative) of ETEAEP affiliates' wages[37] (which form the basis for contribution calculation) and is calculated each year. Hence, the rate of return incorporates the demographic factor, the rate of unemployment of the Fund's affiliates and the level of their income from work, also reflecting the country's fiscal state. (ii) Based on the principle of equivalence, the cumulative future value of contributions at the time of pension calculation shall equal the present value of future pension payments.[38] This is based on expectations regarding the insured's life expectancy at the age of pension take-up and a discount rate of 1.3%.[39] (iii) The annual auxiliary pension indexation is determined by the minimum of the CPI and the difference of the rate of change of the affiliates' income/wages and the rate used for discounting future pension payments (1.3%).[40] Finally, (iv) the balancing mechanism is ensured by not applying a pension indexation in case of deficit; any deficits are covered by the Fund's assets.

5   Some Facts

The social security system in Greece, and the pension system in particular, faced remarkable challenges during the economic crisis and the years of austerity. This was, among other things, due to lower wages and increased unemployment rates that resulted in fewer contributions being paid into the system and to more people wishing to retire (sometimes as an early retirement with reduced pension benefits) in order to overcome the burden of unemployment, resulting, however, in an increased pension bill. Pension reductions[41]

---

37   The notional rate of return is the result of the quotient of the difference of the sum the insured's wages from the calendar year (t) to the year (t+1) divided by the sum of wages at year t.

38   The amount of annual pension (Px) is calculated by the following formula,

$$P_{x,t}^{NDC} = AF_x \sum_{j=1}^{a} Con_j \prod_{k=j}^{a} (1+g_k)$$

39   It is noted that the discount rate, which is used for the annuity calculation, is an important factor in the calculation of the amount of a pension at the date of retirement. The choice of the discount rate also directly affects the scheme's equilibrium and it, therefore, has to be a function of the percentage change in pensionable earnings of all the insured with the Fund and the pensions' indexation. This rate has to be an approximation of the net growth rate of contribution base (inflation notwithstanding).

40   Indexation γ= min (CPI, (g-r)), where g is the rate of change of the affiliates' income/wages and r=1.3%.

41   The cumulative impact of the pension cuts within the period 2009–2012 depends on the conditions under which each pensioner retired (such as their age, whether they receive

introduced would in principle set incentives to work longer; nevertheless, the low labor demand, attributed to the effects of the economic crisis that caused high unemployment and long-term unemployment, has hampered this effect. Based on OECD (2018) calculations, the effective age of retirement has declined from 2006 to 2016 for both men and women (by 0.1 percentage points for men and 0.4 for women), while the employment rate for the age group 50–74 has dropped from 34.7% of the group population in 2006 to 31.7% in 2016.

Recent reform measures that have established a closer link between contributions and pension payments and allow restricted access to early retirement paths are expected to extend individuals' working lives and contributory periods (giving an intertemporal boost to contribution payments into the system), shrinking at the same time the length of retirement intertemporally, thus decreasing pension expenditures.

As was shown by the Hellenic National Actuarial Authority Report on the Financial Development of the majority of the main pension system in the period 2015–2060,[42] although demographic projections (to 2060) are expected to remain unchanged (the ratio of pensioners over the insured in 2060 being 73% in both the pre-reform and the after-reform scenario, higher than the 64% ratio of 2015), main pension expenditure is projected to dramatically fall from 11.86% of GDP in 2015 to 9.21% of GDP in 2060 (lower compared to the pre-2015 reform[43] projection of 10.67% of GDP). On the other hand, in the long run of the reform, the contributory pension part is expected to be almost financed by the revenues from contributions, indicating financial sustainability of the system in the long run.

A later Projection Exercise of the Hellenic National Actuarial Authority[44] based on law 4387/2016[45] projects pension contributions (by employers, employees and the state) at a share of 10.8% of GDP in 2070 exceeding the

---

more than one main pension, whether their pension is due to invalidity etc.); nevertheless OECD estimates (2018) that pensioners drawing a total monthly pension (main plus auxiliary) of 900 euro before the crisis had suffered a total loss of 26%, while the corresponding reduction for those on a total monthly pension of 2,100 euro suffered a pension reduction of 34%.

42   Financial Evolution of the Pension System – Projections 2015–2060 – Greek Parliament.

43   Financial Evolution of the Pension System for IKA-ETAM, OAEE, OGA and the Public Sector. Projections 2015–2060, National Actuarial Authority (Athens, April 2016), Section 7, 16.

44   (Hellenic) National Actuarial Authority Greek Pension System Fiche. Ageing Projections Exercise 2018, European Commission. Economic Policy Committee. Ageing Working Group, http://www.eaa.gr/Portals/o/Greek%20Pension%20System%20Fiche%20 ROUND%202015.pdf (accessed September 19, 2019).

45   Note that the difference in the two reports is the result of, among other factors, different assumptions regarding the demographic and macroeconomic development, the assumed

projected gross total pension expenditures (10.6% of GDP in 2070, of which 9.2% relates to main pension and 1.4% relates to auxiliary pension expenditures). Also, from 2026 onwards the contributory part of main and auxiliary pension benefits is financed by employers' and employees' contributions.

The long-term projected pension spending burden resulting from the post-2016 reforms is estimated at around 1.25% of GDP on average (incorporating subsequent pension reforms and taking into account the situation at the time compared to the 2018 Ageing Report estimate). Recent budgetary data show that from 2011 to 2015, pension expenditures exhibit a decreasing trend despite the increasing number of pensioners, while revenues from contributions exhibit an increasing trend (Figure 4.1). Following the remarkable increase in the difference between contributions paid to the social security funds and pension benefits paid by the funds from 2011 to 2012, the gap between contributions and pensions had remained rather unchanged until 2016. After 2016 and despite the increase in employment levels, the discrepancy between contributions and pension payments increased further[46] (possibly due to vast payments of pension arrears made during the period 2016–2018).

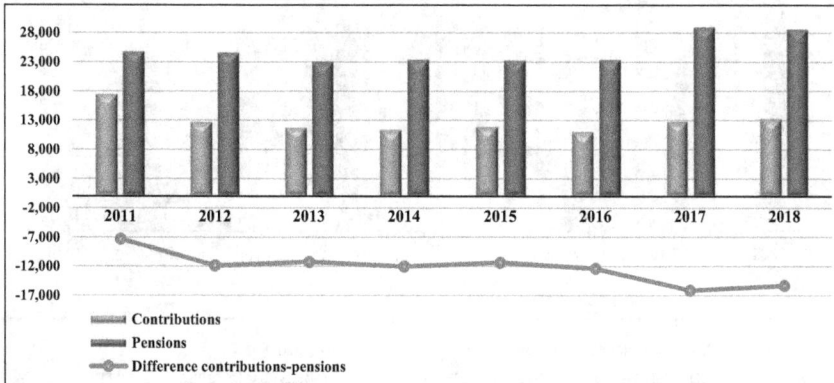

FIGURE 4.1   Pension benefits and contribution payments 2011–2018 (million euro)
SOURCE: UNPUBLISHED DATA FROM THE GREEK MINISTRY OF EMPLOYMENT
AND SOCIAL AFFAIRS, PARTIALLY PUBLISHED BY THE HELLENIC
PARLIAMENTARY BUDGET OFFICE, ELABORATED BY THE AUTHORS.

---

increased pension expenditure in 2016, which is due to a realized further decreased GDP in 2016 and the observed massive retirements.

46   Note that in only one year, pension payments increased from about 23,413 million euros (in 2016) to 28,918 million euro (in 2017); at the same time pension arrears increased from 84 million euro to 511 million.

At the same time (2015–2018), the social security fund budget execution (including grants from the state budget, transfer payments from AKAGE[47] and payments from the special grant to clear arrears) exhibits an improved (small, but positive) balance (Figure 4.2).

According to the projection of the Ageing Report (2018), based on the Eurostat demographic projection,[48] the effect the demographic factor is expected to have on the sustainability of the pension system is hinted at by the fact that the old-age dependency ratio (i.e., the ratio of the population aged at least 65 to the population aged 15–64 years) is expected[49] to increase from 33.4% in 2016 to 63.1% in 2070; that is, 6 in every 10 individuals will be (or will be about to be) pensioners by 2070. This poses financing difficulties for the public pension system. Based on the latest Eurostat[50] demographic projections, the dependency ratio is more favorable for the Greek pension system from 2035 onwards. The next ageing report (round 2021) will be substantiated on Europop 2018.

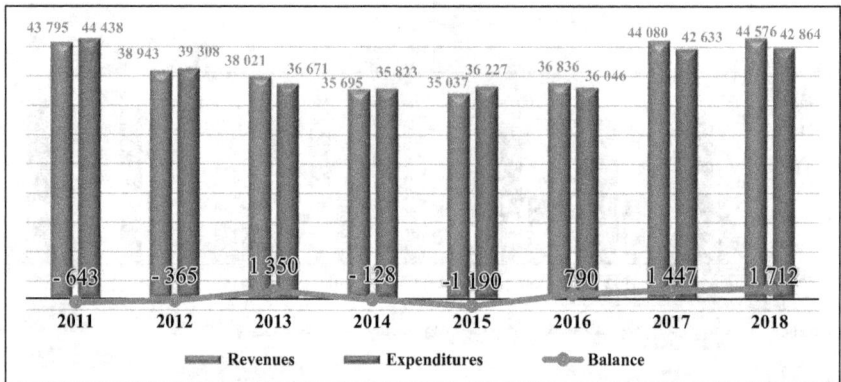

FIGURE 4.2   Social security fund budget execution (million euro)
SOURCE: UNPUBLISHED DATA FROM THE GREEK MINISTRY OF EMPLOYMENT
AND SOCIAL AFFAIRS, PARTIALLY PUBLISHED BY THE HELLENIC
PARLIAMENTARY BUDGET OFFICE, ELABORATED BY THE AUTHORS.

47   AKAGE is a special Intergenerational Solidarity Insurance Account aiming at safeguarding pension benefits.
48   Based on Eurostat's data on population projections of 2015.
49   The 2018 Ageing Report, Economic and Budgetary Projections for the EU Member States (2016–2070), Institutional Paper 079, Economic and Financial Affairs May 2018 (Brussels: European Commission, 2018).
50   Based on Eurostat's data on population projections of 2018.

According to the latest available data from the ILIOS database, the average pension amount (among 2,555,049 pensioners receiving an old-age, invalidity or survivors' pension) in December 2018 was 899.84 euros. At the same time, 1,942,526 pensioners were granted an old-age pension with the average old-age pension benefit being 988.57 euros, the average survivors' pension benefit was 625.57 euros with the number of survivors' pensions being 386,958, while the number of pensioners receiving an invalidity pension were 215,050 and the average invalidity pension benefit was 621.76 euros[51] (Table 4.2). Grouping pensioners on the basis of their age reveals that 59% of pensioners in December 2018 are older than 71 years of age and 37% lie within the age group 51–70. Pensioners aged between 61 and 65 years receive the highest average pension benefits, while, as shown in the following Table 4.2, among pensioners older than 65 years of age the older the pensioner the lower the average pension benefit they receive. This is a result of the continued cuts in pensions during the financial crisis and the non-adjustment of pensions from 2009 to 2023. As issues of pension adequacy may arise gradually and over time, as the Greek economy recovers, the pension system should also be reviewed in this light. Another important element is the asymmetric way in which life-time insurance/contribution records determine pension benefits. Despite the changes in the way the pension benefit is calculated, the generosity of the system favors low earners and those with short contributory periods[52] and may therefore be seen as a disincentive for long careers, putting the system's long-term viability at risk and pension adequacy in doubt.[53]

Migration flows to Greece could possibly help maintain the active population (since it is expected by ELSTAT that they contribute to keep the average age of the population at lower levels) and, provided that migrants are smoothly integrated into society and the labor market, they could help maintain the pension system's ability to provide adequate pensions in the long run (Figure 4.3).

---

51   Average pension benefits in December 2018 are higher compared to December 2017, when the average old-age pension benefit was 979.52 euros paid to 1,967,976 pensioners, the average survivors' pension benefit was 625.73 for 392,237 pensioners and the average invalidity pension benefit was 619.34 paid to 220,178 pensioners. See Ministry of Employment, Social Security and Welfare, Single Pension Control and Payment System "ILIOS" (Ενιαίο Σύστημα Ελέγχου & Πληρωμών Συντάξεων «ΗΛΙΟΣ»), 2013–2018 Editions, http://www.idika.gr/files/ΔΕΚΕΜΒΡΙΟΣ_2018.pdf (accessed September 6, 2019).

52   Also discussed in Milton Nektarios and Tinios Platon, "The Greek Pension Reforms: Crises and NDC Attempts Awaiting Completion".

53   Ministry of Employment, Social Security and Welfare, Single Pension Control and Payment System "ILIOS".

TABLE 4.2   Number of pensioners and average pension benefits by age groups

Age	Number of pensioners	Average monthly pension benefit (€)
< 25	28,318	365.43
26–50	62,574	670.11
51–55	74,572	907.58
56–60	162,698	1,049.61
61–65	312,543	1,114.40
66–70	414,671	1,054.53
71–75	455,213	929.06
76–80	385,095	821.74
81–85	354,984	760.52
86–90	213,613	706.46
91–95	74,547	691.05
> 95	15,606	672.62
TOTAL	2,555,049	899.84

SOURCE: ILIOS, DECEMBER 2018.
[a] Ministry of Employment, Social Security and Welfare, Single Pension Control and Payment System "ILIOS".

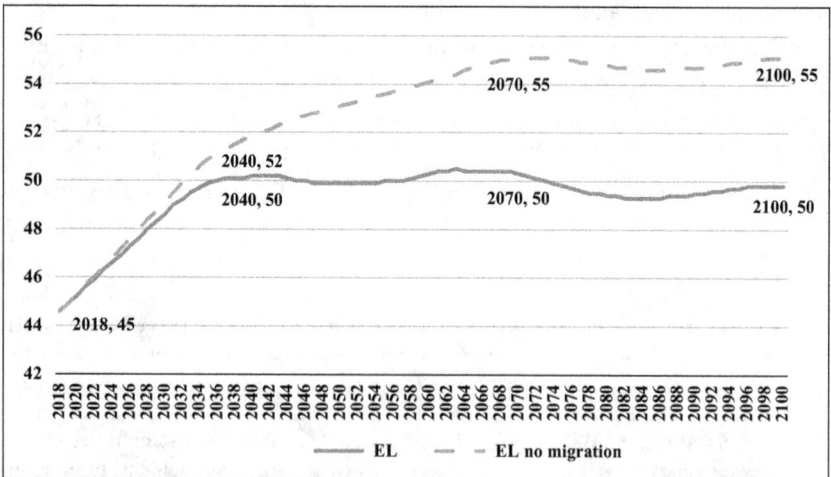

FIGURE 4.3   Average age of the population in Greece with and without migration flows
SOURCE: EUROSTAT (GREECE) "POPULATION ON 1ST JANUARY BY AGE, SEX AND TYPE OF PROJECTION", HTTPS://EC.EUROPA.EU/EUROSTAT/DATABROWSER/VIEW/PROJ_19NP/DEFAULT/TABLE?LANG=EN (ACCESSED JULY 8, 2019).

6   Conclusion

Despite the pension reforms in the last decade in Greece and despite the fact that there are still challenges regarding the pension system's financial sustainability and the future adequacy of pensions, maintaining the financial viability of the pension system and its ability to pay adequate pensions[54] in the long run seems attainable.

The escalation of legal claims for the reversal of past pension cuts and the recent court decisions pose a potentially significant financial burden for the pension system as well as a possible fiscal risk for the economy as a whole.

Besides, the main concern regarding the pension system lies with the demographic factor, given that Greece exhibits a high rate of population ageing (the old-age dependency ratio was expected in 2018[55] to double, from 35.8% in 2016 to 76.3% in 2056), although the most recent Eurostat[56] projections (of 2019) expect a (milder) increase to 62.6% in 2056 and 61.1% in 2100, allowing for a smoother operation of the pension system in the long-run.

Other issues, including undeclared work and low activity rates in the labor market, should also be given attention, despite the efforts in recent years to contain their effects, be it via stricter controls and improved administrative efficiency, or by the implementation of active labor market policies that would increase female labor participation and active ageing for all.

Consolidating the pension system by adopting policy interventions targeting various aspects that affect its fairness, its ability to grant adequate pensions in the future, as well as its financial sustainability is at the center of the new government's announced policies including changes to be imposed by the courts. What remains to be seen is how such announcements will be implemented and how the (exogenous to the pension system) uncertainties regarding the investment returns of pension savings due to the risk of inflation, the capital market fluctuations and the high cost of savings' management will be dealt with. An element that must not be ignored is the reaction of the employed against more pension reforms to the Greek pension system

---

54   For a discussion on whether EU member states can achieve pension adequacy and pension safety see Anne-Sophie Parent, "Can the EU Achieve Adequate, Sustainable and Safe Pensions for All in the Coming Decades?" Pensions International Journal 16, no. 3 (2011): 168–174.

55   Pension Adequacy Report 2018.

56   Eurostat, Projected Old-Age Dependency Ratio, https://appsso.eurostat.ec.europa.eu (accessed October 10, 2019).

and whether people's decision on when to retire would pose financial burdens on the system.

Bibliography

Angelaki Marina, and Leonardo N. Carrera. "Greece and Argentina Show why Pension Reforms should not Be Used as a Quick Fix for Financial Crisis". Accessed January 14, 2020. https://blogs.lse.ac.uk/europpblog/2019/03/01/greece-and-argentina-show-why-pension-reforms-should-not-be-used-as-a-quick-fix-for-a-financial-crisis/.

Colin, Celine, and Bert Brys. Population Ageing and Sub-Central Governments: Long-Term Fiscal Challenges and Tax Policy Reform Options. OECD Working Papers on Fiscal Federalism no 30. November 2019.

EFKA. Accessed September 6, 2019. https://www.efka.gov.gr/el/menoy/kentro-pistopoieses-anaperias-kepa.

Eurostat. Projected Old-Age Dependency Ratio. Accessed October 10, 2019. https://appsso.eurostat.ec.europa.eu.

Eurostat. (Greece) Population on 1st January by Age, Sex and Type of Projection. Accessed July 8, 2019. https://ec.europa.eu/eurostat/databrowser/view/proj_19np/default/table?lang=en.

Hellenic Parliamentary Budget Office. Quarterly Reports 2018–2019. Accessed January 14, 2020. http://www.pbo.gr/Δημοσιεύσεις/Τριμηνιαίες-Εκθέσεις.

(Hellenic) National Actuarial Authority. Financial Evolution of the Pension System for IKA-ETAM, OAEE, OGA and the Public Sector. Projections 2015-2060. Athens, April 2016.

(Hellenic) National Actuarial Authority. Greek Pension System Fiche. Ageing Projections Exercise 2015. European Commission. Economic Policy Committee. Ageing Working Group. Accessed September 19, 2019. http://www.eaa.gr/Portals/0/Greek% 20Pension%20System%20Fiche%20ROUND%202015.pdf.

INE-GSEE. Greek Economy and Employment. Annual Reports 2012–2019. Accessed July 30, 2019. https://www.inegsee.gr/ekdoseis/meletes/ekthesi/.

James, Estelle, Alejandra Cox Edwards, and Rebeca Wong. "The Gender Impact of Pension Reform". Journal of Pension Economics and Finance 2, no. 2 (2003): 181–219. https://doi.org/10.1017/S1474747203001215.

Law 2084 of 1992, Amended. Accessed September 6, 2019. https://www.e-nomothesia.gr/kat-ergasia-koinonikeasphalise/n-2084-1992.html.

Law 3655 of 2008, Amended. Accessed September 6, 2019. https://www.e-nomothesia.gr/suntaksiodotika/n-3655-2008.html?q=3655.

Law 3863 of 2010, Amended. Accessed September 6, 2019. https://www.e-nomothesia.gr/katergasia-koinonike-asphalise/n-3863-2010.html?q=3863.

Law 4052 of 2012. Accessed September 6, 2019. https://www.e-nomothesia.gr/kat
-ergasia-koinonike-asphalise/n-4052-2012.html.

Law 4387 of 2016, Amended. Accessed September 6, 2019. https://bit.ly/3wOvIEf.

Law 4499/2017 (Article 1). Accessed September 6, 2019. https://www.e-nomothesia.gr/
suntaksiodotika/nomos-4499-2017-fek-176a-21-11-2017.html.

Law 4578 of 2018 (Article 1). Accessed September 6, 2019. https://bit.ly/3wVDmwN.

Law 4583/2018 (Article 1). Accessed September 6, 2019. https://www.e-nomothesia.gr/
suntaksiodotika/nomos-4583-2018-phek-212a-18-12-2018.html.

Law 4611 of 2019, Amended. Accessed September 6, 2019. https://www.e-nomothesia
.gr/kat-oikonomia/nomos-4611-2019-phek-73a-17-5-2019.html.

Law 4623. Accessed September 6, 2019. https://bit.ly/3gi8lMT.

Ministerial Decision no. 4241/127/30-1-2019. Accessed September 6, 2019. https://bit
.ly/34IDeof.

Ministry of Employment, Social Security and Welfare. Single Pension Control
and Payment System "ILIOS" (Ενιαίο Σύστημα Ελέγχου & Πληρωμών Συντάξεων
«ΗΛΙΟΣ»). 2013–2018 Editions. Accessed July 30, 2019. http://www.idika.gr/
eseps-mhniaies-ek8eseis.

Mutual Information System on Social Protection. European Commission. Accessed
July 30, 2019. https://www.missoc.org/.

Nektarios, Milton, and Platon Tinios. "The Greek Pension Reforms: Crises and NDC
Attempts Awaiting Completion". World Bank Group Discussion Paper 1906/2019.
World Bank Group, April 2019.

Newspaper of the Government of the Hellenic Republic. Accessed September 6, 2019.
https://bit.ly/3gi8lMT.

Parent, Anne-Sophie. "Can the EU Achieve Adequate, Sustainable and Safe Pensions
for All in the Coming Decades?". Pensions International Journal 16, no. 3
(2011): 168–174.

Pension Adequacy Report 2015. Current and Future Income Adequacy in Old Age
in the EU. Social Protection Committee II. Country Profiles, Brussels: European
Commission, 2015. Accessed January 14, 2019. https://op.europa.eu/en/publication
-detail/-/publication/2a4451ef-6d06-11e5-9317-01aa75ed71a1/language-en.

Pension Adequacy Report 2018. Current and Future Income Adequacy in Old Age
in the EU. Social Protection Committee I. – Country Profiles. Brussels: European
Commission, 2018.

Petmesidou, Maria. "Country document. Update 2014. Pensions, Health and Long-
Term Care, Greece". Analytical Support of the Socio-Economic Impact of Social
Protection Reforms, 2013. Accessed June 29, 2020. https://ec.europa.eu/social/
BlobServlet?docId=12961&langId=en.

Single Pension Control and Payment System "ILIOS" (ΕνιαίοΣύστημα
Ελέγχου&ΠληρωμώνΣυντάξεων «ΗΛΙΟΣ»). Ministry of Employment, Social Security

and Welfare. 2013–2018 Editions. Accessed July 30, 2019. http://www.idika.gr/
    eseps-mhniaies-ek8eseis.
The 2018 Ageing Report. Economic and Budgetary Projections for the EU Member
    States (2016–2070). Institutional Paper 079. Economic and Financial Affairs. May
    2018. (Brussels: European Commission, 2018).

The Current and Future Consistency of the Pension System and Social Security in Romania in the Face of Demographic Changes

Mirela Cristea and Graţiela Georgiana Noja

1 Introduction

Within the social security system, the provision of retirement income as pensions holds a fundamental place and requires special attention and reforms that are introduced to ensure its sustainability, particularly in the context of the difficulties posed by demographic ageing faced by nearly all countries.[1]

In terms of public pensions, most states adopted the social security model introduced in Germany under Chancellor Otto von Bismarck in 1889, through the Old Age and Disability Insurance Law.[2] This pension insurance scheme represents the support provided by the working population (through their social security contributions) to retired people (by covering their pensions) – called the pay–as–you–go (PAYG) system. Given that this system was sustainable by a ratio between pensioners and employees below one (called the old–age dependency ratio), policy makers are seeking to revise/supplement this public pension system, which is linked to the new demographic context, an ageing population. Ageing involves the increasing of life expectancy, while reducing the birth rate, with an impact on the increase of the pensioners to employees dependency ratio, respectively persons within the 65+ age cohorts to the 15–64 age group.[3] Regarding the demographic implications, it is appreciated that "the most underestimated risk is the demographic aging trend of the population +

1 Mihai Daniel Roman, Georgiana Cristina Toma and Gabriela Tuchiluş, "Efficiency of Pension Systems in the EU Countries", Journal for Economic Forecasting 4 (2018): 171.
2 Alexander Hicks, Social Democracy and Welfare Capitalism: A Century of Income Security Politics (New York: Cornell University Press, 2018), 13.
3 Mirela Cristea and Alexandru Mitrică, "Global Ageing: Do Privately Managed Pension Funds Represent a Long Term Alternative for the Romanian Pension System? Empirical Research", Romanian Journal of Political Science 16, no. 1 (2016): 64.

the deficits associated with pension plans and the low level of savings for the years of retirement".[4] In other words, in the long term the PAYG system cannot adequately fulfil the purpose for which it was created, namely to support the payment of current pensioners' pensions from employees' contributions, without affecting their welfare state.

Within this frame of facts, the pension system in Romania faces numerous pitfalls based on the ageing population and mass migration, which make this issue extremely relevant for rigorous scientific research. Moreover, the public pension system in Romania has been modified numerous times, starting in 2001, when different categories of pensions, lengths of service and associated specific conditions were imposed. In this vein Nuta, Zaman and Nuta highlighted that:

> the reform of the Romanian pension system started with the adoption of Law 19/2000, which replaced the former public scheme inherited from the communist period by a new system (Pillar I) based on pension points. Four years later, the Law 411/2004 introduced the second compulsory pillar in the system, which is privately administrated through individual accounts. These initial reforms were completed by the adoption of Law 204/2006, which introduced the third (voluntary) pillar, equally privately administrated.[5]

Hence, the Romanian pension system currently comprises three components (Pillars): Pillar I of public pensions, financed through social security contributions; Pillar II of privately administered pension funds, financed from a certain share of the social security contributions (compulsory for the persons aged less than 35 years, and voluntary for those aged between 35–45 years), introduced in May 2008; and Pillar III of voluntary pension funds, introduced one year earlier than Pillar II (May 2007), in which anyone can contribute with a maximum share of 15% of the gross realized income (with the condition that at least 90 monthly contributions are paid prior to the age of retirement).[6]

4   Ion Stancu, Dragos Haseganu and Alexandra Darmaz-Guzun, "Projections on the Sustainability of the Pension System in Romania", Institute of Financial Studies, no. 28 (2019): 55.

5   Mirela Cristea, Nicu Marcu and Oana-Valentina Cercelaru, "Longer Life with Worsening Pension System? Aging Population Impact on the Pension System in Two Countries: Romania and Croatia", in Economic and Social Development: Book of Proceedings, ed. Marijan Cingula, Rebeka Danijela Vlahov, Damir Dobrinic (Varazdin: Varazdin Development and Entrepreneurship Agency, 2016), 29.

6   Ibid.

The aim of the research endeavor is focused on assessing the Romanian pension system in the face of demographic changes (such as the ageing population, increasing migration, in addition to the wave of people born after 1967, when the 1966 decree prohibiting pregnancy interruptions was adopted – known as the baby boom period – who are set to retire after 2030), and to propose primary strategies and policies for its support. More specifically, we underline how effective the pension system in Romania is in terms of providing a retirement income that replaces the wages before retirement, and how it affects the dependency of the cohort of people aged 65+ on the working population, according to educational background, with further implications on the labor market support of the pension system (grasped through the employment rate, as main provider of social security contributions). These interlinkages are considered from an integrative perspective of direct, indirect and total effects captured through the Structural Equation Modeling (SEM), as methodological endeavor, applied for the period 1990–2017.

To contextualize this assessment, we first provide an overview of the organizational path of the Romanian pension system (after 1990). The hypothesis of our research is that the working population is not able to sustain the long-term PAYG public pension system, given the demographic shortcomings. In these circumstances, we consider that it is essential to supplement public pensions with private ones, at least their mandatory component backdrop of demographic challenges, which will become keener in the coming years. We give asynthesized description of the legislative and organizational path of the pension and social insurance system after 1990. This pathway follows two periods: 1990–2001, and 2001–2019, when major regulatory reassessments were made of the pension system. The endeavor is pursued with the description of data used for the empirical analysis, respectively relevant indicators of the public pension system in combination with the representative demographic factors, followed by the presentation of the research method. The results and discussion section ends not only with the main conclusions and recommendations, but also with a review of labor market integration policies, especially for people aged 55–64. Following the core objective of our research, the empirical analysis sheds important light on the pension system's sustainability in Romania, in the context of global ageing.

2   The Framework of the Pension System in Romania during 1990–
        2019: Organizational Aspects and Representative Indicators

2.1   *The Pattern of the Pension System in Romania*
To shed light on the organizational path of the public pension system in
Romania between 1990–2019, we have defined two time periods that have
brought significant changes on pensions, namely:
–   1990–2001, in which the public pension system was based on a law from
    1977,[7] even though it was constantly revised and further updated, which
    was in force until 2001 (April) when a new law came into force;[8]
–   2001–2019, when the first major revision of the pension system in
    Romania after 1990 was achieved, by mainly changing the way in which
    pensions are established, based on points/scores and the value ascribed
    to a pension point.
Grounded in the difficulties faced by the Romanian public pension system
related to demographic factors and the deficit in the state social insurance
budget,[9] and concomitantly to Romania's accession to the European Union
(EU) (in 2007), it was decided to introduce a private pension system with two
components (pillars), one compulsory for certain age groups, and the other
voluntary. Hence, starting in 2007, the voluntary component (Pillar III) of
Romania's private pension system was configured, following that the second
compulsory component (Pillar II) was enforced in the following year, 2008.[10]
    As a result, the Romanian pension system currently comprises three com-
ponents (Pillars):[11] Pillar I of public pensions, financed through social security contributions; Pillar II of the privately administered pension funds (seven

---

7   Law 3/1977 on The Pensions of State Social Insurance and Social Services, The Official
    Bulletin, no. 82/6 August (Bucharest: The Great National Assembly, 1977), http://legislatie.
    just.ro/Public/DetaliiDocument/440 (accessed March 20, 2019).
8   Law 19/2000 on The Public Pension System and Other Social Insurance Rights, The
    Official Journal of Romania, no. 140/1 April (Bucharest: The Romanian Parliament, 2000).
9   Ingrid-Mihaela Dragota and Emilia Miricescu, "The Public Pension System of Romania
    between Crisis and Reform. The Case of Special Pension System", Theoretical & Applied
    Economics, no. 9 (2010): 99.
10 Mirela Cristea, Nicu Marcu and Raluca Dracea, "Difficulties of the Supporting Pensioners
    by Current Employees - Alternative to Pension Systems at International Level of Empirical
    Analysis in Romania", Theoretical & Applied Economics 21, no. 5, 594 (2014): 54.
11 Mirela Cristea, Nicu Marcu and Oana Valentina Cercelaru "Longer Life with
    Worsening Pension System? Aging Population Impact on the Pension System in Two
    Countries: Romania and Croatia", 54; Alina Cristina Nuta, Constantin Zaman and
    Florian Marcel Nuta, "Romanian Pensions System at a Glance: Some Equity Comments",
    Ekonomska istraživanja 29, no. 1 (2016): 421.

pension funds in 2019), introduced in May 2008; and Pillar III of voluntary pension funds (ten pension funds in 2019), introduced one year earlier than Pillar II (May 2007).[12]

2.2   *Public Pensions and Social Security Contributions during 1990–2001*

In Romania, between 1990–2001 social security pensions comprised the following four pension categories (valid until April 2001): old-age pensions (standard retirement); disability pensions; survivor's pensions; and supplementary pensions, to which the state social insurance pension for farmers was added.[13]

The old-age pension (named by the law the pension for the work deployed and old age) was granted when the following conditions were fulfilled: a seniority (work history) of a minimum of 30 years for men, and 25 years for women; and age 62 years for men, and 57 years for women. Still, one could retire even with a partial seniority of at least ten years, both for men and women. In order to determine the amount of the old-age pension, the calculations were based on the average monthly wages of five consecutive working years, to be chosen from the last ten years of activity.

The disability (invalidity) pension covered the loss of the capacity to work as a result of two distinct situations: through a work accident or a professional disease and outside of the performance of work. The amount of the invalidity pension was established in a differentiated manner for each individual category, and according to the degree of disability (I, II or III), as determined by a medical expertise commission.

The survivor's pension was allocated to the wife and children of deceased persons, by accounting for a series of aspects related to the wife's age, the duration of the marriage, the number of children and their ages (if any), if that person had a disability, the duration of the children's education, and the number of successors.

The supplementary pension was designed to additionally help the pensioners (grounded in the principle of mutuality) over the social security contributions, by applying a percentage to the wage which further represented an income for the "supplementary pension fund"; afterwards, when the pension

---

12   The Financial Supervisory Authority (ASF), Annual Report, 2019, 20, https://asfromania. ro/en/a/970/rapoarte (accessed May 15, 2019).

13   Law 3/1977 on The Pensions of State Social Insurance and Social Services; Marian Preda, Cristina Dobos and Vlad Grigoras, "Romanian Pension System during the Transition: Major Problems and Solutions", Pre-Accession Impact Studies 2, no. 9 (Bucharest: European Institute of Romania, 2004), 25, https://www.econstor.eu/handle/10419/74620 (accessed May 15, 2019).

was calculated, it would have also taken into account the number of years contributions were made to this fund and the percentage granted for this additional financing. The basic contribution to the supplementary pension was
set at between 2–5% from the beginning of 1967 until the end of March 2001,
when Law 19/2000 was enforced, abolishing this contribution.[14]

Regarding the social security contributions required for the payment of
pensions between 1990 – 2001,[15] these were supported only by the employers,
being subsequently divided between employees and employers starting on
April 1, 2001, once Law 19/2000 came into force. Four legal interventions were
designed during that time to set their amount, by increasing them in sequence
from 15%, first to 25% in 1990 (being set at this level in 1973 according to the
activity deployed inside the country or abroad), to 40%, 35% or 30%, established variously in line with the enrolment in working groups in 2000.

As such, for 1990–2001, we highlight several main shortcomings of the public pension system (also relying on the work of Preda, Dobos and Grigoras,[16]
and The National Council of the Elderly),[17] namely:

–   the large difference between men and women in terms of the pension
    age (57 years for women and 62 in the case of men), given the conditions
    of a longer life expectancy for women than men (a difference of over
    seven years in favor of women), which has significantly deepened gender
    inequality;

–   setting the pension based on the average monthly income accomplished
    in the best five consecutive years out of the last ten years before retire-
    ment was not correlated with the period of payment of social security
    contributions. This situation led to inequities between the pension val-
    ues and income evolution over working life, but also to an increase in the

---

14   Law 19/2000 on The Public Pension System and Other Social Insurance Rights. The
     Official Journal of Romania, no. 140/01 April 2000 (Bucharest: The Romanian Parliament,
     2000), http://legislatie.just.ro/Public/DetaliiDocument/21690 (accessed May 4, 2019).

15   Ministry of Labor and Social Justice, Evolution of the Social Security Contributions (CAS),
     the Contribution for the Supplementary Pension and the Contribution for the Pension
     and Social Insurance Fund of the Farmers during 1990–2018 (Evolutiacon tributiei CAS
     si a contributiei pentru pensia suplimentara si contributia pentru fondul de pensii si
     asigurari sociale ale agricultorilor in perioada 1990–2018) Bucharest 2018, http://www.
     mmuncii.ro/j33/images/Documente/protectie_sociala/pensii/2016_Evolutia_valorii-
     cotelor_CAS.pdf (accessed May 12, 2019).

16   Marian Preda, Cristina Dobos and Vlad Grigoras, Romanian Pension System during the
     Transition: Major Problems and Solutions.

17   Evolution of the National Pension System during 1990–2009, National Council of Elderly
     People, 2009, http://cnpv.ro/wp-content/uploads/2020/03/esnp2009.pdf (accessed May
     10, 2019).

deficit of the state social security budget, because of the strategies and policies implemented by employers (with the consent of employees) to pay higher wages only in the final years before retirement, while pushing downsized wages for the earlier years;

– there was no possibility to adjust the incomes representing the pension calculation base depending on inflation. This situation has caused a significant reduction of the pension replacement rate in the years with high levels of inflation in Romania (1991–1994, 1997), nor the possibility to automatically adjust pensions according to inflation, thus leading to their erosion;

– in the situation when the minimum seniority (work history) of 25 years for women and 30 years for men was exceeded, the increase in the pension value for each additional year was descending, since it was granted an extra payment (supplement) of 1% of the average wage used to calculate the pension for each additional year of the first five years, and of 0.5% for the years over these five. Thus, there was no incentive for persons exceeding the standard years of seniority to remain active in the labor market (actively integrated in the labor market), even though they had not reached the retirement age (a cumulative condition of age and seniority for granting the pension being non-existent), hence significantly reducing the incomes of the state social security budget necessary for paying pensions;

– payment of social security contributions only by employers, since employees were covering from their wage only the contribution for the supplementary pension, has led to the impression of both employees and pensioners that the pension was a state obligation and not a benefit that they were entitled to due to the numerous contributions that were paid over the entire working period;

– demographic changes have not been taken into account (increased life expectancy, reduced birth rate, rising old-age dependency rate of persons aged over 65 years on the working population or on those aged less than 18 years); as a result, 1998 was the first year when the dependency rate between pensioners and employees fell below 100, and it has deepened further ever since (Figure 5.1). On the grounds of these pitfalls, the social security contributions were significantly raised starting with February 1999, being 40%, 35%, or 30% respectively for each work category,[18] placing a greater burden on employees and employers.

---

18   Ministry of Labor and Social Justice, Evolution of the Social Security Contributions (CAS), the Contribution for the Supplementary Pension, 2.

2.3   *Public Pensions and Social Security Contributions between 2001–2019*
In 2000, a new law[19] was adopted in order to rebalance the ratio between pension resources and the expenditures arising from their payment. This law came into force in April 2001, lasting until the end of 2010, when another law was introduced,[20] valid from the 1st of January 2011.

Law 19/2000 established the following: essential pension categories, by introducing two new types of pensions, early retirement and partial early retirement pensions, as well as a new regulation to grant them; changing the pension calculation method based on the score achieved for the whole contribution period and the value of the pension point (compared to the previous period when the calculation base was comprised of the monthly wage of the best five consecutive working years, chosen from the last ten years of activity); new contributions to state social insurance, divided between employee and employer; removal of the employee contribution to the supplementary pension; indexation of pensions (of the pension point's value) to inflation; pension correlation and recalculation for the pensioners who retired before 2001.[21]

Consequently, the following types of pensions are granted in Romania through the state pension system established in 2001: old-age pensions; early retirement pensions; partial early retirement pensions; disability pensions; and survivor's pensions.[22] However, in July 2019 a new law was adopted, entering into force in September 2021,[23] that will abolish the partial retirement pension which will become the early retirement pension.[24]

Old age pensions were granted starting in 2001 to those who simultaneously satisfy the following two conditions: having reached the retirement age of 60 years for women and 65 years in the case of men, set to gradually increase until 2015 (previously, from 57 years for women and 62 years for men); minimum retirement contributions/ length of service set at 15 years both for men and women, aimed to increase from ten years until 2015.[25] The full length of service setting was introduced (used to establish the annual average score to

---

19   Law 19/2000 on The Public Pension System and Other Social Insurance Rights, The Official Journal of Romania, no. 140/01 April 2000 (Bucharest: The Romanian Parliament, 2000).
20   Law 263/2010 on The Unitary System of Public Pensions, The Official Journal of Romania, no. 852/20 December (Bucharest: The Romanian Parliament, 2010).
21   Law 19/2000 on The Public Pension System and Other Social Insurance Rights.
22   Ibid.
23   Law 127/2019 regarding The Public Pension System, The Official Journal of Romania, no. 563/9 July (Bucharest: The Romanian Parliament, 2019), http://legislatie.just.ro/Public/DetaliiDocumentAfis/215973 (accessed August 4, 2019).
24   Ibid.
25   Law 19/2000 on The Public Pension System and Other Social Insurance Rights.

which the value of the pension point is applied) at 30 years for women and 35 years in the case of men, set to increase according to forbearance until 2015, starting from 25 years for women, and 30 years for men.

Since January 1, 2011, once Law 263/2010 entered into force,[26] the standard retirement age increased to 63 years in the case of women (from 60 years as set by Law 19/2000) and remained at 65 years for men. Reaching these ages was achieved through a gradual increase until January 2015 for men and is to be reached in January 2030 in the case of women. At present (July 2019), the standard retirement age for women is 61 years and one month (set for the retirement period covering July – September 2019), while in the case of men has reached 65 years. The minimum length of service remained at 15 years both for men and women. Full length of service was set at 35 years for both men, and women. Thus, compared to the legal provisions of Law 19/2000, the full length of service increased by five years only in the case of women.

Nuta, Zaman and Nuta show that "the adoption of the unitary pension system in January 2011 ended up with an increase of the received benefits for about 10% of pensioners, when compared to the average net wage in the economy".[27] Early retirement pensions were granted starting in 2001 for those who are within five years at most before the standard retirement age, if they have surpassed the full length of service by at least eight years. As a result of the implementation of Law 127/2019, from September 2021, the early retirement pensions will become age limit (old-age) pensions, while the early retirement pension category will comprise the partial early retirement pensions of the present time.[28]

Partial early retirement pensions, also established in 2001, are granted at least five years prior the standard retirement age, to those who exceed the full length of service by up to eight years. The amount of the partial early retirement pension is determined by applying 0.75% for each month of time until retirement, until the conditions to reach the age limit pension are met, by reducing it by the number of months by which the standard retirement age has been reduced. When the standard retirement age is reached, the partial early retirement pension is transformed into an age limit pension. Arising from the implementation of Law 127/2019, as of September 2021, the partial early retirement pensions will become early retirement pensions, while the notion of partial early retirement will no longer exist.

---

26   Law 263/2010 on The Unitary System of Public Pensions.
27   Alina Cristina Nuta, Constantin Zaman and Florian Marcel Nuta, "Romanian Pensions System as a Glance: Some Equity Comments", 424.
28   Law 127/2019 regarding The Public Pension System.

Disability pensions are granted according to the degree of disability as set by a medical commission, and the amount is established variously for each of these, by applying it to a score determined for the remaining time until retirement age is reached (being 0.70 points for the first degree, 0.55 points for the second degree, and 0.35 points for the third degree of disability). Starting in September 2021, these scores will be significantly reduced to 0.50 points for the first degree, 0.35 points for the second degree, and 0.15 points for the third degree of disability.

A survivor's pension is given to the children and surviving spouse of the deceased. The children can receive a survivor's pension until the age of 16 years (if they decide to discontinue their education) or until they reach the age of 26 (if they continue their education at higher levels) or through any possible disability of any degree. The husband or wife is entitled to a survivor's pension if the marriage lasted at least 15 years (since 2010), increased from 10 years as had been set in 2001. The amount of the survivor's pension is determined according to the number of successors to the deceased's pension, being of 50% for a single successor, 75% for two successors and 100% in the case of three or more successors.

Most countries have set a certain amount for a guaranteed minimum pension through the state public pension system, as a measure to ensure minimum subsistence incomes for those persons with a very low number of working years. In Romania, the social guaranteed minimum pension has been granted since April 1, 2009, being approximately 148 euro (704 Romanian lei) as of September 1, 2019. However, starting in September 2021, the minimum pension will be determined "in percentages, minimum and maximum, of the gross minimum wage by country guaranteed for payment, according to the length of service".[29] If the resulting pension is under the minimum pension, then the value of the minimum pension will be enforced.

In terms of social security contributions,[30] starting on April 1, 2001, these were established in a differential manner for employers and employees until 2017, after which they have been paid in total by employees. Between 2001–2009, social insurance contributions were successively reduced, from 35% in the case of normal working conditions (employee and employer) in 2001, to 27.5% at the beginning of 2009, when the global economic and financial crisis started to be felt in Romania. After 2009, the social security contribution started to rise again until October 2014, reaching 31.3% for normal working conditions,

29   Law 127/2019 regarding The Public Pension System, Article 91 (1).
30   Ministry of Labor and Social Justice, Evolution of the Social Security Contributions (CAS), the Contribution for the Supplementary Pension.

then dropped again to 25% from 2017 until the present (July 2019). As distinc-tive issues for the 2001–2019 period, we list the following: the employee's con-tribution was capped at 9.5% between 2003–2009, rising to 10.5% between 2009–2016; starting in January 2017, the entire social insurance contribution (of 25%) has been paid only by employees, through increasing their gross sal-aries with the employer's contribution, with certain decreases of net wages at the time of its enforcement.

2.4 Public Pension Indicators and Demographic Credentials in Romania during 1990–2017

Whereas for the payment of public pensions, the number of pensioners has to be supported by the employees paying social security contributions (PAYG system), a significant dimension for the sustainability of public pensions is shown by the number of pensioners related (in counterpart) to the number of employees. Thus, we can see that (Figure 5.1) in Romania, certain distinct periods emerged between 1990 and 2017. Regarding the number of pension-ers, two periods were outlined in their evolution: 1990–2002, an increase (until enforcement of Law 19/2000, which changed the retirement conditions and the way of calculating the pensions, based on scoring during the entire working period); and 2002–2017, a slight decrease. Considering the number of employees, four periods were determined: 1990–2002, with a strong reduction in the number of employees; 2002–2008, with a slight growth; a reduction of employees between 2008–2011 (the period of the economic and financial cri-sis); and a slightly increasing trend between 2011–2017. At the end of 2017, the number of employees was 4,945.87 thousand (which represented about 60% of the number of employees in 1990), and the number of pensioners was 5,228.

We have noticed that 1997 was the last year after 1990 in Romania when the number of pensioners was supported by that of employees, or the depen-dency ratio of pensioners according to the number of employees was sustain-able. Analyzing the values of the monthly average pensions granted during the period 1990–2017, adjusted to the Consumer Price Index (CPI) for 2017 (Figure 5.2), we have discerned four periods of their evolution, following the main legislative changes in the area of pensions, namely: 1990–2000 (2000 being the year in which Law 19/2000 was adopted, which changed the way of determining retirement pensions) that met a significant reduction of the real level of pensions (adjusted to CPI 2017); the period 2001–2009 was marked by an accelerated increase of the average pension values in real values (the pen-sion values increased more than threefold in this period); 2010–2012, by reduc-ing the real pensions, which corresponds to the period of the economic and financial crisis in Romania; and the period 2013–2017, which was characterized

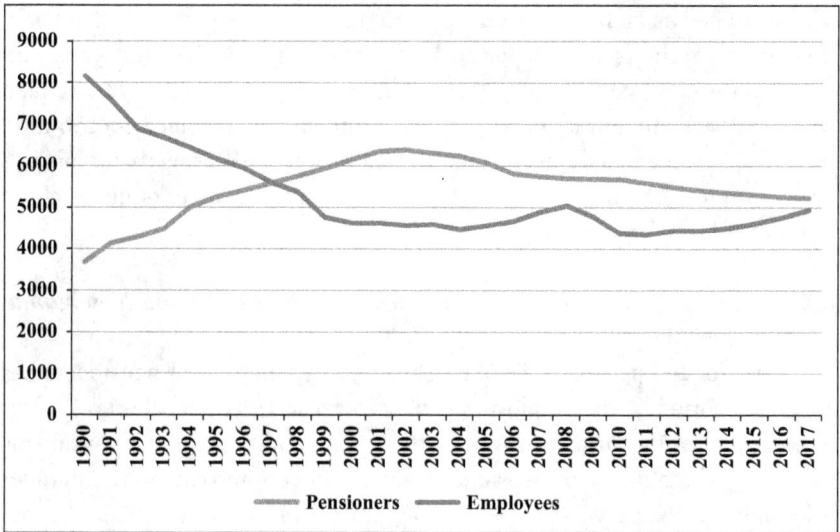

FIGURE 5.1 The evolution of the total number of pensioners and employees in Romania
between 1990–2017
SOURCE: OWN ELABORATION BASED ON NATIONAL INSTITUTE OF STATISTICS
(NIS) IN ROMANIA DATA; "TEMPO-ONLINE DATABASE" HTTP://STATISTICI.
INSSE.RO:8077/TEMPO-ONLINE/#/PAGES/TABLES/INSSE-TABLE (ACCESSED
MARCH 4, 2019).

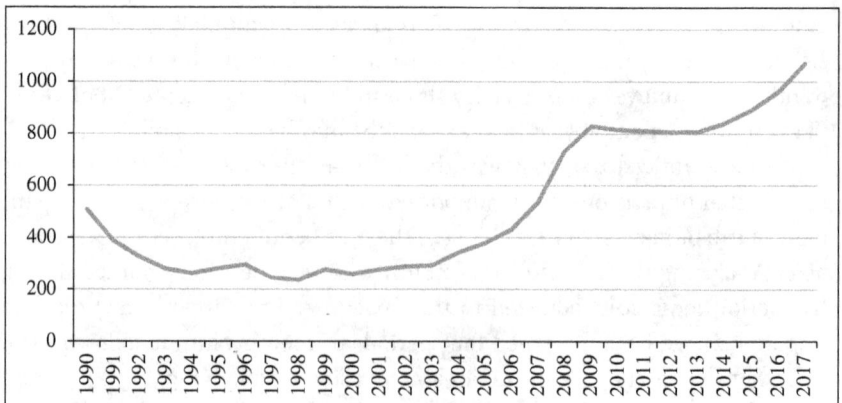

FIGURE 5.2 The average monthly pension (RON adjusted to CPI 2017) between 1990–2017
SOURCE: OWN ELABORATION BASED ON NATIONAL INSTITUTE OF STATISTICS
(NIS) IN ROMANIA DATA; TEMPO-ONLINE DATABASE, HTTP://STATISTICI.
INSSE.RO:8077/TEMPO-ONLINE/#/PAGES/TABLES/INSSE-TABLE (ACCESSED
MARCH 4, 2019).

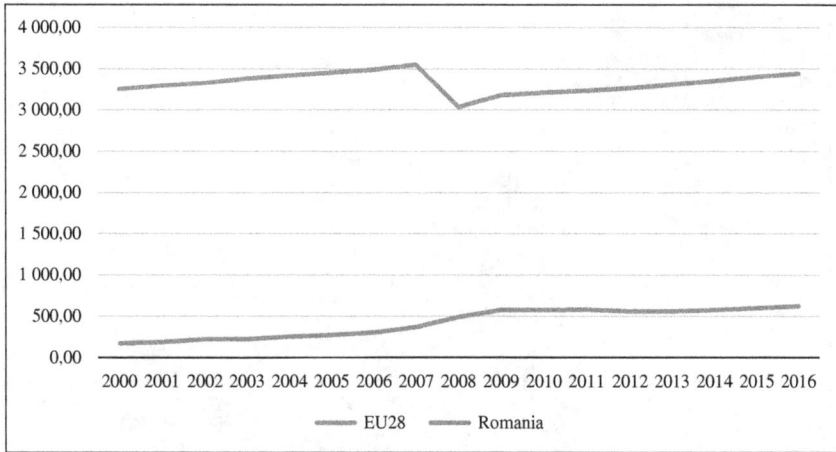

FIGURE 5.3   Average pensions (euro/capita), Romania vs. EU, 2000–2016
SOURCE: EUROSTAT DATABASE, HTTPS://EC.EUROPA.EU/EUROSTAT/DATA/
DATABASE (ACCESSED MAY 5, 2019).

by significant increases in the average values of real pensions, reaching in 2017 the value of 1,069 RON (approximately 240 euro).

We can see that average pensions in Romania are well below the EU average, both in terms of its average per capita (Figure 5.3) and its share of Gross Domestic Product (GDP) (Figure 5.4). In 2000, the lowest average pension in the European countries was recorded in Romania (173.14 euro/inhabitant, compared to 3,252.37 euro/inhabitant on average). As regards pension contributions to GDP, in 2016, Romania recorded 7.9% of GDP, compared to 12.6% at the EU level.

Among the other European countries, the average pension in Romania in 2016 was around 625 euro/inhabitant, ranking fourth from the bottom (Figure 5.5), above Bulgaria, Serbia and North Macedonia.

Rate of replacement of salaries with pensions (net pension replacement rate) is defined as "the individual net pension entitlement divided by net pre-retirement earnings, taking into account personal income taxes and social security contributions paid by workers and pensioners".[31] Over the years (Figure 5.6), the low point of the period, 29.95%, was reached in 1996 and 1998. Afterward, the retirement income allocated to replace the net pre-retirement earnings increased in Romania to slightly more than half of the wage (a peak of 52.15% was achieved in 2011, whereas in 2010 the salaries of those in the budgetary system were reduced by 25%, as the pensions remained unchanged),

31   Pensions at a Glance 2017: OECD and G20 Indicators (OECD Publishing, 2017), 106, http://dx.doi.org/10.1787/pension_glance-2017-en (accessed May 5, 2019).

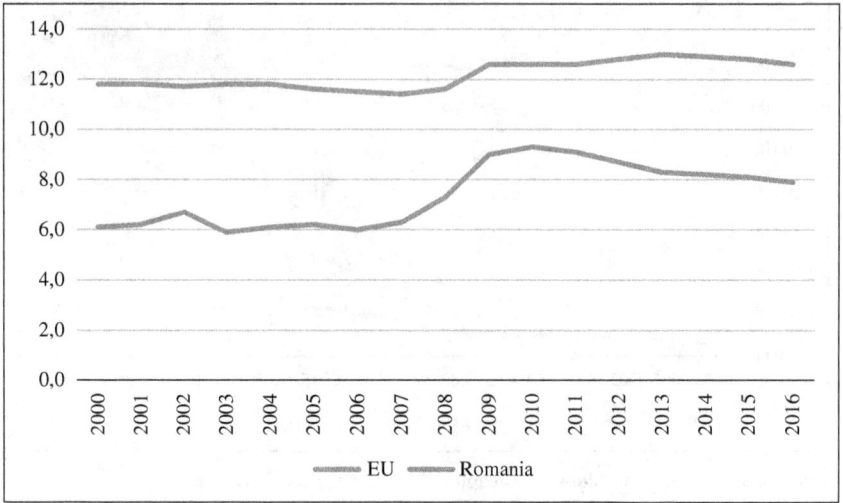

FIGURE 5.4   Average pension of GDP (%), Romania vs. EU, 2000–2016
             SOURCE: EUROSTAT DATABASE, HTTPS://EC.EUROPA.EU/EUROSTAT/DATA/
             DATABASE (ACCESSED MAY 5, 2019).

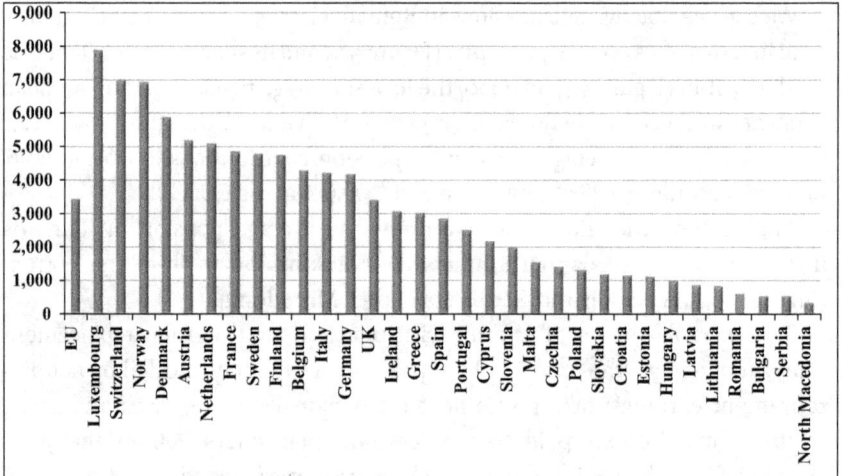

FIGURE 5.5   Average pensions in Europe, 2016 (euro/capita)
             SOURCE: EUROSTAT DATABASE, HTTPS://EC.EUROPA.EU/EUROSTAT/DATA/
             DATABASE (ACCESSED MAY 5, 2019).

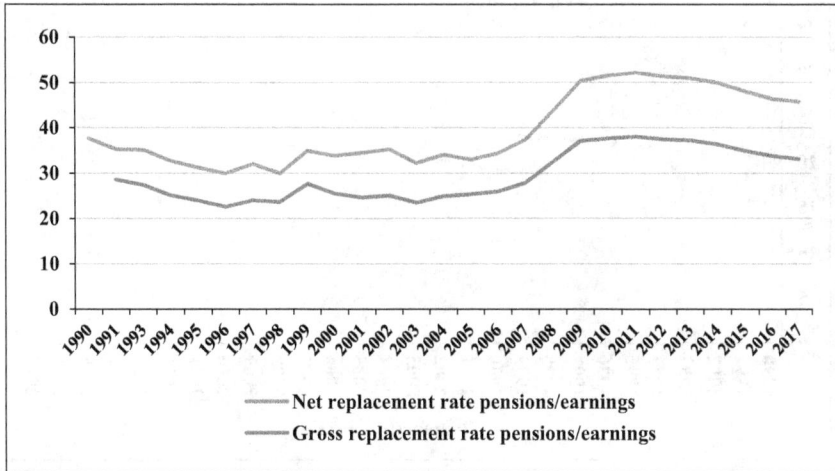

FIGURE 5.6   Net and gross replacement rate pensions/earnings in Romania, 1990–2017
SOURCE: OWN ELABORATION BASED ON NIS OF ROMANIA DATA, TEMPO-
ONLINE DATABASE, STATISTICS IN ROMANIA, HTTP://STATISTICI.INSSE.
RO:8077/TEMPO-ONLINE/#/PAGES/TABLES/INSSE-TABLE (ACCESSED MARCH
4, 2019).

but the pension replacement rate has been on a downward path since then, against a background of a slower increase in earnings compared to pensions in the period following after the economic and financial crisis, reaching 45.72% in 2017 (considering net income), and 33.17%, taking into account gross income.

In both international statistics and the EU,[32] to what extent the population aged over 65 depends on the population aged 15–64 (or 20–64) is determined by the "old-age dependency ratio". The old-age dependency ratio in Romania (Figure 5.7) increased from 15.6% (in 1990) to a maximum of 26.7% (in 2017). The dependency ratio of 65+/(15–64) year olds in Romania followed the evolution recorded by the average of the EU countries (29.9% in 2017), being below this throughout the period. Nonetheless, the birth rate and life expectancy gained too little when compared to the massive emigration, which has significantly affected the labor stock and induced additional imbalances to the sustainability of the Romanian pension system. According to Panzaru,[33] the working-age population (paying contributions to social security funds) declines because of migration, thus stressing the imbalance of the social security system. However,

32   Eurostat database, https://ec.europa.eu/eurostat/data/database (accessed May 5, 2019).
33   Ciprian Pânzaru, "Some Considerations of Population Dynamics and the Sustainability of Social Security System," Procedia – Social and Behavioral Sciences 183 (2015a): 69.

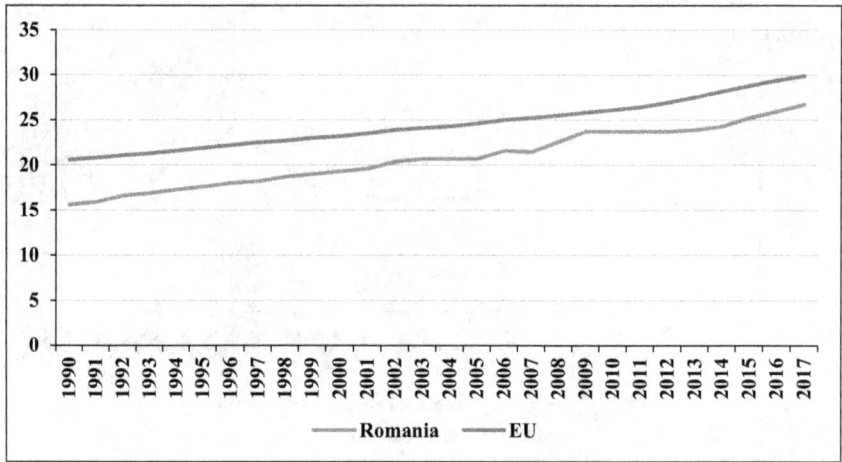

FIGURE 5.7   Old-age dependency rate 65+ in Romania vs. EU, 1990–2017
SOURCE: EUROSTAT DATABASE, HTTPS://EC.EUROPA.EU/EUROSTAT/DATA/
DATABASE (ACCESSED MAY 5, 2019).

between 1990–2017, the birth rate in Romania has somewhat followed its evolution at the EU level (Figure 5.8), massively decreasing from 13.6 persons to 9.3
in 2017. Additionally, life expectancy (Figure 5.9) has increased from 69.56 years
in 1990, to 75.73 years in 2017, also following the EU trend.

3   Data and Applied Methodology

In this frame of reference, we have compiled a dataset on Romania, covering
the timespan from 1990–2017, for several key indicators, namely:
–   pension specific indicators: net pension replacement rate (*PENS_NE*) (%);
–   demographic credentials: old-age-dependency ratio (*OD*) (%); birth rate
      (*Birth_rate*) (number of live births to 1,000 persons); life expectancy (*Life_
      expect*) (years); total number of permanent emigrants (*Emigrants*);
–   labor market and educational indicators: total employment rate (*ER*)
      (%); education enrolment degree (*EDU_enroll*) (%).
The data were extracted from the National Institute of Statistics (NIS) in
Romania database.[34] In order to avoid the stationarity of data, we have

---

34   National Institute of Statistics in Romania, Tempo-online database, http://statistici.insse.
      ro:8077/tempo-online/#/pages/tables/insse-table (accessed March 4, 2019).

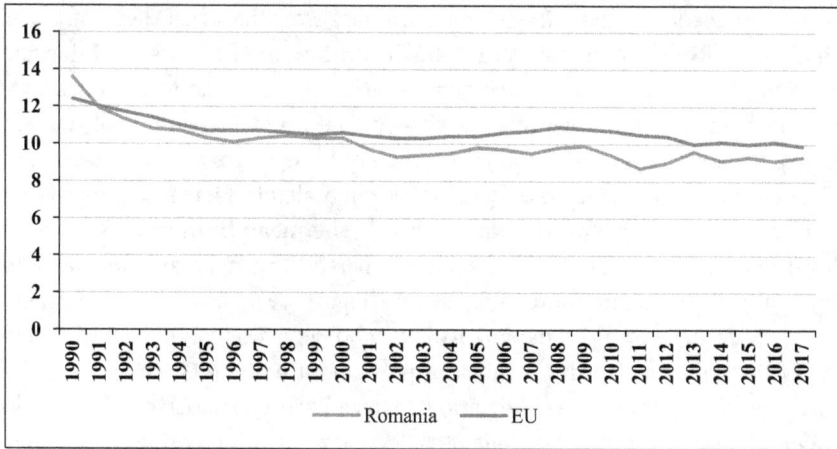

FIGURE 5.8   Birth rate, Romania vs. EU, 1990–2017
SOURCE: OWN ELABORATION BASED ON 'EUROSTAT DATABASE', HTTPS://
EC.EUROPA.EU/EUROSTAT/DATA/DATABASE, AND NIS "TEMPO-ONLINE
DATABASE", HTTP://STATISTICI.INSSE.RO:8077/TEMPO-ONLINE/#/PAGES/
TABLES/INSSE-TABLE (ACCESSED MARCH 4, 2019)

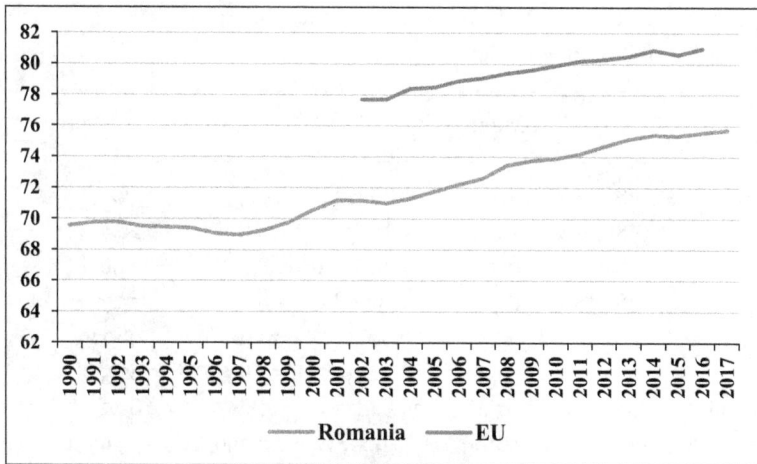

FIGURE 5.9   Life expectancy, Romania vs. EU, 1990–2017
SOURCE: OWN ELABORATION BASED ON 'EUROSTAT DATABASE' HTTPS://
EC.EUROPA.EU/EUROSTAT/DATA/DATABASE AND NIS "TEMPO-ONLINE
DATABASE", HTTP://STATISTICI.INSSE.RO:8077/TEMPO-ONLINE/#/PAGES/
TABLES/INSSE-TABLE (ACCESSED MARCH 4, 2019)

firstly proceeded to logarithm them. Summary statistics of all these variables included within our analysis (crude and logarithm) are presented in Table 5.1.

Thus, the net pension replacement rate (*PENS_NE*), as shown in Figure 5.6 was between a minimum level of 29.95% (in 1998), and a maximum of 52.15 (in 2011), having an average of 39.19% for the entire 1990–2017 period (Table 5.1). The old-age dependency ratio (OD) (presented also in Figure 5.7), registered an average of 20.77% for the whole period. The mean birth rate (*Birth_rate*) over 1990–2017 was ten live births to 1,000 persons, with a maximum value in 1990 of 13.6, and a minimum of 8.7 in 2011 (Figure 5.8). The average life expectancy (*Life_expect*) in Romania between 1990–2017 was 71.91 years (detailed in Figure 5.9). As regards the stock of permanent emigrants (*emigrants*), the average value during the entire period analyzed was 19,654 persons. The working population (employment rate, ER) decreased over the period 1990 – 2013, from 82% to 60.9% within the active population, afterward registering a slight increase to 67.3% in 2017. The minimum value of 59.6% was in 2011, after the economic and financial crises, and the maximum of 82.5% in 1991. The education component represents one of the factors with a positive influence on labor market performance, however, in future years, "the cohorts of more educated

TABLE 5.1   Summary statistics, Romania in 1990–2017

s	N	Mean	Std	Min	Max
PENS_NE	28	39.18929	7.805224	29.95	52.15
OD	28	20.775	3.17719	15.6	26.7
Birth_rate	28	10.00357	1.006454	8.7	13.6
Life_expect	28	71.91143	2.367881	68.95	75.73
Emigrants	28	19654.5	17070.03	7906	96929
ER	28	66.53929	6.843398	59.6	82.5
EDU_enroll	28	46.06536	23.84872	10.6	85.2
log_PENS_NE	28	3.650169	.1920872	3.399529	3.954124
log_OD	28	3.022355	.154256	2.747271	3.284664
log_Birth_rate	28	2.298521	.0935624	2.163323	2.61007
log_Life_expect	28	4.274916	.0327757	4.233382	4.327175
log_Emigrants	28	9.701572	.5470428	8.975377	11.48173
log_ER	28	4.193009	.0980537	4.087656	4.412798
log_EDU_enroll	28	3.660643	.6390103	2.360854	4.445002

workers that have paid more in contributions, during their working years, due to higher wages and salaries, will contribute to rising expenditures within the public pension system".[35] In Romania, the dimension of education, appreciated by the degree of enrolment in of people up to age 19 (EDU_enroll), has registered a substantial increase after 1990 from 10.6% (the minimum value) to 85.2% in 2010, registering 67.6% in 2017, and an average of 46.07% during 1990–2017.

Based on these data, we have applied the SEM (Structural Equations Modeling) technique and developed a model, which captures in a new integrative approach the interlinkages between the pension credentials, demographic factors and labor market (through social security contributions paid) and educational implications. Structural equations are complex methods of data analysis, being configured in this research as the main methodological credentials since they provide the advantage of modeling and testing complex patterns of relationships, including a multitude of hypotheses simultaneously as a whole.

The general configuration of the SEM model is reflected in Equation 1 (presented in Figure 5.10) and Figure 5.11.

$$\begin{cases} b_{11}y_{2t}+....+b_{1m}y_{mt}+c_{11}x_{1t}+...+c_{1n}x_{nt}=\varepsilon_{1t} \\ b_{21}u_{2t}+....+b_{2m}y_{mt}+c_{21}x_{1t}+...+c_{2n}x_{nt}=\varepsilon_{2t} \\ .... \\ b_{m1}u_{mt}+....+b_{mm}y_{mt}+c_{m1}x_{nt}+...+c_{mn}x_{nt}=\varepsilon_{mt} \end{cases}$$

FIGURE 5.10 General configuration of the SEM model (equations)
SOURCE: OWN ELABORATION.

where: t is the number of observed time periods, b_{ij} represents the y_{ij} endogenous variable's parameters, c_{ij} are the x_{ij} exogenous variable's parameters, $i=1$, ..., m, $j=1$, ..., n; ε comprise the error term (residuals).[36]

---

35   Lucian Adrian Sala, "Romania's Population Decline and Demographic Future: Socio-Economic Aspects", Facta Universitatis-Economics and Organization 15, no. 1 (2018): 83.

36   Mirela Cristea and Gratiela Georgiana Noja, "European Agriculture under the Immigration Effects: New Empirical Evidence", Agricultural Economics (Zemědělská Ekonomika) 3, no. 65 (2019): 115.

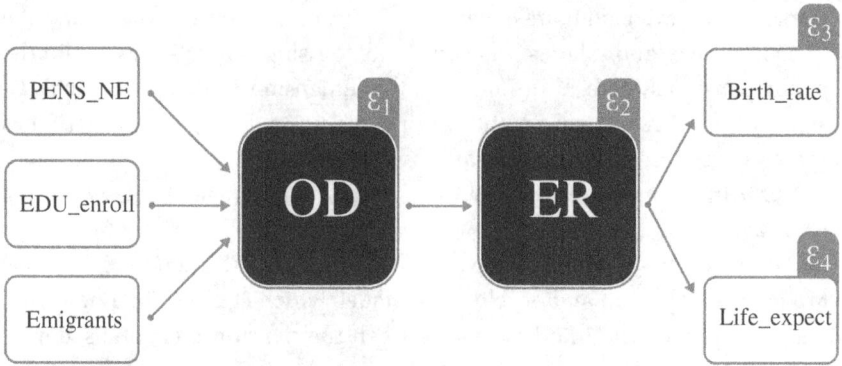

FIGURE 5.11 General configuration of the SEM model
          SOURCE: OWN ELABORATION.

Thus, we are advancing the following hypothesis: *H. The working population (through social security contributions paid) is unable to sustain the PAYG public pension system in Romania in the face of the demographic shortcomings.*

4   The SEM Model in the Case of Romania

The results obtained by the SEM model have revealed that there is a high degree of positive and inverse correlation between all these variables in the case of Romania, as attested by the correlation matrix detailed in Table 5.2. and Figure 5.12.

Romania's employment rate (ER) is negatively correlated with the old-age dependency rate (OD) (-0.7051) (Table 5.2.), meaning that as the old-age dependency rate increases, the total employment rate decreases and inversely, as the country manages to reduce the old-age dependency rate on the working age population, positive outcomes on the labor market will emerge reflected in employment gains. Moreover, there is a strong inverse correlation between the old-age dependency rate (OD) and the net pension replacement rate (PENS_NE), which indicates that as the number of retired people supported by a potential worker increases, the amount of of retirement income compared to net pre-retirement earnings will significantly decrease. Education enrolment (*EDU_enroll*) and emigrant stocks (*Emigrants*) also affect the old dependency dimension in terms of a strong correlation.

The SEM model was processed through the Maximum Likelihood estimation method (MLE) and thus we were able to store several types of results/

TABLE 5.2   Correlation matrix of SEM variables (items), Romania, 1990–2017

	Log_ER	Log_OD	Log_PENS_NE	Log_EDU_enroll	Log_Emigrants	Log_Birth_rate	Log_Life_expect
Log_ER	1.0000						
Log_OD	-0.7051	1.0000					
Log_PENS_NE	-0.3470	-0.7728	1.0000				
Log_EDU_enroll	-0.8430	-0.9431	-0.6795	1.0000			
Log_Emigrants	0.7703	-0.4938	-0.1372	-0.6607	1.0000		
Log_Birth_rate	0.8117	-0.8393	-0.4703	-0.8622	0.7141	1.0000	
Log_Life_expect	-0.5087	0.9427	0.8929	0.8527	-0.3034	-0.6883	1.0000

SOURCE: OWN ELABORATION IN STATA PROGRAM.

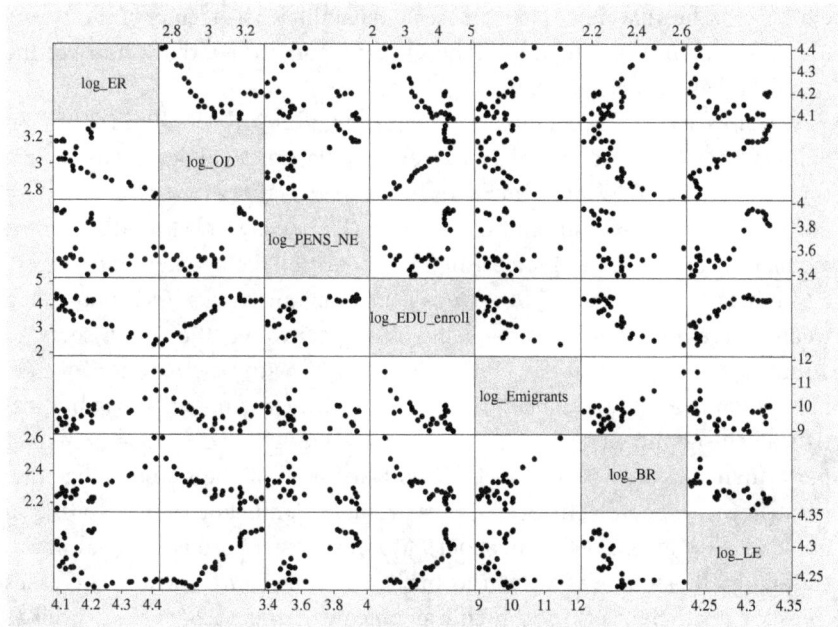

FIGURE 5.12 Correlation matrix of the variables included in the SEM model
SOURCE: OWN ELABORATION IN STATA PROGRAM.

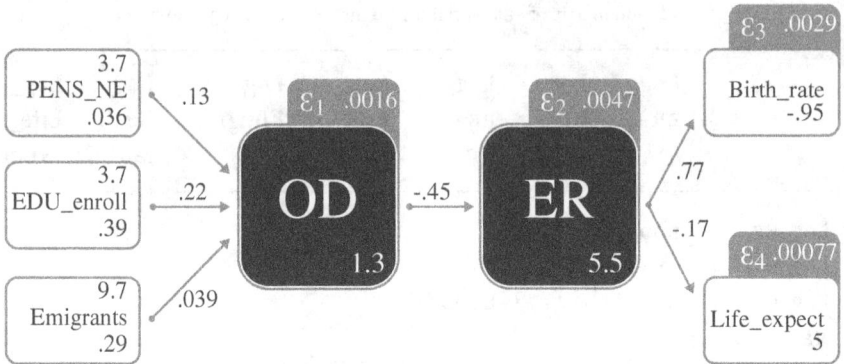

FIGURE 5.13 Results of the SEM model
SOURCE: OWN ELABORATION IN STATA PROGRAM

effects, both direct (shown in Figure 5.13), as well as indirect and the total effects are detailed in Table 5.3.

In order to ensure a high level of robustness of the estimations, we have applied numerous tests, like the Wald test, equation level and overall goodness of fit tests (e.g., Likelihood ratio, Information criteria, Comparative fit index (CFI), Tucker-Lewis index (TLI), Standardized root mean squared residual (SRMR), Coefficient of determination (CD), along with Cronbach's alpha associated with the SEM model to attest scale reliability). The results of these tests are presented in the Appendix: Tables 5.4–5.6 and outline the validity of the model and associated estimations.

We can see that the coefficient of determination (CD) of all of these variables is 0.929 (Appendix: Table 5.5), meaning that 92.9% of demographic factors (birth rate and life expectancy) is influenced by these variables. When we considered the direct and indirect impacts (Figure 5.13), we found empirical evidence to attest that an increase in the net pension replacement rate (*PENS_NE*), education enrolment (*EDU_enroll*) and emigrant stocks (*Emigrants*) lead to an increase in the old dependency rate (positive coefficients associated with *PENS_NE* variable of 0.13, significant at 0.5%, with an *EDU_enroll* of 0.22, highly significant at the 0.1% threshold, and with *Emigrants* at 0.039 but statistically insignificant). There is a further negative impact on the labor market performance as reflected in a significant decrease of the employment rate (*ER*) (negative coefficient of -0.448, extremely significant from a statistical point of view at the 0.1% threshold). Moreover, there are additional implications of these advances on the birth rate (*Birth_rate*), which increases (positive coefficient of 0.775, highly significant at the 0.1% level), as well as

TABLE 5.3   Indirect and total effects grasped by the SEM model results

Indirect effects	Coef. (Std. err.)	p-value	Total effects	Coef. (Std. err.)	p-value
log_OD<-			log_OD<-		
log_PENS_NE	0 (no path)		log_PENS_NE	0.133 (0.0669)	0.047
log_EDU_ enroll	0 (no path)		log_EDU_ enroll	0.223 (0.0265)	0.000
log_Emigrants	0 (no path)		log_ Emigrants	0.038 (0.0229)	0.090
	log_ER<-		log_ER<-		
log_PENS_NE	-0.059 (0.320)	0.063	log_PENS_NE	-0.059 (0.0320)	0.063
log_EDU_ enroll	-0.0997 (0.0224)	0.000	log_EDU_ enroll	-0.099 (0.0224)	0.000
log_Emigrants	-0.0174 (0.0108)	0.107	log_ Emigrants	-0.017 (0.0108)	0.107
log_Birth_ rate<-			log_Birth_ rate<-		
log_OD	-0.347 (0.0659)	0.000	log_OD	-0.347 (0.0659)	0.000
log_ER	0 (no path)		log_ER	0.774 (0.1053)	0.000
log_PENS_NE	-0.046 (0.0256)	0.072	log_PENS_NE	-0.046 (0.0256)	0.072
log_EDU_ enroll	-0.772 (0.0203)	0.000	log_EDU_ enroll	0.077 (0.0202)	0.000
log_Emigrants	-0.014 (0.0086)	0.115	log_ Emigrants	-0.014 (0.0086)	0.115
log_Life_expect<-			log_Life_expect<-		
log_OD	0.076 (0.0145)	0.000	log_OD	0.076 (0.0145)	0.000
log_ER	0 (no path)		log_ER	-0.170 (0.0544)	0.002
log_PENS_NE	0.010 (0.0063)	0.110	log_PENS_NE	0.010 (0.0063)	0.110
log_EDU_ enroll	0.017 (0.0066)	0.010	log_EDU_ enroll	0.017 (0.0066)	0.010
log_Emigrants	0.003 (0.0020)	0.152	log_ Emigrants	0.003 (0.0020)	0.152

SOURCE: OWN ELABORATION IN STATA PROGRAM.

upon life expectancy (*Life_expect*), which however decreases under all these implications (negative coefficient of -0.17, statistically significant at the 0.5% threshold).

These shortcomings are further enhanced and reconfirmed by the indirect and total effects captured by the SEM estimations (Table 5.3). As statistically significant (p-value under 0.05) impacts on the employment rate (*ER*) and birth rate (*Birth_rate*), we can see that educational degree (*EDU_enroll*) has an unfavorable impact on these two variables, while favorable effects were induced on life expectancy (*Life_expect*), both as indirect, and total effects. Moreover, the old-age dependency rate (*OD*) has induced negative spillovers on the birth rate, and positive ones upon life expectancy, both indirect, and total impacts. These results involve the reconsideration of the education component in order to enhance the labor market integration and birth rate.

Thus, our hypothesis, *H, the working population (through social security contributions paid) is unable to sustain the PAYG public pension system in Romania in the face of the demographic shortcomings,* is confirmed.

A relatively high old dependency ratio placed under the influence of pension replacement rates, education enrolment and migration flows has negative effects on the Romanian economy, since it slows down economic growth through lower tax revenues (an additional burden on the working age population to pay tax), lower pension funds due to an increased number of pensioners (and hence possible reduced retirement earnings), and greater pressures to raise the retirement age, increased inequality and diminished competitiveness. The patterned linked impact on employment in Romania is devastating, all of these credentials inducing negative effects on labor market support and further consequences on socio-economic welfare (reduced life expectancy). Therefore, new tailored strategies and labor market policies should be designed to increase the labor stock and working-age population in Romania and mitigate the negative effects of mass emigration (negative net migration).[37] Panzaru also attested that "migration is the only solution to sort out the labor market deficit during the next 50 years, [...], the Romanian labor force should be supplemented till 2060 yearly with 200,000 to 500,000 immigrants".[38]

---

37   Nicu Marcu, Georgeta-Madalina Meghisan and Mihaela-Cristina Ciobanu, "Research on Romanian Labor Market Dynamics", Revista de Chimie 66, no. 9 (2015): 1543.

38   Ciprian Pânzaru, "On the Sustainability of the Romanian Pension System in the Light of Population Declining", Procedia – Social and Behavioral Sciences no. 183 (2015): 77.

5   Conclusion

This research endeavor aims to portray the pension system framework in Romania, related to the awareness of the demographic shortages, and to propose the main strategies and policies for its support. In this vein, the empirical analysis seeks to elucidate the implications of net pension replacement rates (as the main advocacy of pensioners' welfare), educational background and migration outflows on the old-age dependency ratio and labor market support on social security (grasped through the employment rate, as providers of social security contributions), as well as the subsequent spillovers on other demographic fundamentals, namely the birth rate and life expectancy (ageing dimensions). The results obtained have validated that the working population (through social security contributions paid) is unable to sustain the PAYG public pension system in Romania in the face of the demographic shortcomings, unless targeted strategies and policies are implemented in a timely manner.

Moreover, in 2019, policy makers in Romania adopted a regulation[39] that places the second component of the private pension pillar (based on 3.75% from 25% of the social security contributions of employees) under the prospect of uncertainty and instability due to a number of factors. First is the possibility that the participants in the privately managed pension funds, Pillar II, may voluntarily withdraw, remaining only with the public pension (Pillar I). Second is the indebtedness of the private pension fund administrators, Pillar II, to increase the share capital by a percentage of the total contributions of the participants of 5%, 7% or 10%, applied differentiated according to the total assets, which will lead to possible mergers of certain administrators (the disappearance of some of the seven administrators found on the private pensions market, Pillar II, at the end of 2018), Third is the exemption of those employed in construction from paying social security contributions for privately managed pension funds for a period of ten years, resulting in a reduction in the assets of these pension funds. Fourth is the massive reduction of the commissions of private pension fund administrators, alongside with the redistribution of some part to the institution that manages public pensions, Pillar I.

Thus, along with the unfavorable implications of the demographic factors, the legislative measures that undermine the private pensions market, the

---

39   The Romanian Parliament, Emergency Ordinance no. 114/28 December 2018 regarding The Establishment of Measures in the Field of Public Investments and Fiscal-Budgetary Measures, the Modification and Completion of Some Normative Acts and the Extension of Certain Terms, the Official Journal of Romania, no. 1116/29 December 2018.

pension received through the public system will depend on the policy extant at the time of retirement. Dragota and Miricescu attested that the main issue of the public pensions is "the deficit of the public social insurance budget",[40] since the social security system in Romania has undergone several crises. The same authors highlighted that an important moment of severe unbalance was in 1995, when the revenues to the social security budget (measured as a percentage of GDP) were surpassed by social security expenditures (with the same measurement unit as % of GDP). This deficit was constantly maintained until 2005, while 2006 and 2007 were the only two years without a deficit over the entire 1995–2010 period. As a consequence, the public pension system needed significant financial transfers, thus raising several inquiries as to its sustainability, even more so in the face of the demographic challenges. In addition to these factors, further components eroding the pensioners' support, such as the retirement of a massive population cohort, starting with 2030 for women, and 2032 for men, born after 1967,when a birth rate boom occurred (when 27 live births were registered per 1,000 people), the largest in Europe at that time,[41] as a consequence of the prohibition of the interruption of pregnancy by Decree No. 770 of October 1, 1966,[42] and the relatively high poverty rate in Romania compared to other EU member states, 35.7% in 2017, being the second country after Bulgaria (38.9%) and well over the EU average of 22.4%.[43] This will only worsen due to the increase in the old-age dependence rate 65+ compared to the working age group (15–64 years). In addition, the poverty rate for people over 65 was 17.8% at the end of 2017, rising from 11.9% in 1995.[44]

Given these facts, it is necessary to also analyze the implications of private pension funds, the second pillar, in sustaining pensioners' welfare.[45] Against this backdrop, we recommend Romania to maintain privately managed pension funds (Pillar II), representing an additional retirement income, besides

---

40   Ingrid-Mihaela Dragota and Emilia Miricescu, "The Public Pension System of Romania between Crisis and Reform. The Case of Special Pension System".

41   European Commission, Eurostat database, https://ec.europa.eu/eurostat/data/database (accessed May 5, 2019).

42   Mirela Cristea, Nicu Marcu and Oana-Valentina Cercelaru, "Longer Life with Worsening Pension System? Aging Population Impact on the Pension System in Two Countries: Romania and Croatia".

43   Eurostat database, https://ec.europa.eu/eurostat/data/database (accessed May 5, 2019).

44   Ibid.

45   Elaine Fultz and Kenichi Hirose, "Second-Pillar Pensions in Central and Eastern Europe: Payment Constraints and Exit Options", International Social Security Review 72, no. 2 (2019): 13.

the public pension, for which the participants do not pay additional money (being part of the social security contributions, of 25%). The high poverty rate in Romania does not allow many people to contribute extra financial resources to supplement their public pension. As explained by Allot et al. "the private pension systems seem to represent the main solution in this respect, and the experience of Central and Eastern Europe with fully capitalized pension funds provides encouraging results".[46]

In addition, besides strategies to further support the birth rate, the integration of young people into the labor market, it is also recommended to promote the concept of 'active aging' applied at the EU level starting in 2012,[47] which encourages people over 55 to contribute to the economy and society.[48] Thus, strategies are needed to support the increase in the employment rate of people aged 55–64 through the setting up of centers that support and guide them according to their abilities and skills, different from those of the younger cohorts, as those applied in the Nordic countries (Denmark, Sweden, Finland).[49] Moreover, in the present context of the global crisis brought about by the Covid-19 pandemic, educational support for the acquisition of digital skills and training people to adapt to online working have become essential tools for reducing unemployment and emigration (Romania has the biggest number of emigrants in Europe). The implementation of Active Labor Market Policies (ALMPs) and Passive Labor Policies (PLMPs) in the labor market, the involvement of older people over 65 in volunteer, political and other social activities, are other main directions of active ageing activities. At the EU level, an Active Ageing Index (AAI) was established, which comprises 22 indicators on the employment rate of people 55–74 years, their participation in society through volunteer and political activities, family care, health, involvement in lifelong learning activities, increasing life expectancy, use of

46   Allot Atomi et al., "Private Pension Systems in Central and Eastern Europe", Milliman Research Report, 2010, 62.

47   Decision 940/2011/EU. The European Year for Active Ageing and Solidarity between Generations (Strasbourg: The European Parliament and the Council of The European Union, 2012).

48   European Commission, Active Ageing Index at the Local Level. Peer Review in Social Protection and Social Inclusion 2015–2016 (Berlin: Directorate-General for Employment, Social Affairs and Inclusion, Population Unit of the UNECE and the European Centre for Social Welfare Policy and Research, 2016), 6, https://ec.europa.eu/social/main.jsp?-catId=1024&langId=en&newsId=2333&furtherNews=yes (accessed 10 June, 2019).

49   Ageing and Employment Policies: Denmark 2015. Ageing and Employment Policies (Paris: OECD Publishing, 2015), https://doi.org/10.1787/9789264235335-en (accessed 10 June, 2019).

technology, information and communication (TIC) and others.[50] AAI was determined for 2010, 2012, 2014, 2016 and 2018, for which Romania achieved in 2018 a score of 30.4, compared to the EU average of 35.8, and Sweden's highest score of 46.9.[51]

The main limits of our research arise from the low availability of indicators starting in 1990. The future research directions are to include Romania in the Central and Eastern European group of developing countries for a comparative analysis with the developed Member States (the EU-15), as regards the phenomenon of ageing, pension support, the labor market and economic development.

6   Appendix

TABLE 5.4   Wald tests and equation level goodness of fit for the SEM model, Romania, 1990–2017

Wald tests for equations				Equation-level goodness of fit		
Variables	Chi2	Df	p-value	R-sq	mc*	mc2**
OD	366.36	3	0.0000	0.9289	0.9638	0.9289
ER	27.69	1	0.0000	0.4971	0.7051	0.4971
Birth_rate	54.09	1	0.0000	0.6588	0.8117	0.6588
Life_expect	9.77	1	0.0018	0.2587	0.5086	0.2587

H_0: all coefficients excluding the intercepts are 0.
We can thus reject that null hypothesis for each equation.

Note: *correlation between the dependent variable and its prediction; **Bentler-Raykov squared multiple correlation coefficient
SOURCE: OWN ELABORATION IN STATA PROGRAM.

50   UNECE/European Commission. 2018 Active Ageing Index: Analytical Report, Brussels 2019, https://www.unece.org/fileadmin/DAM/pau/age/Active_Ageing_Index/Stakeholder_Meeting/ACTIVE_AGEING_INDEX_TRENDS_2008-2016_web_cover_reduced.pdf (accessed 10 September, 2019), 13; Eleftherios Thalassinos, Mirela Cristea and Gratiela Georgiana Noja, "Measuring Active Ageing within the European Union: Implications on Economic Development", Equilibrium. Quarterly Journal of Economics and Economic Policy 14, no. 4 (2019): 593–594.
51   UNECE/European Commission. 2018 Active Ageing Index: Analytical Report.

TABLE 5.5 Overall goodness-of-fit tests for the SEM model, Romania, 1990–2017

Fit statistic	Value	Description
Likelihood ratio		
chi2_ms(12)	148.350	model vs. saturated
$p>$ chi2	0.000	
chi2_bs(18)	280.161	baseline vs. saturated
$p>$ chi2	0.000	
Information criteria		
AIC	-308.978	Akaike's information criterion
BIC	-290.327	Bayesian information criterion
Baseline comparison		
CFI	0.680	Comparative fit index
TLI	0.420	Tucker-Lewis index
Size of residuals		
SRMR	0.020	Standardized root mean squared residual
CD	0.929	Coefficient of determination

SOURCE: OWN ELABORATION IN STATA PROGRAM.

TABLE 5.6 Cronbach's alpha associated with the SEM model, Romania, 1990–2017

Variables	Test scale = mean (standardized items), average					
	Obs	Sign	Item-test correlation	Item-rest correlation	Average interitem Correlation	alpha
Log_OD	28	+	0.9564	0.9378	0.6361	0.9130
Log_ER	28	-	0.8371	0.7742	0.6835	0.9284
Log_Birth_rate	28	-	0.9042	0.8650	0.6569	0.9199
Log_Life_expect	28	+	0.8711	0.8199	0.6700	0.9241
Log_PENS_NE	28	+	0.7219	0.6249	0.7293	0.9417
Log_EDU_enroll	28	+	0.9807	0.9722	0.6265	0.9096
Log_Emigrants	28	-	0.6849	0.5787	0.7440	0.9457
Total scale					0.6780	0.9365

SOURCE: OWN ELABORATION IN STATA PROGRAM.

Bibliography

Ageing and Employment Policies: Denmark 2015. Ageing and Employment Policies. Paris: OECD, 215. https://doi.org/10.1787/9789264235335-en.

Allott, Adrian, Cristina Atomi, Paul Ernest, Beata Golembiecka, Marcin Krzykowski, Anna Mazerant, and Olexander Ofutin. "Private Pension Systems in Central and Eastern Europe". Milliman Research Report, (2010): 1–64.

Cristea, Mirela, and Alexandru Mitrică. "Global Ageing: Do Privately Managed Pension Funds Represent a Long-Term Alternative for the Romanian Pension System? Empirical Research". Romanian Journal of Political Science 16, no. 1 (2016): 63–106.

Cristea, Mirela, and Gratiela Georgiana Noja. "European Agriculture under the Immigration Effects: New Empirical Evidence". Agricultural Economics (Zemědělská Ekonomika) 3, no. 65 (2019): 112–122.

Cristea, Mirela, Nicu Marcu, and Oana-Valentina Cercelaru. "Longer Life with Worsening Pension System? Aging Population Impact on the Pension System in Two Countries: Romania and Croatia". In Economic and Social Development: Book of Proceedings, edited by Marijan Cingula, Rebeka Danijela Vlahov, Damir Dobrinic. Varazdin: Varazdin Development and Entrepreneurship Agency, 2016, 28–37.

Cristea, Mirela, Nicu Marcu, and Raluca Dracea. "Difficulties of the Supporting Pensioners by Current Employees-Alternative to Pension Systems at International Level: Empirical Analysis in Romania". Theoretical & Applied Economics 21, no. 5 (594) (2014): 51–68.

Decision 940/2011/EU. The European Year for Active Ageing and Solidarity between Generations. Strasbourg: The European Parliament and the Council of The European Union, 2012.

Dragota, Ingrid-Mihaela, and Emilia Miricescu. "The Public Pension System of Romania between Crisis and Reform. The Case of Special Pension System". Theoretical & Applied Economics 17, no. 9 (2010): 97–116.

European Commission. "Active Ageing Index at the Local Level. Peer Review in Social Protection and Social Inclusion 2015–2016". Directorate-General for Employment, Social Affairs and Inclusion, Population Unit of the UNECE and the European Centre for Social Welfare Policy and Research, Berlin, 2016. Accessed 10 June, 2019.

Eurostat database. Accessed May 5, 2019. https://ec.europa.eu/eurostat/data/database.

Evolution of the National Pension System during 1990–2009. National Council of Elderly People, 2009. Accessed 5 May, 2019. http://cnpv.ro/wp-content/uploads/2020/03/esnp2009.pdf.

Fultz, Elaine, and Kenichi Hirose. "Second-pillar Pensions in Central and Eastern Europe: Payment Constraints and Exit Options". International Social Security Review 72, no. 2 (2019): 3–22.

Hicks, Alexander. Social Democracy and Welfare Capitalism: A century of Income Security Politics. New York: Cornell University Press, 2018.

Law 3/1977 on The Pensions of State Social Insurance and Social Services, The Official Bulletin, no. 82/6 August 1977. Accessed March 20, 2019. http://legislatie.just.ro/Public/DetaliiDocument/440.

Law 127/2019 regarding The Public Pension System, The Official Journal of Romania, no. 563/9 July. The Romanian Parliament, 2019. Accessed August 4, 2019. http://legislatie.just.ro/Public/DetaliiDocumentAfis/215973.

Law 19/2000 on The Public Pension System and Other Social Insurance Rights, The Official Journal of Romania, no. 140/1 April 2000. The Romanian Parliament, 2000.

Law 263/2010 on The Unitary System of Public Pensions, The Official Journal of Romania, no. 852/20 December. The Romanian Parliament, 2010.

Marcu, Nicu, Georgeta-Madalina Meghişan, and Mihaela-Cristina Ciobanu. "Research on Romanian Labor Market Dynamics". Revista de Chimie 66, no. 9 (2015): 1540–1544.

Ministry of Labor and Social Justice. Evolution of the Social Security Contributions (CAS), the Contribution for the Supplementary Pension and the Contribution for the Pension and Social Insurance Fund of the Farmers during 1990–2018 (Evolutia contributiei CAS si a contributiei pentru pensia suplimentara si contributia pentru fondul de pensii si asigurari sociale ale agricultorilor in perioada 1990–2018), Bucharest 2018. Accessed May 12, 2019. http://www.mmuncii.ro/j33/images/Documente/protectie_sociala/pensii/2016_Evolutia_valorii-cotelor_CAS.pdf.

National Institute of Statistics in Romania. Tempo-online database. National Institute of Statistics in Romania. Accessed March 4, 2019. http://statistici.insse.ro:8077/tempo-online/#/pages/tables/insse-table.

Nuta, Alina Cristina, Constantin Zaman, and Florian Marcel Nuta. "Romanian Pensions System at a Glance: Some Equity Comments". Economic Research – Ekonomska istraživanja 29, no. 1 (2016): 419–433.

Pânzaru, Ciprian. "On the Sustainability of the Romanian Pension System in the Light of Population Declining". Procedia – Social and Behavioral Sciences 183 (2015): 77–84.

Pânzaru, Ciprian. "Some Considerations of Population Dynamics and the Sustainability of Social Security System". Procedia – Social and Behavioral Sciences 183 (2015): 68–76.

Pensions at a Glance 2017: OECD and G20 Indicators. Paris: OECD Publishing, 2017. Accessed March 4, 2019. http://dx.doi.org/10.1787/pension_glance-2017-en.

Preda, Marian, Cristina Dobos, and Vlad Grigoras. "Romanian Pension System during the Transition: Major Problems and Solutions". Pre-Accession Impact Studies 2, no. 9 (Bucharest: European Institute of Romania, 2004). Accessed May 15, 2019. https://www.econstor.eu/bitstream/10419/74620/1/503069485.pdf.

Roman, Mihai Daniel, Georgiana Cristina Toma, and Gabriela Tuchiluş. "Efficiency of Pension Systems in the EU Countries". Journal for Economic Forecasting 4 (2018): 161–173.

Sala, Lucian Adrian. "Romania's Population Decline and Demographic Future: Socio-Economic Aspects". Facta Universitatis-Economics and Organization 15, no. 1 (2018): 73–84.

Stancu, Ion, Dragos Haseganu, and Alexandra Darmaz-Guzun. "Projections on the Sustainability of the Pension System in Romania". Scientific Papers 0028, Institute of Financial Studies 2019.

Thalassinos, Eleftherios, Mirela Cristea and Gratiela Georgiana Noja. "Measuring Active Ageing within the European Union: Implications on Economic Development". Equilibrium. Quarterly Journal of Economics and Economic Policy 14, no. 4 (2019): 591–609. https://doi.org/10.24136/eq.2019.028.

The Financial Supervisory Authority (ASF). Annual Report, 2019. Accessed May 15, 2019. https://asfromania.ro/en/a/970/rapoarte.

The Romanian Parliament. Emergency Ordinance no. 114/28 December. 2018 regarding The Establishment of Measures in the Field of Public Investments and Fiscal-Budgetary Measures, the Modification and Completion of some Normative Acts and the Extension of Certain Terms, the Official Journal of Romania, no. 1116/29, 2018.

UNECE/European Commission. 2018 Active Ageing Index: Analytical Report. Brussels, June 2019. Accessed 10 September, 2019. https://www.unece.org/fileadmin/DAM/pau/age/Active_Ageing_Index/Stakeholder_Meeting/ACTIVE_AGEING_INDEX_TRENDS_2008-2016_web_cover_reduced.pdf.

The Pension System in Bulgaria: The Complexity of Socioeconomic Development towards Sustainable Social Security

Dorota Domalewska and Irina Mindova Docheva

1 Introduction

Bulgaria is one of the poorest EU states by GDP per capita in both nominal terms and purchasing power parity (PPP),[1] with a rapid demographic decline[2] and a rising emigration rate.[3] It is a former communist state that in late 1989 began implementing radical structural reforms in order to transform itself into a pluralistic, market-based democracy. Before the transformation, Bulgaria provided an all-embracing social safety net, including a comprehensive pension scheme and disability allowances, full employment, healthcare, worker's compensation, and tuition-free education. Unemployment benefits were unnecessary because both full employment and social insurance provided systemic support for families. During the period of transformation, Bulgaria experienced a sharp decline in output and real wages, along with rising unemployment rates[4] and considerable foreign debt (10.7 billion USD in 1989).[5] These factors constituted a significant challenge for social policy, especially in terms of ensuring the existing social safety net effectively reached the poor. Furthermore, because Bulgaria relied heavily on trade with Council of Mutual Economic Assistance (CMEA) economies and other countries (Libya, Iraq, and the Federal Republic of Yugoslavia), which were affected by UN sanctions, the

---

1   Eurostat, GDP per capita in PPS (Luxembourg: Eurostat, 2020), https://ec.europa.eu/eurostat/tgm/table.do?tab=table&init=1&language=en&pcode=tec00114&plugin=1 (accessed March 5, 2020).

2   Eurostat, Population on 1 January by Age and Sex (Luxembourg: Eurostat, 2020), https://appsso.eurostat.ec.europa.eu/nui/show.do?dataset=demo_pjan&lang=en (accessed March 5, 2020).

3   Eurostat, Emigration by Age and Sex (Luxembourg: Eurostat, 2020).

4   Ekaterina Arabska, "Problems of Employment and Unemployment in Bulgaria: Is Sustainable Development Possible?", Journal of Tekirdag Agricultural Faculty 12, no. 3 (2015): 7–8.

5   Vesna Nikolic-Ristanovic, Social Change, Gender and Violence. Post-Communist and War Affected Societies (Berlin: Springer, 2002), 9, https://doi.org/10.1007/978-94-015-9872-9.

country experienced in its transition what was possibly the largest external demand shock among Eastern and Central European economies. The lower output and income levels it has endured proved to be some of the most severe among the former CMEA countries.[6] This immense drop in output between 1989 and 1993 (amounting to a cumulative decrease in GDP of about one-third) has been followed by steady growth since 2000. More recently, the GDP has increased 3.5% (from 2018 to 2019, year-on-year), following 3.7% growth in the previous quarter.[7]

Bulgaria implemented liberalization and stabilization programs in 1989 and accelerated the structural political and economic reform in 1991. Bulgaria's state sector also underwent retrenchment as output continued to fall and unemployment skyrocketed from only 1.6% in 1990 to 10.4% in 1991, reaching an all-time high of 19.27% in 2001. In 2020 the unemployment rate was 5.9%.[8]

Finally, it has been difficult for Bulgaria to establish a viable social safety net.[9] Although the country has established unemployment compensation and social assistance programs, reaching a consensus on how these programs should be targeted has proven to be a challenge.[10] Some small reforms have been made to the pension scheme, but overhauling the system has been politically difficult, financially straining, and unfortunately inadequate when it comes to serving the needy. Additionally, since the transformation many people have lost their jobs and others have decided to emigrate for better prospects. The number of retirees enrolled in the program has also risen substantially. The system dependency ratio peaked at 82.7% in 1994 and the pension system is permanently dependent on subsidies from the treasury, while average replacement rates had dropped by 1997 to only 29% of the average monthly salary.[11]

The upward trend in individuals living on social security benefits was halted in late 1989, but it then accelerated alongside a significant decrease in GDP

---

6   Fareed M. A. Hassan and R. Kyle Jr. Peters, "The Structure of Incomes and Social Protection during the Transition: The Case of Bulgaria," Europe-Asia Studies 48, no. 4 (1996): 634.

7   Trading Economics, Bulgaria GDP Annual Growth Rate (Trading Economics, 2020), https:// tradingeconomics.com/bulgaria/gdp-growth-annual (accessed March 5, 2020).

8   Trading Economics, Bulgaria GDP Annual Growth Rate (Trading Economics).

9   Robert Ackrill et al., "Social Security, Poverty and Economic Transition: An Analysis for Bulgaria 1992–96", Economics of Planning 35, no. 1 (2002): 35.

10   Venelin Terziev et al., "The Social Assistance System in Bulgaria," IJASOS- International E-Journal of Advances in Social Sciences 5, no. 15 (December 29, 2019): 1260, https://doi.org/10.18769/ijasos.592086 (accessed February 18, 2020).

11   OECD, Reforming Public Pensions. Sharing the Experiences of Transition and OECD Countries (Paris: OECD, 2013), 29–30.

and household income (by nearly 30% between 1990 and 1992).[12] In 2012, the number of unemployed people over 15 years of age came to over three million, i.e. almost half of the working-age population remained outside the labor market, though they still participated in the consumption of income in the form of pensions, benefits, or other funds they were entitled to.[13] A majority (57%) of the unemployed are female. A large proportion is comprised of the Roma, the less educated, the unskilled, or those with a disability.[14] The rising rate of disabilities can be put down to the quality of healthcare as well as working and living conditions. As can be expected, over 40% of economically inactive people are 65 years of age or older.[15]

The current Bulgarian pension system was instituted under the Mandatory Social Insurance Code on January 1, 2000 (later renamed the Social Insurance Code in 2003). The reform sought primarily to stabilize the existing public insurance system (first pillar), and to provide an opportunity for Bulgarians to increase their own pensions by contributing to the second and third pillars of the pension system.

The aim of the chapter is to investigate general issues concerning the pension system in Bulgaria and the economic, demographic, and social determinants that affect its sustainability. Desk research was used to collect resources and available data on the status of the Bulgarian pension system. Furthermore, descriptive analysis of data was carried out, including pension system financing and the socioeconomic background of social security in Bulgaria. The chapter provides an overview of the modern Bulgarian pension system and investigates the reforms that are being implemented in order to provide sustainable and adequate social protection in old age. This is followed by an outline of key economic, demographic, and social features that affect the Bulgarian pension system and drive social policy reforms to enable social quality in old age.

---

12   Fareed M. A. Hassan and R. Kyle Jr. Peters, "The Structure of Incomes and Social Protection during the Transition: The Case of Bulgaria", 635.

13   Katya Vladimirova, Human Resource Management: Policies on Resource or Potential for Development and Social Progress (Sofia: University of National and World Economy, 2012), 97–99.

14   Katya Vladimirova, Employment Strategies and Equal Opportunities for Men and Women (Sofia: University of National and World Economy, 2008), 14–16.

15   Tihomira Trifonova and Kamellia Lillova, "Bulgaria", in Extended Working Life Policies, ed. Ni Leime A. et al. (Cham: Springer International Publishing, 2020), 178, https://doi.org/10.1007/978-3-030-40985-2_11.

2 The Bulgarian Pension System

The pension system in Bulgaria is transforming from a state-funded model to a mixed model, which is also present in other counties in the Balkans.[16] Table 6.1 displays the key features of the pension system operating in Bulgaria.

The contemporary model of the Bulgarian pension system is based on two main legislative acts: the first, the Social Insurance Fund Act, which was adopted in 1996 (SG 104/1995, canceled SG 110/1999) paved the way for a system of self-financing according to which social expenses are covered primarily by the payments of the people insured. The second act, the Mandatory Social Insurance Code (SG 110/1999, since January 1, 2000), which at present is known as the Social Insurance Code (name change as of SG 67/2003) paved the way for a three-pillar pension system that combines the advantages of both the cost-covering system of the first pillar and the capital systems of the second and third pillars.

Social insurance is based on the principles of general and obligatory insurance, solidarity among the people insured, equal rights of the people insured, social dialogue in the management of the social insurance system and the fund-based organization of resources (Art. 3, Social Insurance Code).

At present, the Bulgarian pension system is based on three pillars:

> Pillar 1 – a statutory state pension based on the cost-covering system and the principle of solidarity among generations, due to which the currently insured and self-insured people pay for the pensions of present retirees. In this pillar, a problem of great concern is the worsening of the demographic structure of society. The resources of the state public insurance concerning pensions are separated into the following funds: Pensions, Pensions of people under Article 69, and Pensions not connected with labor activity. This pillar is administered by the National Social Security Institute and is financed by the payments of three categories of people insurers, insured people, and self-insured people. The contribution of each group is legislatively mandated and there is a trend to increase the payments of insured people for the 'Pension' fund in 2017 and 2018 by 1 percent annually: 17.8% in 2016, 18.8 % in 2017, and 19.8% in 2018 for those born before January 1, 1960, and from 12.8% to 13.8 % to 14.8% for those born after December 31, 1959. There is a special provision for the armed forces, the police, and other security services: payments are paid in full by the insurers, amounting to 60.8% for people born before January 1, 1960 and 55.8% for people born

---

16   See other articles in this volume.

TABLE 6.1 Key features of the Bulgarian pension system

Pillar	Target group	Institution	Participation	Contributions	Financing	Target gross replacement rate
0	70-year-old citizens with an annual income less than the guaranteed minimum income	Means-tested social pension	Universal	non-contributory	Budget	min. 84.12 BGN per month
1	61-year-old women with social insurance cover of 35 years and 8 months; 64-year-old men with social insurance cover of 38 years and 8 months	Social Security managed by the National Social Security Institute (NSSI) and the National Revenue Authority (NRA)	Mandated	17.8% (60:40)	pay-as-you-go pension plan with a defined benefit pension	40%
2	61-year-old women and 64-year-old men born after 1959 and insured through the public pension insurance	Universal Pension Funds managed by pension insurance companies (PIC) and the NRA	Voluntary	5% (60:40)	defined contribution earning-based	20%

TABLE 6.1   Key features of the Bulgarian pension system (*cont.*)

Pillar	Target group	Institution	Participation	Contributions	Financing	Target gross replacement rate
	55-year-old workers with 10 years' work experience in arduous jobs	Professional Pension Funds managed by PIC s and the NRA	Mandated	5% (100:0)	defined contribution	N/
3	61-year-old women and 64-year-old men insured through private pension insurance	Voluntary personal and occupational pension funds managed by PIC s	Voluntary	N/A	defined contribution	N/A

SOURCE: GREGORIO IMPAVIDO, EFFICIENCY AND PERFORMANCE OF BULGARIAN PRIVATE PENSIONS (WASHINGTON DC: INTERNATIONAL MONETARY FUND, 2008), 6; INTERNATIONAL MONETARY FUND, BULGARIA. SELECTED ISSUES PAPER (WASHINGTON DC: INTERNATIONAL MONETARY FUND PUBLICATION SERVICES, 2016), 25–26; VENELIN TERZIEV, "MAIN CHARACTERISTICS OF THE PENSION SYSTEM IN BULGARIA," IJASOS – INTERNATIONAL E-JOURNAL OF ADVANCES IN SOCIAL SCIENCES 5, NO. 13 (2019), HTTP://IJASOS.OCERINTJOURNALS.ORG/EN/DOWNLOAD/ARTICLE-FILE/704972 (ACCESSED FEBRUARY 16, 2020).

after December 31, 1959.[17] The first pillar provides the following types of pensions: pensions for pensionable service and retirement age, the basic one, pensions for disabled people, inheritance pensions, and pensions not connected with labor activity. The right to a pension depends on the following, interconnected factors: age, social insurance payment history, and work under a certain category of labor conditions.

Pillar 2 – a mandatory supplementary pension scheme with universal and professional pension funds and the teacher's professional fund, which is mandatory for the early retirement of workers in arduous jobs (contributions amount to 12% or 7% of the wages paid by employers), but with an opt-out option for citizens born after 1959.[18] This second pillar is obligatory for people born after December 31, 1959. This is a capital pillar and it is based on individual savings, which constitutes the main difference between this and the first pillar. Since 2000, professional funds for early pensions have been obligatory for employees that work under the first and second categories of labor conditions (hard and unhealthy labor conditions), regardless of their age. This insurance is entirely covered by the employer.

Pillar 3 – voluntary supplementary personal pension scheme and occupational pension fund based on voluntary contributions paid to PIC s.

The minimum age for retirement in 2020 is 64.3 years for men and 61.6 years for women, though retirement can be postponed. Once an individual gains the right to a pension, it cannot be taken away. The national pension insurance fund provides special incentives for people who defer their retirement, since extending one's working life encourages potential economic growth and increases the labor supply.[19] In the funded pension insurance, contracts are based on the funds accrued in individual accounts, the technical interest rates, and biometric tables approved by the regulatory body.

The individual pension savings insurance and occupational pension schemes provide the foundation for an adequate and sustainable pension. Given the budgetary pressure on pension funding and the rising old-age

---

17   National Social Security Institute, Annual Actuarial Report (Sofia, National Social Security Institute, 2019), 13. https://www.noi.bg/images/bg/about/statisticsandanalysis/analysis/ActuarialReport_2019.PDF (accessed January 15, 2020).

18   Elaine Fultx and Kenichi Hirose, "Bulgaria, Croatia, Estonia, Latvia, Macedonia, Romania, Slovakia", in Reversing Pension Privatizations. Rebuilding Public Pension Systems in Eastern Europe and Latin America, ed. Isabel Ortiz et al. (Geneva: International Labour Organization, 2018), 309.

19   Dirk Muir and Anke Weber, Fiscal Multipliers in Bulgaria: Low but Still Relevant (Washington DC: International Monetary Fund, 2013).

dependency ratio, private pensions seem to be the best instrument for ensuring more generous pensions in the future.[20] Unfortunately, Bulgaria has yet to develop a personal pension insurance system. The number of contributors to the personal pension scheme is 600,000, with accumulated assets of 880 million BGN in 2016. This number is low in comparison to the total workforce of 3,032,000 workers, which inhibits its efficiency.[21] Table 6.2 below shows

TABLE 6.2 People insured by funds for supplementary insurance, by age and gender, as of December 31, 2019

Gender	Total number	15–24 years	25–34 years	35–44 years	45–54 years	55–64 years	Above 64	Average age (years)
Universal pension funds								
Men	1,960,206	142,262	456,408	578,500	551,660	231,376	-	40.8
Women	1,845,339	123,806	415,634	535,230	535,177	235,492	-	41.2
Total	3,805,545	266,068	872,042	1,113,730	1,086,837	466,868		41.0
Professional pension funds								
Men	254,748	3,156	32,707	71,584	87,536	46,741	13,024	46.7
Women	42,438	784	5,098	9,553	14,816	7,450	4,737	48.0
Total	297,186	3,940	37,805	81,137	102,352	54,191	17,761	46.9
Voluntary pension funds								
Men	365,718	3,389	28,317	68,329	110,957	89,258	65,468	52.3
Women	274,387	1,870	19,290	53,039	82,337	70,294	47,557	52.3
Total	640,105	5,259	47,607	121,368	193,294	159,552	113,025	52.3
Funds of voluntary professional pension schemes								
Men	2,711	47	682	938	641	312	91	42.2
Women	5,942	141	1,744	2,036	1,292	662	67	40.8
Total	8,653	188	2,426	2,974	1,933	974	158	41.3

SOURCE: OWN ELABORATION BASED ON FINANCIAL SUPERVISION COMMISSION, OSIGURENI LITSA VAV FONDOVETE ZA DOPALNITELNO PENSIONNO OSIGURYAVANE PO POL I VAZRAST KAM 30.09.2019 G., (FINANCIAL SUPERVISION COMMISSION, 2019), HTTPS://WWW.FSC.BG/ BG/PAZARI/OSIGURITELEN-PAZAR/STATISTIKA/STATISTIKA-I-ANALIZI/2019/ (ACCESSED FEBRUARY 21, 2020).

20   Venelin Terziev, "Main Characteristics of the Pension System in Bulgaria", IJASOS – International E-Journal of Advances in Social Sciences 5, no. 13 (2019), 369–370, http:// ijasos.ocerintjournals.org/en/download/article-file/704972 (accessed January 18, 2020); Lubomir Christoff, "DvePensii Ili Edna?", SSRN Electronic Journal, March 9, 2016, https:// doi.org/10.2139/ssrn.2740262.
21   Stanislav Dimitrov, "Readiness of Bulgaria to Participate in the System of a Pan-European Personal Pension Product", VUZF REVIEW 2 (2017): 75, https://doi.org/10.5281/zenodo.3376556.

age- and gender-specific information about the number of Bulgarians insured by funds for supplementary insurance.

The Bulgarian Financial Supervision Commission announced a negative minimum income of -2% for the professional pension funds for the period from December 29, 2017 to December 31, 2019 and a minimum income of -1.93% for the universal pension funds. The Commission makes these announcements on a quarterly basis. Income is an important value because it depends on the kind of activities in which the accumulated financial resources are invested in.

3   Reform Trends

There is an ongoing reform to increase the pensionable age for all categories of workers, which was adopted in 2015 and whose main aim was to financially secure pension benefits.[22] The general case for obtaining the right to a pension for pensionable service and the retirement age of men and women working under the third category of labor conditions is regulated by Art. 68 (1) and (2) of the Social Insurance Code.[23] In 2020, men must reach the age of 64.3 years and have a social insurance-payment record of 38 years and 10 months; women must be 61.6 years old and have a social insurance-payment record of 35 years and 10 months. The general idea of the legislation is that by 2037 men and women will obtain the right to a pension at the same minimum age of 65 years, but with different length-social-insurance-payment records required: 37 years for women and 40 years for men. There is an option for people who have the necessary amount of social insurance payments but have not reached the minimum age to obtain the right to a pension one year earlier, but with a reduced pension.

For people who do not have the necessary years of social insurance experience, Article 68 (3) of the Social Insurance Code[24] provides an exception – in order to obtain the right to a pension in 2020 both women and men must reach the age of 66 years and 6 months and must have real social insurance experience of 15 years. Each year, this age will rise by two months, reaching 67 years (for both men and women) in 2023.

---

22   Natalie Pitheckoff, "Aging in the Republic of Bulgaria", The Gerontologist 57, no. 5 (2017): 811, https://academic.oup.com/gerontologist/article/57/5/809/3859739 (accessed January 18, 2020); Boyan Zahariev, The Hectic Restart of the Long-Awaited Bulgarian Pension Reform. Brussels, Belgium (Brussels: European Commission, European Social Policy Network, 2015).

23   Code of Social Insurance (Title Amend. – SG 67/03), Article 68 (1–2), https://www.noi.bg/images/en/legislation/SIC_2019.pdf (accessed January 25, 2020).

24   Code of Social Insurance (Title Amend. – SG 67/03), Article 68 (3), https://www.noi.bg/images/en/legislation/SIC_2019.pdf (accessed January 25, 2020).

This exception is a double-edged sword. On the one hand, it provides the opportunity for a pension, which in 2020 amounts to 212.20 BGN (110 EUR) per month. On the other hand, it has a demotivating effect because men with 38 years and 10 months of social insurance experience who have received at least the minimum salary for these years will receive a pension of 250 BGN, and the difference that 17 years' social insurance experience makes is 38 BGN per month.[25]

Exceptions have been introduced in the law for certain categories of employees in the security sector and the armed forces to obtain the right to a pension: the Social Security Code in 2015 and Article 69 – members of the armed forces, state servants of the Ministry of the Interior, the National Intelligence Agency, the State Agency of National Security, the State Commission of Countering Corruption, the Chief Directorate 'Security' and Execution of Punishments General Directorate of the Ministry of Justice, investigators, and certain others. This category of employees (both men and women) obtains the right to a pension at an early age and with fewer years of social insurance payments: in 2020 the minimum age is 53 years and 6 months and 27 years total social insurance payments, of which 18 years were specialized social insurance experience, are required. The trend established by the legislation for this category of employees is to raise the minimum age by 2 months each year until it reaches 55 years in 2029, with no change in the amount of social insurance experience required. There is a special sub-category of employees who serve in the security services and armed forces as pilots, crew members, divers, and paratroopers obtain the right to a pension in 2020 at the age of 43 years and 6 months (for both men and women) and a special social insurance experience of 15 years. For this sub-category the trend is to raise the minimum age by 2 months annually until it reaches 45 years in 2029.[26]

Another very important category of employees with exceptions in terms of pensions are teachers. They obtain the right to a pension under Art. 69B of the Social Insurance Code, and in 2020 at the minimum age of 58 years and 6 months for women with 25 years and 8 months of teacher's social insurance experience and at 61 years and 3 months for men with 30 years and 8 months of teacher's social insurance experience.[27] The trend for this category of

25   Evgeniya Marinova, „Ot 1 yuli srednata pensiya stava 412 lv., minimalnata – 250 lv", Investor. bg, https://www.investor.bg/ikonomika-i-politika/332/a/ot-1-iuli-srednata-pensiia-stava-412-lv-minimalnata-250-lv-306840/ (accessed March 18, 2020).

26   Code of Social Insurance (Title Amend. – SG 67/03) Art. 69, https://www.noi.bg/images/en/legislation/SIC_2019.pdf (accessed January 25, 2020).

27   Code of Social Insurance (Title Amend. – SG 67/03) Art. 69B, https://www.noi.bg/images/en/legislation/SIC_2019.pdf (accessed January 25, 2020).

employees is to raise the minimum age by 2 months annually until it reaches 60 years for women and 62 years for men in 2029, and after that to raise the age by three months annually for women until it reaches an equal age for both men and women in 2037.[28]

For a two-year period (between 2018 and 2019), the judges, prosecutors, and investigators who constitute the judiciary obtained the right to a pension after 35 years of social insurance experience, two-thirds of which was special experience, with no requirement for a minimum age. As of 2020, this regulation no longer exists.

The main problem with the legal provisions establishing exceptions for early retirement is the opportunity given by the law to obtain the right to a pension without retiring and to keep the same position simultaneously. This leads to the formation of different groups of retirees. The first group consist of retirees whose only source of income is their pension. For this group of people, there are two problematic questions. There is no legal basis for recalculating their pensions (there is only a legal option to actualize or index the pension according to Art. 100 of the Social Insurance Code),[29] and over the years their pension is very close to the legal minimum. On the other hand, Bulgaria has decided to put a cap on pensions, which slightly raises it: according to the State budget law, the cap for 2020 is 1,200 BGN (600 EUR). The only people exempt from this cap are those who have held high office and had been barred by law from taking up additional employment. In 2012, the European Court of Human Rights released the decision that Bulgaria's cap on pensions does not violate Article 14 of the European Convention of Human Rights, and that there is no discriminatory treatment of different groups of retirees.[30]

The next group of retirees are those who have obtained their right to a pension, retired, and started working again in a different position in the third category of labor conditions. The pensions of this group are recalculated, and their additional social insurance experience is added.

---

28   National Social Security Institute, "Rules of Pension for Teachers", (National Social Security Institute, Sofia 2020), https://www.noi.bg/pensions/uchpf/1902-ordpensteachers (accessed January 15, 2020).

29   According to art. 100 Social Insurance Code, pensions allowed up till 31 December of previous year are actualized annually as of 1 July with a decision of National Social Security Institute with a percentage equal to 50 % of the rising of social insurance income and 50% of the index of consumer prices for the previous year. If the sum is negative, there is no actualization.

30   European Court of Human Rights (Fourth Section), Case of Valkov and others v. Bulgaria (Strasbourg: European Court of Human Rights, 2012), https://international.vlex.com/vid/valkov-and-others-v-564786950 (accessed March 17, 2020).

The third group concerns those who retire especially early, such as people working in the armed forces, the security sector, teachers, etc. They obtain the right to a pension earlier and have the legal right to exercise it without leaving their job, because there is a difference between the pensionable age and the maximum age for service: according to the Social Insurance Code (Article 69),[31] members of the armed forces obtain the right to a pension at the age of 53.6 years for both for men and women in 2020. However, according to Art. 160 of the Law of Defense and the Armed Forces of the Republic of Bulgaria (SG 35/2009, last amended SG 94/2019),[32] the maximum age of service is 55 years (sergeants and officers up to lieutenant colonels), 56 (for colonels), 57 (for colonels who are professors), 58 (for brigadier generals and major generals), 59 (for lieutenant generals) and 62 (for generals). Art. 226 (1) 1 of the Law for the Ministry of the Interior (SG 53/2014, last amended SG 58/2019) sets the maximum age of service for government workers at 60. Currently, the Council of Ministers submitted a draft amendment to the the Law of Defense and the Armed Forces of the Republic of Bulgaria to the National Assembly[33] with the aim of raising the maximum age of service for those members of the armed forces who have not exercised their right to a pension. As an argument, the Council of Ministers emphasize that at the moment two types of staff members on active duty exist: one that has exercised the right to a pension and another which has not, because there is no such example in the armed forces of the EU and NATO member states. Another argument for the amendment is the expected negative impact on the defense budget: raising the pension cap to 1,200 BGN on July 1, 2019 and the number of armed forces personnel who exercised their right to a pension by the end of 2018 has led to a significant increase in the expense for pension payments, and the budget deficit of the "pensions under article 69" fund has risen from 99.94 million BGN in 2019 to 147.54 million BGN in 2020. The Council of Ministers expects that this process will continue until 2029.[34]

31   Code of Social Insurance (Title Amend. – SG 67/03), Article 69, https://www.noi.bg/images/en/legislation/SIC_2019.pdf (accessed January 25, 2020).

32   Law of Defense and the Armed Forces of the Republic of Bulgaria (SG 35/2009, last amended SG 94/ 2019), http://vp.mod.bg/documents/Republic_of_Bulgaria_Defence_and_Armed_Forces_Act_en.pdf (accessed February 6, 2020).

33   "Zakonoproekt za izmenenie i dopalnenie na Zakona za otbranata i vaoragenite sili na Republica Bulgaria", https://www.parliament.bg/bg/bills/ID/157337/ (accessed March 2, 2020).

34   Start.bg, "Voennite vzemat po-golemi pensii, no zhiveyat dosta po-malko", https://svodka.start.bg/%D0%90%D0%B2%D0%B3%D1%83%D1%81%D1%82+%2816-31%29-19613 (accessed February 4, 2020).

Since a temporary freeze during the global financial crisis, when revenues in the social security system were lower, a weighted indexation formula has been applied. The raising of the pensionable age enacted in 2015 is projected to stabilize the budget of the mandatory social security system, assuming that the government continues to fund approximately half of the benefits annually from general taxes.[35] Since the beginning of 2017, the indexation has favored length of service over age. This measure is meant to reward longer contribution in the labor market.[36]

A plan to increase the pensionable age has been gradually introduced in recent years and it coincided with an overall stimulation of the labor market following an economic upturn. For these reasons it is difficult to determine if the results are potentially due to the ongoing reforms, especially among people immediately before and after retirement age. It will become clear in the future how the reforms will impact careers.

One of the most controversial changes to the pension system, among those introduced in a series of amendments in July 2015, allows an insured person to opt in and out of the second pillar of the system multiple times.[37] Although some felt that the decision could further weaken public trust in the private pension funds which operate the mandatory pension schemes considering there is a general lack of experience with such schemes in Bulgaria, and considering their performance and high fees there has been no noticeable, statistically significant impact on participation rates. The year-on-year growth in people participating in the schemes was similar for the periods 2012–2014 (the last year before the reform) and 2014–2016 (5.6% and 4.5%, respectively), which indicates the passivity of the participants (which is also visible in their choice of funds). According to data from the Financial Supervision Commission, 217,500 people exercised their right to transfer assets from an individual account in 2019. The proportion of people making withdrawals to the average number of people insured in universal funds is 5.35%, of those using professional funds 4.63%, and 0.25% in the case of voluntary funds.[38]

---

35   Lubomir Christoff, "(Ne)Adekvatnost Na Pensiite v Bulgarija", SSRN Electronic Journal, August 24, 2016, https://doi.org/10.2139/ssrn.2825011.

36   Code of Social Insurance (Title Amend. – SG 67/03), Article 100, https://www.noi.bg/images/en/legislation/SIC_2019.pdf (accessed January 25, 2020).

37   Nikola Altiparmakov, "Another Look at Causes and Consequences of Pension Privatization Reform Reversals in Eastern Europe", Journal of European Social Policy 28, no. 3 (2018): 231, https://doi.org/10.1177/0958928717735053.

38   Окончателни резултати от дейността по допълнително пенсионно осигуряване за 2019 г. (Final results of the supplementary pension insurance activity for 2019), Financial

The adequacy of pensions lies in fighting old-age poverty. Bulgaria has implemented comprehensive social security policies to prevent poverty and social exclusion. Apart from pension policies, in 2017 the government raised the minimum pension by a considerable amount. On July 1, 2017 the minimum pension increased from 161.38 BGN (82.5 EUR) to 180 BGN (92 EUR) monthly, which represents an increase of 11.5 percent. On October 1, 2017 there was a further increase of 11.1 percent, bringing the minimum pension to 200 BGN (102.3 EUR) per month. Such reforms not only fight poverty, but also promote social inclusion, intergenerational fairness, and equality in the context of aging populations.

4   Socioeconomic and Demographic Challenges to the Pension System

Bulgaria is one of the fastest-aging societies in the European Union due to falling fertility rates, emigration, and increasing life expectancy, as illustrated in Table 6.3. The old-age dependency ratio, which was 30.4% in 2016, is predicted to double by 2050.[39]

As the demographic indicators presented in Table 6.3 prove, the population of Bulgaria is both declining and aging, with the median age steadily increasing and the fertility rate dropping. Migratory flow, a demographic factor which shapes the population structure over time,[40] also affects the progressive aging of the population. At present, the net migration flow is negative. The age dependency ratio in Bulgaria reached 55.32% in 2018, since 2000 has increased by 7.71 points (the age dependency ratio amounted to 47.61% in 2000 and 50.36% in 1990).[41] The population pyramid (Figure 6.1) clearly shows the progressive aging of the population.

There is a large number of men and women aged 25–44, a cohort born from the late 1970s through the early 1990s, who will be gradually shifting into retirement. Taking into consideration the falling fertility rate, the proportion of elderly people will grow, placing a strain on the public pension system.

Supervision Commission, 2020, https://www.fsc.bg/en/news/okonchatelni-rezultati-ot
-deynostta-po-dopalnitelno-pensionno-osiguryavane-za-2019-g9935.html (accessed July 15, 2020).

39   World Bank, Bulgaria, 2016, https://data.worldbank.org/country/bulgaria (accessed July 15, 2020).

40   Jana Fingarova, Agency in Transnational Social Protection. Practices of Migrant Families between Bulgaria and Germany (Berlin: Frank & Timme, 2019).

41   World Bank, Age Dependency Ratio (% of Working-age Population) – Bulgaria (World Bank, 2019), https://data.worldbank.org/indicator/SP.POP.DPND?locations=BG (accessed January 4, 2020).

TABLE 6.3   An overview of the demographic developments in Bulgaria, 1955–2020

Year	Population	Yearly change (%)	Migrants (net)	Median age (years)	Fertility rate
2020	6,948,445	-0.74	-4,800	44.6	1.56
2015	7,199,741	-0.61	-4,894	43.4	1.52
2010	7,199,741	-0.69	-16,748	42.3	1.52
2005	7,686,962	-0.79	-17,100	41.1	1.25
2000	7,997,957	-0.93	-26,765	39.7	1.20
1995	8,379,308	-1.07	-71,293	38.2	1.55
1990	8,841,458	-0.30	-36,829	36.5	1.95
1985	8,975,361	0.22	-4,469	35.3	2.01
1980	8,878,791	0.32	-18,974	34.2	2.19
1975	8,738,392	0.54	-8,679	33.7	2.16
1970	8,507,551	0.68	-1,285	33.2	2.13
1965	8,222,589	0.84	-287	32.0	2.22
1960	7,885,607	0.84	-8,693	30.4	2.30
1955	7,561,493	0.84	-20,179	28.9	2.53

SOURCE: OWN ELABORATION BASED ON WORLDOMETER, BULGARIA POPULATION, HTTPS://WWW.WORLDOMETERS.INFO/WORLD-POPULATION/BULGARIA-POPULATION/ (ACCESSED MARCH 30, 2020).

The declining population has a significant effect on budgetary expenditures and revenues because an aging population requires increased allocations to both old-age pensions and public healthcare and long-term care. Unlike pensions and healthcare, the potential impact of demographic changes on other types of spending (e.g., education) tends to be uncertain.

Budgetary revenue also tends to undergo changes as a result of demographic changes.[42] Most importantly, personal income and consumer spending patterns change over one's lifetime: individuals tend to spend more at the beginning of one's working life. The spending pattern remains roughly constant until 50 years of age, then declines.[43] Governmental budgetary revenue reflects this shift which, with an aging and less active population, indicates lower

---

42   European Commission, Pension Schemes and Pension Projections in the EU-27 Member States – 2008–2060 (Brussels: European Commission, 2009), https://doi.org/10.2765/54270.

43   Gianluca Violante, "Special Issue: Cross-Sectional Facts for Macroeconomists", Review of Economic Dynamics 13, no. 1 (2010).

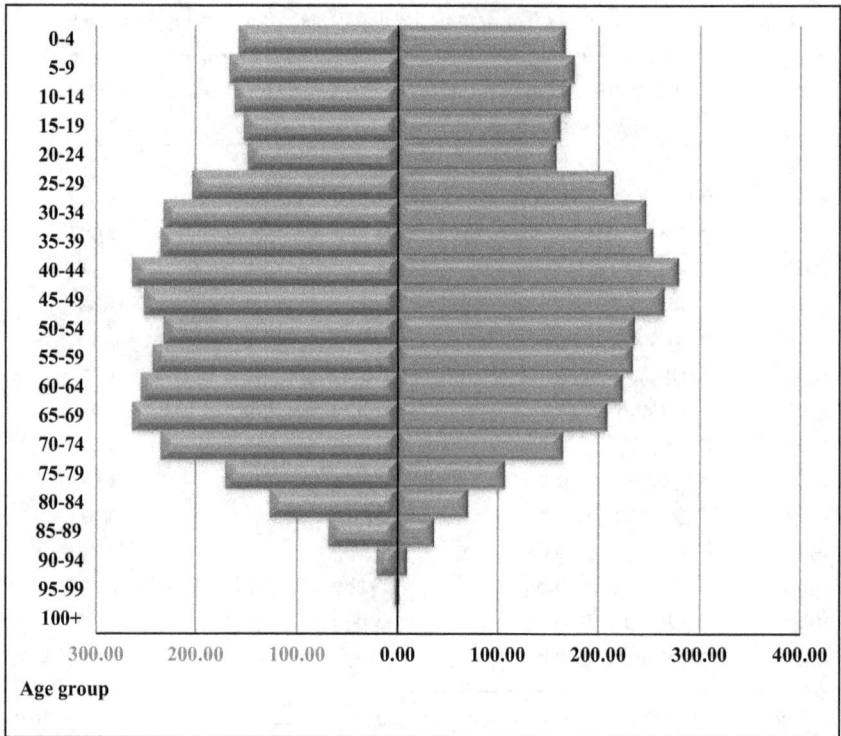

FIGURE 6.1   Population pyramid of Bulgaria
SOURCE: NATIONAL STATISTICAL INSTITUTE, POPULATION BY STATISTICAL
REGIONS, AGE, PLACE OF RESIDENCE AND SEX, (NATIONAL STATISTICAL
INSTITUTE, 2017), HTTPS://WWW.NSI.BG/EN/CONTENT/6706/POPULATION
-STATISTICAL-REGIONS-AGE-PLACE-RESIDENCE-AND-SEX (ACCESSED APRIL
8, 2020).

revenues and economic slowdown. This projection calls for policy reforms.
Nevertheless, the Bulgarian economy is keeping up with the change, as it has
entered a more advanced phase of expansion, where the growth is gradually
shifting from consumption to investment. However, at the same time, there are
noticeable increased regional disparities in socioeconomic indicators, unemployment rates, and investment.[44] Another problem that increases the fiscal

44   European Commission, Labor Market Information – Bulgaria (Brussels:
      European Commission, 2019), https://ec.europa.eu/eures/main.jsp?catId=9366&acro
      =lmi&lang=en&countryId=BG&regionId=BG0&nuts2Code=null&nuts3Code=null&
      regionName=NationalLevel (accessed March 16, 2020).

challenge is the inefficient Bulgarian healthcare system, which results from deficiencies, particularly in preventative measures and diagnosis, excessive use of expensive inpatient care, inefficient pharmaceutical pricing, problems with long-term care services, regional health inequalities, and the brain drain of medical doctors.[45] As medical expenses increase with age, retirees are at risk of falling into poverty. In 2016, more than 22.9% of the population lived below the poverty line, which was approximately 314 BGN (157 EUR).[46]

According to the written response of the Minister of Labor and Social Affairs to a parliamentary control question from the National Assembly from December 1, 2016, 1,491,371 retirees live on a basic monthly pension of less than 314 BGN (below the poverty line).[47]

Age-related public spending is related to fiscal sustainability. Bulgaria shows quite favorable financing conditions; therefore, significant fiscal adjustment is not required. The reason for improved financial stability in Bulgaria is related to the low level of public debt in relation to GDP and the reforms of the pension scheme, such as the raising of the retirement age, the restrictive pension indexation rules, and the extension of the basic entitlement period for police officers and members of the military.[48] However, it needs to be taken into account that certain factors pose risks to the financial stability of Bulgaria, such as the bank-dominated financial system that was shaken by the collapse of the country's fourth largest bank in 2014, a flagging economy, less foreign investment, and growing geopolitical tensions in the Balkan region.[49]

45   Antoniya Dimova et al., "Bulgaria. Health System Review", Health Systems in Transition 20, no. 4 (2018).
46   National Statistical Institute, Mapping of Poverty in Bulgaria (Sofia: National Statistical Institute, 2018) 13, https://www.nsi.bg/sites/default/files/files/publications/povmap.pdf (accessed April 8, 2020).
47   National Assembly of the Republic of Bulgaria, Written Answer to Parliamentary Question Nos. 654-06-1950 (Sofia: National Assembly of the Republic of Bulgaria, 2016), https://www.parliament.bg/pub/PK/248950654-06-1950.pdf (accessed April 16, 2020).
48   Kamila Bielawska, "Pension Reforms and Long-Term Sustainability of Public Finances in the Central Eastern European Countries", in Social Security Systems in the Light of Demographic, Economic and Technological Challenges, ed. Marek Szczepański (Poznań: Publishing House of Poznan Univeristy of Technology, 2015); Nikolay Nichev and Venelin Terziev, "Key Features of Pension Insurance of Military Personnel in Bulgaria", Union of Scientists in Bulgaria-Smolyan Scientific Research 2 (2016): 132–40.
49   International Monetary Fund, Bulgaria. Selected Issues Paper (Washington DC: International Monetary Fund Publication Services, 2016), 25–26.

5   Conclusion

The Bulgarian pension system has undergone several radical transformations. Firstly, major structural reforms were implemented at the end of 1989 during the post-Communist transformation to a pluralistic, market-based democracy. Secondly, the Mandatory Social Insurance Code was launched on January 1, 2000 (later renamed the Social Insurance Code in 2003). The reform sought primarily to stabilize the existing public insurance system (first pillar), and to provide an opportunity for Bulgarians to increase their own pensions by contributing to the second and third pillars of the pension system. Finally, a series of amendments to the legislation were introduced in 2015 to modify the retirement age and to allow individuals to repeatedly opt in and out of the second pillar of the pension system. The objective of the multiple reforms was to meet the socioeconomic and demographic challenges that Bulgaria is facing. However, further reforms are still necessary to alleviate poverty, promote social inclusion, and support sustainable growth.[50]

The progressive aging of the population, increasing longevity, and declining fertility lead to a rising old-age dependency ratio and a shrinking working-age population. Therefore, these demographic changes are putting financial pressure on the pension system. Policymakers need to take into account the fiscal risks resulting from demographic developments in order to ensure the long-term sustainability of the pension system. Structural and parametric changes need to be implemented to secure efficient pension schemes. As Terziev argues, a sustainable pension scheme needs to be based on contributions, taxes, and private savings; therefore "the methods of funding, eligibility conditions, and conditions on the labor market must be adapted in such a way as to achieve a balanced relationship between contributions and entitlements, the number of employed contributors of security and that of retired beneficiaries".[51] Private pension funds also ensure adequate pensions by releasing the pressure on the state budget to finance pensions. Only a sustainable and adequate pension scheme is able to withstand the grim demographic challenge. Bulgaria needs

---

50   Nikolay Nichev and Venelin Terziev, "Key Features of Pension Insurance of Military Personnel in Bulgaria", 132–40; Dragos Adascalitei, "From Austerity to Austerity: The Political Economy of Public Pension Reforms in Romania and Bulgaria", Social Policy & Administration 51, no. 3 (2017): 464–87, https://doi.org/10.1111/spol.12173.

51   Venelin Terziev, "Main Characteristics of the Pension System in Bulgaria", IJASOS – International E-Journal of Advances in Social Sciences 5, no. 13 (2019), http://ijasos.ocer-intjournals.org/en/download/article-file/704972 (accessed February 16, 2020).

to institute pension reforms faster in order to meet this challenge and to provide adequate and sustainable pensions, especially for the most economically
vulnerable retirees. Furthermore, age-related public spending on pensions,
healthcare, and long-term care needs to be more efficient to secure the stability of projected expenditures, and this can only be done once public finance is
sustainable.

Bibliography

Ackrill, Robert, Rumen Dobrinsky, Nikolay Markov, and Steven Pudney. "Social Security,
Poverty and Economic Transition: An Analysis for Bulgaria 1992–96". Economics of
Planning 35, no. 1 (2002): 19–46.

Adascalitei, Dragos. "From Austerity to Austerity: The Political Economy of Public
Pension Reforms in Romania and Bulgaria". Social Policy & Administration 51, no. 3
(2017): 464–487. https://doi.org/10.1111/spol.12173.

Altiparmakov, Nikola. "Another Look at Causes and Consequences of Pension
Privatization Reform Reversals in Eastern Europe". Journal of European Social
Policy 28, no. 3 (2018): 224–41. https://doi.org/10.1177/0958928717735053.

Arabska, Ekaterina. "Problems of Employment and Unemployment in Bulgaria: Is
Sustainable Development Possible?". Journal of Tekirdag Agricultural Faculty 12, no.
3 (2015): 6–19.

Bielawska, Kamila. "Pension Reforms and Long-Term Sustainability of Public
Finances in the Central Eastern European Countries". In Social Security Systems
in the Light of Demographic, Economic and Technological Challenges, edited
by Marek Szczepański, 21–32. Poznań: Publishing House of Poznan Univeristy of
Technology, 2015.

Christoff, Lubomir. "(Ne)Adekvatnost Na Pensiite v Bulgarija". SSRN Electronic Journal,
August 24, 2016. https://doi.org/10.2139/ssrn.2825011.

Christoff, Lubomir. "DvePensii Ili Edna?". SSRN Electronic Journal, March 9, 2016.
https://doi.org/10.2139/ssrn.2740262.

Code of Social Insurance (Title Amend. – SG 67/03 (68, 69, 69B, 100)). Accessed January
25, 2020. https://www.noi.bg/images/en/legislation/SIC_2019.pdf.

Dimitrov, Stanislav. "Readiness of Bulgaria to Participate in the System of a Pan-
European Personal Pension Product". VUZF Review 2 (2017): 69–78. https://doi.org/
10.5281/zenodo.3376556.

Dimova, Antoniya, Maria Rohova, Stefka Koeva, Elka Atanasova, Lubomira Doeva-
Dimitrova, Anne Kostadinova, and Todorka Spranger. "Bulgaria. Health System
Review". Health Systems in Transition 20, no. 4 (2018).

European Commission. Labor market information – Bulgaria. Brussels: European Commission, 2019. Accessed March 16, 2020. https://ec.europa.eu /eures/main. jsp?catId=9366&acro=lmi&lang=en&countryId=BG&regionId=BG0&nuts2Code= null&nuts3Code=null&regionName=NationalLevel.

European Commission. Pension Schemes and Pension Projections in the EU-27 Member States – 2008–2060. Brussels: European Commission, 2009. https://doi. org/10.2765/54270.

European Court of Human Rights (Fourth Section). Case of Valkov and others v. Bulgaria. Strasbourg: European Court of Human Rights, 2012. Accessed March 17, 2020. https://international.vlex.com/vid/valkov-and-others-v-564786950,

Eurostat. GDP per capita in PPS. Luxembourg: Eurostat, 2020. Accessed March 5, 2020. https://ec.europa.eu/eurostat/tgm/table.do?tab=table&init=1&language=en&p-code=tec00114&plugin=1.

Eurostat. Population on 1 January by age and sex. Luxembourg: Eurostat, 2020. Accessed March 5. 2020. https://appsso.eurostat.ec.europa.eu/nui/show.do?data-set=demo_pjan&lang=en.

Eurostat. Emigration by Age and Sex. Luxembourg: Eurostat, 2020.

Financial Supervision Commission, 2019. Osigurenilits avavfondovete zadopalnitelno pensionno osiguryavanepo pol ivazrastkam 30.09.2019 g., Accessed February 21, 2020. https://www.fsc.bg/bg/pazari/osiguritelen-pazar/statistika/statistika-i -analizi/2019/.

Fingarova, Jana. Agency in Transnational Social Protection. Practices of Migrant Families between Bulgaria and Germany. Berlin: Frank & Timme, 2019.

Fultx, Elaine, and Kenichi Hirose. "Bulgaria, Croatia, Estonia, Latvia, Macedonia, Romania, Slovakia". In Reversing Pension Privatizations. Rebuilding Public Pension Systems in Eastern Europe and Latin America, edited by Isabel Ortiz, Fabio Duran-Valverde, Stefan Urban, and Veronika Wodsak. Geneva: International Labour Organization, 2018, 303–338.

Hassan, Fareed M. A., and R. Kyle Jr. Peters. "The Structure of Incomes and Social Protection during the Transition: The Case of Bulgaria". Europe-Asia Studies 48, no. 4 (1996): 629–46.

Impavido, Gregorio. Efficiency and Performance of Bulgarian Private Pensions. Washington DC: International Monetary Fund, 2008.

International Monetary Fund. Bulgaria. Selected Issues Paper. Washington DC: International Monetary Fund Publication Services, 2016.

Law of Defense and the Armed Forces of the Republic of Bulgaria (SG 35/2009, last amended SG 94/2019). Accessed February 6, 2020. http://vp.mod.bg/documents/ Republic_of_Bulgaria_Defence_and_Armed_Forces_Act_en.pdf.

Marinova, Evgeniya. „Ot 1 yuli srednata pensiya stava 412 lv., minimalnata – 250 lv." Investor.bg. Accessed March 18, 2020. https://www.investor.bg/ikonomika-i-politika/332/a/ot-1-iuli-srednata-pensiia-stava-412-lv-minimalnata-250-lv-306840/.

Muir, Dirk, and Anke Weber. Fiscal Multipliers in Bulgaria: Low but Still Relevant. Washington DC: International Monetary Fund, 2013.

National Assembly of the Republic of Bulgaria. "Written Answer to Parliamentary Question Nos. 654-06-1950", 2016. Accessed April 16, 2020. https://www.parliament. bg/pub/PK/ 248950654-06-1950.pdf.

National Social Security Institute. "Annual Actuarial Report". Sofia, 2019. Accessed January 15, 2020. https://www.noi.bg/images/bg/about/statisticsandanalysis/analysis/ActuarialReport_2019.PDF.

National Social Security Institute. "Rules of Pension for Teachers". Sofia, 2020. Accessed January 15, 2020. https://www.noi.bg/pensions/uchpf/1902-ordpensteachers.

National Statistical Institute. "Mapping of Poverty in Bulgaria" 2018. Accessed April 8, 2020. https://www.nsi.bg/sites/default/files/files/publications/povmap.pdf.

National Statistical Institute. "Population by Statistical Regions, Age, Place of Residence and Sex" 2017. Accessed April 8, 2020. https://www.nsi.bg/en/content/ 6706/population-statistical-regions-age-place-residence-and-sex.

Nichev, Nikolay, and Venelin Terziev. "Key Features of Pension Insurance of Military Personnel in Bulgaria". Union of Scientists in Bulgaria-Smolyan Scientific Research 2 (2016): 132–140.

Nikolic-Ristanovic, Vesna. Social Change, Gender and Violence. Post-Communist and War Affected Societies. Berlin: Springer, 2002. https://doi.org/10.1007/ 978-94-015-9872-9.

Окончателни резултати от дейността по допълнително пенсионно осигуряване за 2019 г. (Final results of the supplementary pension insurance activity for 2019), Financial Supervision Commission, 2020. Accessed July, 2020. https://www.fsc .bg/en/news/okonchatelni-rezultati-ot-deynostta-po-dopalnitelno-pensionno -osiguryavane-za-2019-g9935.html.

OECD. "Reforming Public Pensions. Sharing the Experiences of Transition and OECD Countries". Paris: OECD, 2013.

Pitheckoff, Natalie. "Aging in the Republic of Bulgaria". The Gerontologist 57, no. 5 (2017):809–815.AccessedJanuary18,2020.https://academic.oup.com/gerontologist/ article/57/5/809/3859739.

Start.bg. "Voennite vzemat po-golemi pensii, no zhiveyat dosta po-malko". Accessed February 4, 2020. https://svodka.start.bg/%D0%90%D0%B2%D0%B3%D1%83% D1%81%D1%82+%2816-31%29-19613.

Terziev, Venelin. "Main Characteristics of the Pension System in Bulgaria". IJASOS – International E-Journal of Advances in Social Sciences 5, no. 13 (2019). Accessed January 18, 2020. http://ijasos.ocerintjournals.org/en/download/article-file/704972.

Terziev, Venelin, Margarita Bogdanova, Dimitar Kanev, Marin Georgiev, and Simeon Simeonov. "The Social Assistance System in Bulgaria". IJASOS – International E-Journal of Advances in Social Sciences 5, no. 15 (December 29, 2019): 1259–1265. https://doi.org/10.18769/ijasos.592086.

Trading Economics. Bulgaria GDP Annual Growth Rate (Trading Economics). https://
    tradingeconomics.com/bulgaria/gdp-growth-annual.

Trifonova, Tihomira, and Kamellia Lillova. "Bulgaria". In Extended Working Life
    Policies, edited by Ni Leime A. Cham: Springer International Publishing, 2020.
    https://doi.org/10.1007/978-3-030-40985-2_11.

Violante, Gianluca. "Special Issue: Cross-Sectional Facts for Macroeconomists." Review
    of Economic Dynamics 13, no. 1 (2010).

Vladimirova, Katya. Employment Strategies and Equal Opportunities for Men and
    Women. Sofia: University of National and World Economy, 2008.

Vladimirova, Katya. Human Resource Management: Policies on Resource or Potential
    for Development and Social Progress. Sofia: University of National and World
    Economy, 2012.

World Bank. "Bulgaria". World Bank, 2016. Accessed July 15, 2020. https://data.world-
    bank.org/country/bulgaria.

World Bank. Age Dependency Ratio (% of Working-age Population) – Bulgaria (World
    Bank, 2019). Accessed February 4, 2020. https://data.worldbank.org/indicator/
    SP.POP.DPND?locations=BG.

Zahariev, Boyan. The Hectic Restart of the Long-Awaited Bulgarian Pension Reform.
    Brussels: European Commission, European Social Policy Network, 2015.

Zakonoproekt za izmenenie i dopalnenie na Zakona za otbranata i vaoragenite sili na
    Republica Bulgaria. Accessed March 2, 2020. https://www.parliament.bg/bg/bills/
    ID/157337/.

PART 3

Social Security Evolution and Economic Recession

∴

CHAPTER 7

The Evolution of the Social Security System in Greece

Nikos Kourachanis

1   Introduction

This chapter aims to give a macroscopic view of reforms in the Greek social security system. Emphasis will be placed on the changes that have occurred in the last ten years of the crisis and austerity policies, in line with the international framework of social policy transformations. A fundamental argument is that, despite the significant divergences in the stages of development of the social security system in Greece compared to the welfare states of the Western Europe, the deregulation policies adopted in the wake of the economic crisis have led to a process that is effectively a race to the bottom.[1]

Social security is the backbone of every country's social protection system. Therefore, examining its morphology and structure highlights the complexity of social interventions in each case study. It also indicates how social policy is developed in each country and provides useful data for its interpretation. This chapter will seek to trace aspects of the operation of the social security system in Greece, comparing it with the trends in social policy transformation in Western European countries. To achieve this, a brief outline of the transformations of social citizenship and the welfare state in the countries of Western Europe will be provided in the following section. The institutional evolution of the Greek social security system from its foundation to the crisis will then be presented. The next part of this chapter offers an interpretative description of the changes brought about by the crisis in the Greek social security system. It argues that, despite significant divergences in its developmental stages compared to the welfare states of Western Europe, economic crisis management policies contribute to a race to the bottom.

At the level of methodology, this chapter elaborates primary and secondary data. The scholarly literature on the theoretical transformations of social

---

1   Barbara Vis, Kees van Kersbergen, and Tom Hylands, "To what Extent did the Financial Crisis Intensify the Pressure to Reform the Welfare State?", Social Policy & Administration 45, no. 4 (2011): 338–353.

citizenship and the welfare state is addressed. Then, through the use of scientific books and articles, laws, reports and statistics, it seeks to map the historical evolution of the Greek social security system up to the 2008 financial crisis. It then examines the impact of the crisis on the reforms of the social security system over the last decade by drawing on laws, reports and statistics from European and national organizations. The conclusions of this paper provide the key findings from the use of all these sources.

2   Transformations in Social Citizenship and the Welfare State

The theoretical framework of this chapter attempts to elaborate on the current transformations in social citizenship and the welfare state. A fundamental argument is that the modern form of social policy fails to adequately provide cover for decent living conditions, as formulated in T.H. Marshall's approach.[2] Instead, it focuses more on managing extreme poverty within a strong culture of the privatization of social services. This is a trend that had been milder since the late 1970s but became more pronounced during the Great Recession of 2008.

T.H. Marshall's approach[3] to social citizenship formed the framework for the protection and development of the post-war welfare state.[4] This protection benefited the need for the de-commodification of social benefits.[5] Marshall correlated citizenship with the working class in order to alleviate class inequalities. The establishment of social rights was not aimed at alleviating poverty; instead, the fight against social inequality in Marshall's theory was linked to living a 'civilized life'. This would be achieved by spreading the values and privileges held, until then, by a small group of affluent bourgeoisies across the broad spectrum of citizens.[6]

The post-war welfare state constituted the historical spread of the bourgeois state into the social field. In particular, it embodied the extension of state activity to an area of intervention previously covered by fragmented informal

---

2 Thomas Humphrey Marshall, Citizenship and Social Class (Cambridge: Cambridge University Press, 1950).
3 Ibid.
4 Lawrence Mead ed., Beyond Entitlement: The Social Obligations of Citizenship (New York: Free Press, 1986).
5 Gosta Esping-Andersen, The Three Worlds of Welfare Capitalism (Polity: Cambridge, 1990).
6 Thomas Humphrey Marshall and Tom Bottomore, Citizenship and Social Class (Athens: Gutenberg, 1992).

social care initiatives.[7] The dominant perception of the post-war welfare state was that the government holds collective responsibility for the well-being of its citizens[8] while the main sources of funding for these services were state taxation and public insurance.[9]

In the years that followed these economic, technological and ideological changes, there came criticisms of the Marshallian approach. It was accused of constructing a typology of a linear evolutionary form of rights that had no real impact.[10] Social rights have also been viewed as the highest evolutionary stage of rights, thus excluding the emergence of new forms of rights.[11] Marshall's theory has not sufficiently developed the dimension of the balance-of-rights measure.[12] A number of broader factors that influence the access and participation of vulnerable social groups in social rights, such as status and employment, marital status and age, were not included.[13] Finally, other forms of inequality, other than the classical, for example cultural causes such as gender, race, or religion, have been silenced.[14]

The oil crisis of the 1970s and its consequences in terms of the economic downturn challenged the Keynesian model of the welfare state. The prevalence of neoliberal ideology from the mid-1970s onwards coincided with the revival of economic liberalism.[15] In the wake of the structural reconstruction of the post-war welfare state, fundamental social rearrangements took place. Significant reductions in social spending have resulted in the emergence of new poverty phenomena.[16]

---

7   Paul Spicker, The Welfare State: A General Theory (London: Sage Publications, 2000).

8   Ramesh Mishra, The Welfare State in Crisis (Hemel Hempstead: Harvester Wheatsheaf, 1984).

9   Robert Pinker, The Idea of Welfare (London: Heinemann, 1980).

10   Bryan Turner, "Citizenship Studies: A General Theory", Citizenship Studies 1, no. 1 (1997): 14.

11   Dann Hoxsey, "Debating the Ghost of Marshall: A Ctitique of Citizenship", Citizenship Studies 15, no. 6–7 (2011): 919.

12   Lale Yalsin-Heckman, "Introduction: Claiming Social Citizenship", Citizenship Studies 15, no. 3–4 (2011): 434.

13   Julia O'Connor, "Understanding the Welfare State and Welfare States: Theoretical Perspectives", in Political Sociology: Canadian Perspectives, ed. Douglas Baer (Oxford: Oxford University Press, 2002), 12.

14   Tony Fitzpatrick, Welfare Theory: An Introduction (London: Palgrave Macmillan, 2001), 61; Bryan Turner, "Citizenship Studies: A General Theory", Citizenship Studies 1, no. 1 (1997): 14.

15   Peter Taylor-Gooby, "Postmodernism and Social Policy: A Great Leap Backwards?", Journal of Social Policy 23, no. 3 (1994): 385–404.

16   Vicente Navarro, "Neoliberalism, 'Globalization', Unemployment, Inequalities, and the Welfare State", International Journal of Health Services: Planning, Administration, Evaluation 28, no. 4 (1998): 607–82.

Vulnerable social groups from the weaker socioeconomic strata that could not cope with the new economic pressures have grown impoverished and dependent on social welfare benefits.[17] The one-dimensional focus of the dominant discourse of social policy on the new extremely excluded groups has resulted in the creation of a dichotomous construction: those within and outside the 'walls'. The formulation of this discourse implied that the non-socially excluded body was unified, compact and homogeneous, while silencing the multiple and significant inequalities within it.[18]

In the decades that followed, the grounds for a more comprehensive restructuring of the philosophy of European welfare states were cultivated in a gentle, yet systematic, way through the process of the 'Europeanization' of social policy. Strongly influenced by Giddens' 'third way' approach and the popular phrase 'no rights without responsibilities', establishing a balance between rights and obligations was considered imperative. According to this view, social reforms needed to create a form of residual social benefits for non-workers and reciprocal social rights for workers.[19] The impact of such a philosophy has contributed to the transition from the institutional and redistributive to a capitalist insurance system, as well as to a form of residual social welfare for those who fail to have insurance coverage.[20]

The transition to active social policies has been identified with the progressive domination of the active citizenship approach. Active citizenship implies greater individual responsibility for protection against social risks and for receiving welfare.[21] Increasingly, social rights are linked to obligations and conditions, which, above all, usually fail to meet the needs of citizens from the weaker socio-economic strata. A parallel development to this phenomenon was the prevalence of the concept of welfare pluralism.[22] Welfare pluralism as

---

17   Hartley Dean ed., The Ethics of Welfare: Human Rights, Dependency, and Responsibility (Bristol: Policy Press, 2004).

18   Ruth Levitas, "The Concept of Social Exclusion and the New Durkheimian Hegemony", Critical Social Policy 16, no. 2 (1996): 5–20.

19   Anthony Giddens, The Third Way: The Renewal of Social Democracy (Cambridge: Polity Press, 1998).

20   Leah Rogne, Carroll Estes, Brian Grossman, Brooke Hollister, and Erica Solway, eds. Social Insurance and Social Justice: Social Security, Medicare and the Campaign Against Entitlements (New York: Springer, 2009).

21   Kathleen Lynch, Michael Kalaitzake, and Mags Crean. Research Report on the Conceptualization of European Solidarity, SOLIDUS Project (Dublin: UCD, 2018), 18.

22   Maurizio Ferrera and Anton Hemerijck. "Recalibrating Europe's Welfare Regimes", in Governing Work and Welfare in a New Economy: European and American Experiments, ed. Jonathan Zeitlin J. and David Trubeck (Oxford: Oxford University Press, 2003).

a concept argues that prosperity can be offered by pillars other than the state, such as by civil society and the private sector.[23]

The 2008 crisis is what provided the necessary impetus to accelerate the pre-existing tendency toward social policy deregulation and to legislate new labor and social standards.[24] State backing of social policy has been legalized. In this context, the multiplicity of actors becomes an indispensable prerequisite for the fulfillment of the new context of social rights. Neoliberalism establishes the blend of welfare pluralism as a dominant model of social intervention.

The real impact of these developments is to accelerate the process of the decentralization of social services. It also intensifies the introduction of private sector administrative practices into the public sector through the New Public Management philosophy. This is a philosophy that perceives users of public services as customers / consumers and emphasizes the dimensions of efficiency, competitiveness and outsourcing at the implementation stage.[25]

In the context of the legalization of the residual welfare state, citizenship is increasingly linked to the growing commodification of social protection systems. The legal basis of citizenship is replaced by a version of economic citizenship or consumer citizenship.[26] This means that citizens can exercise their rights as long as they are able to comply with market rules. In this version of 'self-responsibilized individualism' the ideal citizen is the one who must for themselves provide social insurance, health protection and the promotion of his / her own well-being. However, this commodification of social protection results in an expansion of social inequalities, with new phenomena of social, work and insurance insecurity.

For those groups that cannot satisfy market rules and, therefore, fail to fulfill the criteria of economic citizenship, there is a residual benefit network, with charitable characteristics, on the margins of abject poverty. Since they cannot take care of their own welfare, the only care offered may come from other responsible citizens who volunteer to alleviate extreme poverty. Non-state solidarity initiatives have been developed in recent decades and were intensified during the crisis as a substitute for residual state intervention. Large

23   Norman Johnson ed., Mixed Economies of Welfare: A Comparative Perspective (London: Routledge, 2014).

24   Stephen McBried, Rianne Mahon and Gerard Boychuk eds., After '08: Social Policy and the Global Financial Crisis (Vancouver: UBC Press, 2016).

25   Joel Aberbach and Tom Christiansen, "Citizens and Consumers: An NPM Dilemma", Public Management Review 7, no. 2 (2005): 226.

26   John Clarke, Janet Newman, Nick Smith, Elizabeth Vidler and Louisse Westmarland, Creating Citizen – Consumers: Changing Publics and Changing Public Services (London: Sage, 2007).

charities, NGOs and Corporate Social Responsibility practices are expanding their social activities to alleviate the adverse social consequences of the recession.[27] Indeed, the state, in the face of the apparent residualization of its social actions, has formed partnerships with actors from the above welfare pillars (Civil Society and Private Sector).[28]

3   The Evolution of the Social Security System in Greece prior to the Economic Crisis

The development of the Greek welfare state differs significantly from the developmental stages of the welfare states of Western Europe, as has been the case in the other Southern European countries too.[29] The Greek social security system has been characterized by strong fragmentation and obvious forms of inequality in terms of paid contributions and the quality of benefits.[30]

Until recently, the social insurance system was organized on the basis of sectoral fragmentation, the vertical segmentation of the insurance agencies and the expansion of their oversight. This has been a major reason for reinforcing the uneven distribution of existing liabilities and entitlements in terms of funding, and peak benefits in the case of the pension system.[31] In this context, the social insurance system has been demarcated by over-fragmentation, the lack of meaningful social dialogue, political attrition before political costs, the abuse of pension fund reserves, selfish trade union interests and inequalities in the privileges and benefits between different professional groups.

The social assistance system was the poor relative of the Greek social security system. The social care services themselves were developed in a fragmented manner and with particular delay.[32] The safety net they offered was

---

27   Eddy Hogg and Susan Baines, "Changing Responsibilities and Roles of the Voluntary and Community Sector in the Welfare Mix: A Review", Social Policy and Society 10, no. 3 (2011): 341–352.

28   Rob Macmillan, The Third Sector Delivering Public Services: An Evidence Review (Birmingham: TSRC, 2010).

29   Maurizio Ferrera, "The Southern Model of Welfare in Social Europe", Journal of European Social Policy 6, no. 1 (1996): 17–37.

30   Maria Petmesidou and Elias Mossialos eds., Social Policy Developments in Greece (London: Routledge, 2006).

31   Xenophon Contiades, Introduction to Social Administration and Social Security Institutions (Athens: Papazisi, 2008).

32   Maria Petmesidou, "Social Care Services: Catching up", in Social Policy Developments in Greece, ed. Petmesidou Maria and Mossialos Elias (Aldershot: Ashgate, 2006), 319.

insufficient. In such conditions, the institution of the family substituted for the limited welfare functions.[33] These two key dimensions will be summarized below, in an attempt to understand the form they had until the outbreak of the 2008 financial crisis.

3.1 The Evolution of the Greek Social Insurance System until the Financial Crisis

From the 19th century until the 1920s, there was a fragmented establishment of mutual aid funds by trade unions. The state was not involved in these ventures. The first legislative attempt by the Greek state was Law 2868/1922, which established the obligation of social insurance for employees working in urban centers. In spite of its generalist spirit, this first institutional intervention did not repair the fragmented framework of the many mutual aid funds. Thus, the 'anarchic' insurance regime that began in the mid-19th century ended up being institutionalized in law.[34]

With Law 5733/1932, the Liberal government pursued a second major reform effort. The law sought to integrate insurance policy through the establishment of the Social Insurance Institute (IKA), to be responsible for sickness, invalidity, old age and death insurance. Pressure groups, such as doctors, employers, trade unions and the opposition reacted strongly to the law, and this led to its annulment.[35] Two years later, the Populist government introduced Law 6298/1934, which was a more conservative version of Law 5733/1932. The Law of 1934 was marked by a very compromising attitude to the resolution of existing problems and the basic principles laid down for the IKA were strongly influenced by the Bismarckian tradition. Law 6298/1934 was eventually implemented in 1937 by the Metaxas dictatorship.[36]

In the early post-war period, efforts were made to control the already existing fiscal deficits of the Greek social insurance system. Law 1846/1951 reorganized health and unemployment insurance and introduced legislation requiring trilateral financing of the IKA with state participation. The most important event, however, in the field of social insurance in the early postwar years was the coverage of the hitherto uninsured agricultural population with the establishment of the Agricultural Insurance Agency (OGA) under Law 4169/1961. OGA's

---

33   Maurizio Ferrera, "The Southern Model of Welfare in Social Europe", 17–37.

34   Dimitris Venieris, "The Social Insurance System in Greece: A Historical Exploration", Social Security Law Review 10, no. 442 (1995): 577–584.

35   Antonis Liakos, Labor and Politics in Interwar Greece. The International Labor Office and the Emergence of Social Institutions (Athens: MIET, 1993).

36   Dimitris Venieris, "The Social Insurance System in Greece: A Historical Exploration".

benefits were initially based on the Beveridge insurance model, funded by general taxation, so no contributions from pensioners were required.

Following the institutionalization of the OGA, the two decades that followed did not produce any radical legislative intervention in the area of pensions. Laws 825/1978 and 1305/1982 introduced the permanent and automatic indexation of IKA benefits and resources, increased pensions and expanded IKA insurance coverage throughout Greece.[37] Although they reflected a policy of social fairness, the large increases to pensions introduced by the first Socialist government (1981–1985) reinforced the fiscal deficits of the insurance system. As a result, since the early 1980s, the IKA has faced sustainability issues.[38]

The assumption of power by Constantinos Mitsotakis, the leader of the Liberals, was linked to a major three-year insurance reform aimed at reducing economic deficits. Law 1902/1990 sought to raise the retirement age, create retirement ceilings, tackle tax evasion and increase required contributions. After fierce political reactions, the government was forced to withdraw the politically painful provisions of the bill, postponing it for a second phase. Law 2084/1992 presented a breakthrough in the modern institutional development of the insurance system. It consolidated many fragmented funds, set up provisions for collecting funds, and attempted pension and benefit cuts. Most importantly, however, it introduced a new retirement scheme for those entering the labor market after 1993, with the provision of a single system of social security contributions, trilateral financing and a general retirement age of 65 years.

The Social Democrats' modernization program of 1996–2004 aimed at a new insurance reform. Following a dialogue with the social partners in 1999, a law was passed that was designated a 'mini-insurance program'. Law 2676/1999 focused more on administrative modifications than on touching upon the burning issues that had arisen in the previous years.

The Social Democrats' second election victory in 2000 gave impetus to wider changes in social insurance. A new law focused on extending the insurance problem for about 20 years. Specifically, the provisions provided for an increase in the retirement age to 65, a reduction of 60% in the rate of retirement, a calculation of the average retirement pension of the best ten of the last fifteen years, the introduction of a fictional premium for women with children and maintaining the OGA pension as a basic social benefit for the uninsured.[39]

---

37   Xenophon Contiades, Introduction to Social Administration and Social Security Institutions.

38   Dimitris Venieris, "The Social Insurance System in Greece: A Historical Exploration", 580.

39   Theodoros Sakellaropoulos, Social Policy Issues (Athens: Dionikos, 2006), 86.

After strong political and social reactions, the government backtracked by adopting a much softer law. Law 3029/2002 established occupational insurance funds, which had not been foreseen until then, increased occupational life to 35 years, set uniform retirement rules, and planned to secure the financial solvency of the IKA by the year 2030.

Law 3655/2008 of the Liberal government was the last before the onset of the financial crisis. It essentially sought to eliminate the bureaucratic system of 133 insurance agencies, reduce the waste of resources and tax evasion and reduce the unequal treatment of insurers by different professional bodies. The reform plan was designed to put in place five main insurance bodies, six subsidiary insurance bodies and two welfare agencies. The total number of insurance companies would be concentrated to just 13.

It follows from the above that the evolution of the Greek insurance system up to the economic crisis involved specific weaknesses and pathogens for which there has not been adequate political courage to tackle. In the face of strong reactions, political costs and the lack of effective social dialogue, Greek governments have opted for mild – and sometimes timid – reform interventions with extremely limited results in the face of increasing social and fiscal challenges. A central dimension from the Greek interwar period until the insurance law of 2008 was the attempt to unify a secular, fragmented and unequal insurance system through professional groups. An initiative that was started at the administrative level with the insurance reform of 2008, but also at the fiscal level, did not produce any real results. The outbreak of the financial crisis, as will be seen below, has foreshadowed a new chapter on the form and aims of social security in Greece.

3.2   The Evolution of the Greek Social Assistance System until the Financial Crisis

The evolution of the social assistance system in Greece does not depart from the fragmented spirit that characterizes wider social policy measures. Until World War II, social assistance services were extremely limited, with strong elements of stigmatization and social control practices.[40] Some forms of government-initiated welfare action occurred in the first half of the 20th century with the establishment of various institutions and public bodies.[41]

What can be considered a milestone in the evolution of social assistance in Greece is the establishment of the Patriotic Institute for Social Protection and

---

40   Maria Petmesidou and Elias Mossialos eds., Social Policy Developments in Greece, 320.
41   Antonis Liakos, Labor and Politics in Interwar Greece.

Perception (PIKPA) in 1914. PIKPA was established to meet the needs of the wounded in the Balkan wars and to care for the families of poor soldiers. Law 4062/1930 entrusted PIKPA with the operation of soup kitchens. PIKPA was later reorganized by Law 1950/1939, which defined its responsibilities and purposes, in particular tasks and purposes such as the protection of motherhood and childhood, the operation of soup kitchens and the provision of any care necessary for the afflicted and needy.

In the post-war period, a more organized social assistance policy was sought, compared to its pre-war form. Social Assistance Centers were established in 1945 in each county, while two years later the National Social Assistance Organization was established. During the 1950s, important social assistance agencies such as Mitera Hospital were established. In 1973, a single system of income support for the economically weak was introduced.[42]

The 1980s saw the will to reorganize the social assistance system and to expand the types of vulnerable groups that could receive benefits in kind and in cash.[43] Measures such as subsidies for disabled people, the retirement of uninsured elderly people, and the provision of maternity welfare, etc. were instituted at that time.[44]

The foundation of the National Health System (ESY) with Law 1397 1983 was one of the milestones of social policy in Greece. The creation of the ESY aimed at eliminating the fragmented framework of public health interventions, based on the universality of the Beveridge model.[45] In this way, access to health care for the whole population was achieved.

Concerning targeted non-income support, social assistance policy focused mainly on three vulnerable populations. The first focus was on the creation of family and child protection by providing care services through nurseries and kindergartens but also focusing on making them available for orphanages and poor children. Secondly, care was provided for the elderly through the setting up of the Elderly Care Centers (KAPI). Third, for people with disabilities, there were actions for forms of institutional care and vocational education and training programs.[46] The institutional reform of the social assistance system

---

42   Xenophon Contiades, Introduction to Social Administration and Social Security Institutions.

43   Maria Petmesidou and Elias Mossialos eds., Social Policy Developments in Greece.

44   Xenophon Contiades, Introduction to Social Administration and Social Security Institutions.

45   Charalambos Economou, Health Policies in Greece and European Communities (Athens: Dionicos, 2004).

46   Andreas Feronas, Poverty and Social Exclusion in Europe and Greece (Athens: Sakkoula, 2004).

was finally formally carried out in 1992 for the purpose of reforming the administrative structure of the public welfare system and introducing new social protection institutions.

The culmination of reform efforts that began in 1980 was the establishment of the National Social Care System (ESKF) with Law 2646/1998. The ESKF aspired to eliminate the outdated social assistance framework in the country, which was characterized by a lack of uniform planning and prioritized actions for individuals and objectives, lack of an informed development of programs, inefficiencies in the utilization of social spending, poor coordination with the ESY and low standards of the culture of voluntarism as a vehicle for assisting welfare activities.[47]

The ESKF was structured on two levels: that of planning and coordination, as well as the level of service provision. Four general groups were designated as beneficiaries of the ESKF programs: first, families, children and the youth; second, the elderly; third, people with disabilities; and fourth, vulnerable population groups and groups in need of emergency care. In the context of the reform, there was also a rationale for merging traditional providers of care, such as PIKPA, Mitera and the National Social Assistance Organization, under the auspices of the National Social Care Organization (EOKF).[48] At the same time, in 1998 the Social Solidarity Pensioners Allowance (EKAS) for the Financial Support of Elderly People with Low Retirement Benefits was introduced.

The establishment of the National Center for Emergency Social Assistance (EKAV) in 2003 aimed at coordinating the network of social support services for sections of the population experiencing emergency situations. In 2005 it was renamed the National Center for Social Solidarity (EKKA).[49] That same year, Law 3329/2005, which seeks to establish the Regional Health and Social Solidarity System, was adopted.

Until the economic crisis, the social assistance system in Greece was extremely residual. The founding of the first social assistance institutions was strongly influenced by the model of charitable organizations. After the war, the establishment of an early social assistance system legalized and instituted a repressive and socially inadequate logic. The 1980s set the stage for the expansion and institutional reorganization of social assistance policies in Greece by

---

47   Theodoros Sakellaropoulos ed., The Reform of the Social State (Athens: Kritiki, 1999), 289–290.

48   Gabriel Amitsis, Principles of Organization and Functioning of the Social Welfare System (Athens: Papazisi, 2001), 377–378, 383.

49   Xenophon Contiades, Introduction to Social Administration and Social Security Institutions.

developing targeted interventions for vulnerable social groups. As part of the European integration process, the welfare system has undergone new reform initiatives aimed at unifying and decentralizing institutions. However, the goal of providing adequate social protection for vulnerable social groups has never been achieved.

4   The Greek Social Security System during the Economic Crisis

4.1   *The Impact of the Crisis on Exacerbating Poverty and Social Exclusion*

During the period of the economic crisis, there were a number of adverse developments that led to the conclusion that the phenomena of poverty and social exclusion were significantly and abruptly exacerbated.[50] According to Eurostat data,[51] Greek government debt increased from 103% of GDP in 2007 to 127% in 2009 and, following the MoU, to 177% in 2015. Since 2010, Greece has had to resort to programs of financial adjustment (Memorandums) offered by the European Union, the European Central Bank and the International Monetary Fund. The implementation of the measures to date has been compounded by negative impacts on the income and taxation of Greek citizens, exacerbating inequalities within Greek society.[52]

Social policy is a victim of these fiscal cuts and the framework for protecting households from poverty has been further weakened. Substantial cuts to pensions, social assistance and family benefits, as well as the weakening of social services are just some of the widespread changes made to the Greek social security system during the crisis. Additionally, structural changes in the field of employment have placed even more strain on the weaker sections of society.[53]

According to Eurostat (2019) data,[54] within Greek society there has been a significant deterioration of social indicators. The poverty risk and social exclusion rates from 27.7% in 2010 increased to 35.7% in 2016, unemployment rates from 9.6% in 2009 jumped to 27.5% in 2013, long-term unemployment rates

50   Ioannis Kouzis, Constantine Dimoulas and Panagiotis Karlaganis, The Social Impact of Memoranda in Greece, GUE/LEFT (Athens: European Parliament, 2019).

51   Eurostat Database, http://ec.europa.eu/eurostat/data/database (accessed August 8, 2019).

52   Tasos Giannitsis and Stavros Zografakis, Greece: Solidarity and Adjudgement in Times of Crisis (Berlin: Hans Böckler Foundation, 2015).

53   Constantine Dimoulas and Ioannis Kouzis eds., Crisis and Social Policy, Deadlocks and Solutions (Athens: Topos, 2018).

54   Eurostat Database, http://ec.europa.eu/eurostat/data/database (accessed August 8, 2019).

from 3.9% in 2008 to 18.2% in 2015, material deprivation rates from 21.8% in 2008 to 40.7% in 2016, while the housing burden on poor households ranged from 18.1% in 2010 to 40.9% in 2016.

In an unfavorable social context, as will be discussed below, the policies of the social security system, rather than being expanded to adequately protect the growing groups of the vulnerable, have produced a residualization process.[55] In other words, the distorted, fragmented and inefficient Greek social security system, instead of being overhauled – in the light of social justice – is undergoing a major restructuring process aimed at managing extreme poverty.[56] This is a target compatible with the wider developments in the pursuit of neoliberal social policy internationally.[57]

4.2 Reforms in the Social Insurance System during the Crisis

One of the main goals of the austerity reforms was to reduce pension spending.[58] Pension expenditures decreased from 33 billion euros in 2010 to 22 billion euros in 2014. At the same time, the state subsidy to the insurance system in 2011 was 21 billion euros while in 2014 it had decreased to 8.6 billion euros. Negative side effects such as high unemployment (26%), significant wage cuts (40–45%), debts to insurance funds (26 billion euros), PSI (12 billion losses) and high rates of uninsured/ undeclared labor have contributed to this backdrop. It is noteworthy that pensions themselves have fallen sharply, with 44.8% of pensioners receiving a monthly pension below 650 euros.[59]

The parameter of the crisis is, therefore, the trigger for a series of disruptions to the social insurance system. These changes are taking place abruptly, with a major tendency to enhance the privatization of the social insurance institution by reducing its redistributive structure and enhancing its capitalization.[60] The specific spirit of the insurance changes in the Memorandum years seeks to create a mixed insurance protection economy by reducing the public pension system, reducing replacement rates, increasing contributions

---

55   Maria Petmesidou, "Is Social Protection in Greece at a Crossroads?", European Societies 15, no. 4 (2013): 597–616.
56   Christos Papatheodorou, "Economic Crisis, Poverty and Deprivation in Greece. The Impact of Neoliberal Remedies", Greek Capitalism in Crisis: Marxist Analyses, ed. Stavros Mavroudeas (London: Routledge, 2014).
57   Stephen McBride, Rianne Mahon and Gerard Boychuk, G. eds., After '08: Social Policy and the Global Financial Crisis (Vancouver: UBC Press, 2015).
58   Angelos Stergiou, Social Insurance Law (Athens: Sakkoula, 2017).
59   Savvas Robolis and Vasilis Betsis, The Insurance Odyssey (Athens: Livani, 2016), 81, 85.
60   Dimitris Venieris, Crisis Social Policy and Social Justice: The Case for Greece, GreeSE Paper no. 69 (London: LSE, 2013).

and required insurance years, making continuous cuts to pensions and pension benefits and the establishment of private-public partnerships.[61]

The first phase of insurance reformso in the years of the crisis came with Law 3863/2010 for the private sector and Law 3865/2010 for the public sector. The PASOK government attempted to establish a new framework in the architecture of the insurance system. The key points of the insurance reform were basically three: first, the establishment of uniform rules for all insured persons; second, the new structure of the pension system; third, the continuation of the task of integrating social insurance providers.

With regard to the first point, it was envisaged that it would apply a uniform way of calculating pensions for all insured persons from 2013 onwards. The required general insurance limits would increase from 37 years to 40. The retirement age would be 65 for insured men and 60 for women. Correspondingly, the ages would be 60 and 55 years respectively for those insured in difficult and unhealthy occupations. The new pension structure would be divided into two main strands: first, the basic pension of 360 euros per month, which would be provided to those over 65 on a time and income basis; secondly, a contributory type of pension that would depend on the total life of the insured person with an approximate rate of retirement of 60%. The third point concerned the continuation of the consolidation process that had begun under the insurance law of 2008. Now, insurance funds would be merged from thirteen to three, through the creation of three large funds: salaried workers, the self-employed and farmers.[62]

In the spirit of unification, there were two other health-related interventions for insured persons. Law 3863/2010[63] established the Disability Certification Center (KEPA) to provide a single health assessment of the degree of disability for all insurance funds by removing the previous multi-split disability health certification committees.

Law 3918/2011 established the National Health Service Organization (EOPYY) with the aim of reorganizing the administrative structures of the health system. Despite its unifying rationale, its operation has encountered several problems, due to the limitation of cost-saving insurance coverage, its inherent fiscal

---

61   Evangelos Koumarianos, "The Greek Social Insurance during the Crisis", in Crisis and Social Policy. Deadlocks and Solutions, ed. Constantine Dimoulas and Ioannis Kouzis (Athens: Topos, 2018).

62   New Insurance System and Related Provisions, Labor Relations Regulations, 2010 and State Pension System Reform and Related Provisions, 2010, https://www.taxheaven.gr/law/3863/2010 (accessed August 8, 2019).

63   Ibid.

deficits resulting from the transfer of the debts of the consolidated pension funds, and other issues.[64]

In 2012, Law 4046[65] provided for the reduction of employer contributions to the IKA by five percentage points in order to enhance competitiveness and entrepreneurship and reduce non-wage labor costs. The establishment of an "Insurance System Support Fund" (ETEA) was also foreseen for the utilization of the assets of the insurance funds. Law 4052/2012 establishes the Single Subsidiary Insurance Fund, which includes public and private supplementary pension funds and operates henceforth with individual accounts of defined contribution capital (NDC).

Law 4093/2012[66] introduced new changes to retirement age limits, pension reductions, and the abolition of Christmas and Easter extra pension allowances. In particular, the establishment of a pension entitlement was defined as a general age limit of sixty-seven and a minimum period of insurance of fifteen years. Also, from 2013, forty years of insurance and a minimum age of sixty-two were defined as a general requirement for retirement. With regard to pension reductions, it was foreseen that from 2013 any pension of more than 1,000 euros would be cut by 5–20% (corresponding to the scales of 1,000–1,500, 1,501–2,000, 2,001–3,000 and 3,000 euros and above respectively).

The second phase of the insurance reform was initiated by the SYRIZA-ANEL government with Law 4387/2016.[67] This law established the United Social Insurance Agency (EFKA), which merged all insurance institutions. Thus, the EFKA is now the sole main payer with uniform rules for all insured persons (even freelancers). At the same time, and by the same law, the United Subsidiary Insurance and Single Benefit Fund (ETEAEP) was established, to consolidate all supplementary insurance and one-off funds. The same logic applies to uniform contributions rules for all insured persons, uniform rules

---

64   Charalambos Economou, "The Impact of the Economic Crisis and the Memoranda on the Greek Health System", in Crisis and Social Policy. Deadlocks and Solutions, ed. Constantine Dimoulas and Ioannis Kouzis (Athens: Topos, 2018).

65   Approval of Draft Financial Facility Agreements between the European Financial Stability Fund (EFSF), the Hellenic Republic and the Bank of Greece, the Draft Memorandum of Understanding between the Hellenic Republic, the European Commission and the Bank of Greece and other urgent provisions to reduce government debt and rescue the national economy, 2012. https://www.taxheaven.gr/law/4046/2012 (accessed August 8, 2019).

66   Adoption of Medium-Term Fiscal Strategy 2013–2016, Immediate Implementation Measures of Law 4046/2012 and Medium-Term Financial Strategy 2013–2016, 2012, https://www.taxheaven.gr/law/4093/2012 (accessed August 8, 2019).

67   Unified Social Security System – Reform of Insurance – Pension System – Income and Gaming Tax Arrangeemnts and Other Provisions, 2016, https://www.taxheaven.gr/law/4387/2016 (accessed August 8, 2019).

for collecting social insurance contributions, and the consolidation of pension benefits. The EFKA will hereafter pay national and contributory pensions. The national pension is awarded to those who have completed at least 15 years of insurance and are funded by the state. The contributory pension is calculated on the basis of the average monthly salary of the insured person over his or her working life and is paid by the insurance institutions. In this context, pensions are recalculated (approximately) with the new method of calculation, while it remains to be determined what will happen with the 'personal difference'.

The fundamental change in the architecture of the social insurance system reveals at least two fundamental rearrangements. On the one hand, the introduction of a single main pension from general taxation establishes a solidarity relationship between citizens, moving away from the solidarity relationship between insured workers. Its level of institutionalization reveals that its main purpose is the management of extreme poverty. On the other hand, the introduction of the conceptual capitalization of defined contributions introduces individual returns and transfers the responsibility for ensuring a decent pension to the insured citizen themselves. In this way, the categories of workers most vulnerable to the risk of unemployment, those in ill-paid and precarious work, are most affected.[68]

The period of the economic crisis and austerity policies, therefore, brought structural breaks in the philosophy of the Greek social insurance system. A series of major consolidations of institutions and insurance rules that have been pending for decades were implemented as a result of the crisis in an abrupt manner and with the purpose, almost exclusively, of reducing pension costs. The new structure of the insurance system is a vehicle for serving the broader contemporary social policy goals and orientations: a residual type of pension coverage for those in extreme poverty and a contributory type for those who can afford insurance services.

4.3   Reforms in the Social Assistance System during the Crisis

The multifaceted adverse effects of the crisis and the implementation of the policies of austerity have had a major impact on social assistance services. In general, further tightening of the performance criteria and extensive funding cuts can be observed. However, the most important measure could be the introduction of the national pension,[69] as described in the previous section. At

---

68   Evangelos Koumarianos, "The Greek Social Insurance during the Crisis", in Crisis and Social Policy. Deadlocks and Solutions.

69   Manos Matsaganis, Social Policy in Difficult Times. Financial Crisis, Austerity, and Social Protection (Athens: Kritiki, 2011).

the same time, the tendency toward the privatization of social services, which had already been emerging, has sharply increased, making civil society itself the most important implementer of social actions.[70]

With Law 3996/2011,[71] the EKAS eligibility criteria have been made stricter, resulting in fewer beneficiaries. Following a series of amendments that deepen the cuts made to it, Law 4387/2016[72] establishes the criteria for eligibility, such as beneficiaries having reached the age of 65 and their total net income not exceeding 7,972 euros. The amount of the allowance varies from 57.50 euros to 230 euros per month although it is expected that the EKAS will be abolished by 2020. The same law provided for the payment of social solidarity allowance to uninsured elderly persons, as long as they have reached the age of 67 and are not eligible for a pension, as well as a number of other conditions for permanent legal residence in the country, including income and property criteria.

At the level of social assistance structures, a first, horizontal form of intervention during the economic crisis was implemented in the context of fiscal adjustment programs. Its purpose was to develop emergency measures to mitigate the extreme social consequences of implementation of the austerity policies. The creation of the "Social Structures to Confront Poverty" with co-financing from the European Social Fund and in collaboration with the implementing agencies of Municipalities and NGOs is typical here. Structures such as social groceries, social clinics, social pharmacies, time banks, sleeping hostels and open homeless daycare centers are being set up to relieve vulnerable groups from the adverse effects of austerity.[73]

At the same time, and also in the context of the implementation of the second memorandum, there is an initiative to streamline family benefits. The aim of rationalization was to combat fragmentation but also to reduce the amount of benefits. Law 4093/2012 introduced a single monthly family allowance of 13 – 40 euros per child, replacing a number of different family allowances. In contrast, the support allowance for families with three or more children of 42 euros per month was retained. In the same context, the universality of family

---

70   Dimitris Sotiropoulo and Dimitris Bourikos, "Economic Crisis, Social Solidarity and the Voluntary Sector in Greece", Journal of Power, Politics and Governance 2, no. 2 (2014): 33–53.

71   Reform of the Labor Inspectorate, Social Insurance regulations and other provisions, 2011, https://www.taxheaven.gr/law/3996/2011 (accessed August 8, 2019).

72   Unified Social Security System – Reform of Insurance – Pension System – Income and Gaming Tax Arrangeemnts and Other Provisions, 2016, https://www.taxheaven.gr/law/4387/2016 (accessed August 8, 2019).

73   Nikos Kourachanis, Homelessness Policies, The Greek Residual Approach (Athens: Papazisi, 2017).

benefits was abolished. Families with an annual household income of up to 30,000 euros would be eligible as would those with three or more children and an annual income of up to 45,000 euros. Law 4512/2018 introduced a second reform that further tightened the criteria for the receipt of benefits and lowered the income coverage range from 30,000 to 15,000 euros. This was done by enhancing the benefits for households experiencing extreme poverty and reducing the benefits for the small and medium-sized households. Indicatively, a household with one child and an annual income of 0-6,000 euros would receive a monthly allowance of 70 euros while those with an annual income of 6,001–10,000 euros would receive a monthly allowance of 42 euros and those with an annual income of 10,001–15,000 euros.[74] From 2017, school lunches were also introduced in selected schools in 63 municipalities around the country.

In 2013, following a series of major changes, one of the last reform initiatives was Law 4109/2013. The Law provided for the merging of the Social Care Units into a United Institution in each region. These institutions have been renamed Social Assistance Centers and they help protect the family, childhood, youth, the elderly, people with disabilities and vulnerable groups.

At the end of 2014, the implementation of actions by the Food Aid Fund for the Disadvantaged (TEVA) was approved. The TEVA is aimed at individuals and families living in extreme poverty with the aim of distributing food and basic material assistance as well as accompanying services. In 2016, Community Centers were set up to form the core of one-stop, expanded services. Their function is to develop a local reference point for the reception, service and interconnection of citizens with all social programs and services implemented in the intervention area.

At the same time, in December 2014, the Ministry of Labor published the National Strategy for Social Inclusion (ESKE). The main aim was to establish a common framework of principles, priorities and objectives for the coordination, monitoring and evaluation of all actions to combat poverty, social exclusion and discrimination at the national, regional and local levels. The basic philosophy of the ESKE is the broader development plan of the Active Welfare State.[75]

---

74   Andres Feronas, "Social Assistance in Crisis Greece: The 'Poor Relative' in the Vortex of Neoliberal Austerity", in Crisis and Social Policy. Deadlocks and Solutions, ed. Constantine Dimoulas and Ioannis Kouzis (Athens: Topos, 2018).

75   Gabriel Amitsis, Flagship Initiatives for the Preservation of Social Cohesion in the Age of the Memorandums. The Model of the National Strategy for Social Inclusion (Athens: Papazisi, 2016).

The beneficiaries of the ESKE were classified into three distinct groups: first, persons living in extreme poverty; second minors in a state of social exclusion; third, persons at increased risk of poverty and social exclusion. The first target group of ESKE beneficiaries were selected from the population who face extreme poverty due to the lack of resources to cover their main needs (nutrition, housing, hygiene, heating, etc.). For this group, the main response to social policy was to institute a minimum guaranteed income. The development of social inclusion policies for children has, in a proclamation, predicted a network of social policies with a focus on preventing the risks of poverty and social exclusion and combating social disadvantages in the first years of one's life.

The institutional interventions of the SYRIZA-ANEL government (2015–2019) have established a more systematic framework for managing extreme poverty with a set of actions to address the 'humanitarian crisis'. Article 3 of Law 4320/2015 provided for an annual food subsidy, in the form of vouchers, for extremely poor households. With Article 2 of Law 4320/2015, the government granted an annual rent allowance of up to 70–220 euros to 30,000 individuals and families living in extreme poverty and who were not able to live in a privately-owned property in their place of permanent residence. The housing allowance was reinstated in 2019 for 260,000 households at 70 euros per beneficiary and 35 euros for each additional member of the household, with a subsidy ceiling of 210 euros per month. In addition, Law 4368/2016 established the right of free access to all public health structures for the provision of nursing and medical care to the uninsured and vulnerable social groups. Finally, with Article 93 of Law 4387/2016, the Social Solidarity Benefit of the Uninsured Elderly of 360 euros per month was established.[76]

The most fundamental social assistance change in times of crisis relates to the institutionalization of social solidarity income (SSI) (a form of minimum guaranteed income). The design of this program is based on three pillars:
- income support (with an allowance below the poverty line of 200 euros per month for one-person households 300 euros for two-person households, and 350 euros for households with three persons);
- interconnection with social inclusion services;
- interconnection with activation services aimed at integrating or reintegrating beneficiaries into the labor market and social reintegration.[77]

---

76 Nikos Kourachanis, Homelessness Policies.
77 Constantine Dimoulas, "The Implementation of Social Solidarity Income in Greece", Social Policy. Hellenic Social Policy Association 7 (2017): 7–24; Varvara Lalioti, Minimum Guaranteed Income. The Chronicle of a Proposed Measure (Athens: Gutenberg, 2017).

– From the limited research evaluation to date, it has been shown that the ssi fails to address extreme poverty. On the contrary, it provides the material conditions necessary for its beneficiaries to survive, as only the income support pillar has been fully implemented to date. In such an implementation context, the creation of welfare dependency conditions is quite possible, as the beneficiaries remain for long periods in the program without being able to make themselves autonomous.[78]

The area of social assistance in Greece remains to this day obsolete in both its services and income support. Even before the crisis erupted, the safety net was perforated and unprepared for the management of its aftermath. This is due to the diverse gaps left by a number of vulnerable social groups such as the long-term unemployed, new entrants to the labor market, insecure workers, the self-employed in need, poor families, etc.[79] Based on relevant analyses, the needs of vulnerable groups for specialized services have not been sufficiently met. The need to strengthen the social safety net so that it can mitigate the social consequences does not seem to be understood by policy makers[80]; nor, by extension, does it seem to be a priority for the government to fill in the gaps in social protection.

5   Conclusions

The post-war welfare state was founded in the countries of Western Europe based on social citizenship and state social policy aimed at ensuring social cohesion. From the 1970s onwards, its contention has led to significant restructuring and regressions in state social policy. The transition to extreme poverty management and the privatization of social services took place in a gentle but systematic way until the Great Recession, and in a sharper and more intense manner over the last decade. The case of the Greek social security system diverges from this temporal fluctuation, but it does converge with its modern

---

78   Theodoros Sakellaropoulos, Varvara Lalioti and Nikos Kourachanis, "The Social Impact of the 'Social Solidarity Income' in Greece: A Qualitative Interpretation", Social Cohesion & Development 13, no. 2 (2019): 1–23.

79   Manos Matsaganis, Social Policy in Difficult Times. Financial Crisis, Austerity, and Social Protection (Athens: Kritiki, 2011), 186–187.

80   Manos Matsaganis, "Social Policy in Hard Times: The Case of Greece", Critical Social Policy 33, no. 2 (2012): 417.

manifestations. It is a process for the residualization of social policy, imposed by the dominant neoliberal ideology.

The Greek social security system was built on slender foundations and with inherent pathologies as regards the fragmentation of institutions and services, inequalities in access to social benefits across different professional and social groups, customer networks, the absence of bold reform in the face of political resistance, social inequalities, the inefficiency of social spending in tackling poverty, and the distorted and financially unstable structure of the insurance system social assistance structures.

On the one hand, the evolution of the social insurance system has been characterized by the over-fragmentation of insurance providers, the abuse of their reserves, the inequality of access to insurance for the benefit of pro-fessional groups with political influence, the lack of a social dialogue culture, and fear of the political cost of reforms. Over time, the focus has come to rest on tackling the proliferation of insurance agencies, something that was not achieved in the years before the financial crisis.

On the other hand, in the Greek example, the institution of social assistance has experienced underdevelopment over time. Its dominant features were its overstretched role within the social security system, its ineffectiveness in pov-erty reduction and a pervasive charitable dimension in the ways in which its benefits were distributed. The Europeanization of social assistance since the late 1990s has given impetus to the unification of institutions and the decen-tralization of the system, with limited social effects.

The economic crisis has had a double negative social impact on Greek soci-ety. At a time when social problems are sharply increasing, the social security system is being dismantled. The consequence of this double negative devel-opment is the exposure of more and more citizens to the risk of poverty and social exclusion. Now, the provision of the Greek social security system has shifted solely to the management of extreme poverty. It is about the cutting away of a distorted, unequal and inefficient – but existent – system of social security in a state of residualization. All the universal types of social benefit actions are designed to help the extreme poor not to die.

Major reversals are taking place in the architecture of the social insurance system, which is being transformed on the one hand into a residual-type national pension, the level of which is below the poverty line for all. On the other hand, a contributory type of pension is now added to the national one, the amount of which depends on the total life of the insured.

The increasing effects of poverty and social exclusion in times of crisis have resulted in a more structured reorganization of the social assistance system. A range of actions focusing on the material support of those who are vulnerable and cannot meet their very basic needs has been activated. But these are actions that do not depart from the philanthropic mindset of the past and are essentially fulfilled by civil society and the growing corporate social responsibility ventures. An important development is the creation of a social solidarity income, the amount of which also does not go beyond the needs of extreme poverty and, therefore, does not seek to alleviate it.

The reforms undertaken in the Greek social security system during the period of the economic crisis have led to a philosophy of convergence in social policy profiles with the wider transformations that are occurring in the European welfare states. However, this is a downward convergence process. A race to the bottom. The consolidation of a framework of residual social assistance policies for the extremely poor and the development of a privatized model of insurance coverage for those workers who are not able to obtain it are central features of modern developments internationally. The financial crisis and its management policies are the vehicle for implementing these deregulations, which follow a social policy that does not guarantee, and does not serve, the dignity of citizens.

Bibliography

Aberbach, Joel, and Tom Christiansen. "Citizens and Consumers: An NPM Dilemma". Public Management Review 7, no. 2 (2005): 225–245.

Adoption of Medium-Term Fiscal Strategy 2013–2016 – Immediate Implementation Measures of Law 4046/2012 and Medium-Term Financial Strategy 2013–2016, 2012. Accessed August 8, 2019. https://www.taxheaven.gr/law/4093/2012.

Amitsis, Gabriel. Flagship Initiatives for the Preservation of Social Cohesion in the Age of the Memorandums. The Model of the National Strategy for Social Inclusion. Athens: Papazisi, 2016.

Amitsis, Gabriel. Principles of Organization and Functioning of the Social Welfare System. Athens: Papazisi, 2001.

Approval of Draft Financial Facility Agreements between the European Financial Stability Fund (EFSF), the Hellenic Republic and the Bank of Greece, the Draft Memorandum of Understanding between the Hellenic Republic, the European Commission and the Bank of Greece and other urgent provisions to reduce government debt and rescue the national economy, 2012. Accessed August 8, 2019. https://www.taxheaven.gr/law/4046/2012.

Clarke, John, Janet Newman, Nick Smith, Elizabeth Vidler, and Louise Westmarland. Creating Citizen – Consumers: Changing Publics and Changing Public Services. London: Sage, 2007.

Contiades, Xenophon. Introduction to Social Administration and Social Security Institutions. Athens: Papazisi, 2008.

Dean, Hartley, ed. The Ethics of Welfare: Human Rights, Dependency, and Responsibility. Bristol: Policy Press, 2004.

Dimoulas, Constantine, and Ioannis Kouzis, eds. Crisis and Social Policy. Deadlocks and Solutions. Athens: Topos, 2018.

Dimoulas, Constantine. "The Implementation of Social Solidarity Income in Greece. Social Policy". Hellenic Social Policy Association 7 (2017): 7–24.

Economou, Charalambos. Health Policies in Greece and European Communities. Athens: Dionicos, 2004.

Economou, Charalambos. "The Impact of the Economic Crisis and the Memoranda on the Greek Health System". In Crisis and Social Policy. Deadlocks and Solutions edited by Constantine Dimoulas, and Ioannis Kouzis, 231–252. Athens: Topos, 2018.

Esping-Andersen, Gosta. The Three Worlds of Welfare Capitalism. Polity: Cambridge, 1990.

Feronas, Andreas. "Social Assistance in Crisis Greece: The 'Poor Relative' in the Vortex of Neoliberal Austerity". In Crisis and Social Policy. Deadlocks and Solutions edited by Constantine Dimoulas, and Ioannis Kouzis. Athens: Topos, 2018.

Feronas, Andreas. Poverty and Social Exclusion in Europe and Greece. Athens: Sakkoula, 2004.

Ferrera, Maurizio, and Anton Hemerijck. "Recalibrating Europe's Welfare Regime". In Governing Work and Welfare in a New Economy: European and American Experiments edited by Jonathan Zeitlin, and David Trubeck, 88–128. Oxford: Oxford University Press, 2003.

Ferrera, Maurizio. "The Southern Model of Welfare in Social Europe". Journal of European Social Policy 6, no. 1 (1996): 17–37.

Fitzpatrick, Tony. Welfare Theory: An Introduction. London: Palgrave Macmillan, 2001.

Giannitsis, Tasos, and Stavros Zografakis. Greece: Solidarity and Adjudgement in Times of Crisis. Berlin: Hans Böckler Foundation, 2015.

Giddens, Anthony. The Third Way: The Renewal of Social Democracy. Cambridge: Polity Press, 1998.

Hogg, Eddy, and Susan Baines. "Changing Responsibilities and Roles of the Voluntary and Community Sector in the Welfare Mix: A Review". Social Policy and Society 10, no. 3 (2011): 341–352.

Hoxsey, Dann. "Debating the Ghost of Marshall: A Ctitique of Citizenship". Citizenship Studies 15, no. 6–7 (2011): 915–932.

Johnson, Norman, ed. Mixed Economies of Welfare: A Comparative Perspective. London: Routledge, 2014.

Koumarianos, Evangelos. "The Greek Social Insurance during the Crisis". In Crisis and Social Policy. Deadlocks and Solutions, edited by Constantine Dimoulas, and Ioannis Kouzis, 151–172. Athens: Topos, 2018.

Kourachanis, Nikos. Homelessness Policies. The Greek Residual Approach. Athens: Papazisi, 2017.

Kouzis, Ioannis, Constantine Dimoulas, and Panagiotis Karlaganis. The Social Impact of Memoranda in Greece, GUE/LEFT. Athens: European Parliament, 2019.

Lalioti, Varvara. Minimum Guaranteed Income. The Chronicle of a Proposed Measure. Athens: Gutenberg, 2017.

Levitas, Ruth. "The Concept of Social Exclusion and the New Durkheimian Hegemony". Critical Social Policy 16, no. 2 (1996): 5–20.

Liakos, Antonis. Labor and Politics in Interwar Greece. The International Labor Office and the Emergence of Social Institutions. Athens: MIET, 1993.

Lynch, Kathleen, Michael Kalaitzake, and Margaret Crean. Research Report on the Conceptualization of European Solidarity, SOLIDUS Project. Dublin: UCD, 2018.

Macmillan, Rob. The Third Sector Delivering Public Services: An Evidence Review. Birmingham: TSRC, 2010.

Marshall, Thomas Humphrey. Citizenship and Social Class. Cambridge: Cambridge University Press, 1950.

Marshall, Thomas Humphrey, and Tom Bottomore. Citizenship and Social Class. Athens: Gutenberg, 1992.

Matsaganis, Manos. "Social Policy in Hard Times: The Case of Greece". Critical Social Policy 33, no. 2 (2012): 406–421.

Matsaganis, Manos. Social Policy in Difficult Times. Financial Crisis, Austerity, and Social Protection. Athens: Kritiki, 2011.

McBride, Stephen, Rianne Mahon, and Gerard Boychuk, eds. After '08: Social Policy and the Global Financial Crisis. Vancouver: UBC Press, 2016.

Mead, Lawrence, ed. Beyond Entitlement: The Social Obligations of Citizenship. New York: Free Press, 1986.

Mishra, Ramesh. The Welfare State in Crisis. Hemel Hempstead: Harvester Wheatsheaf, 1984.

Navarro, Vicente. "Neoliberalism, 'Globalization', Unemployment, Inequalities, and the Welfare State". International Journal of Health Services: Planning, Administration, Evaluation 28, no. 4 (1998): 607–82.

New Insurance System and Related Provisions, Labor Relations Regulations, 2010 and State Pension System Reform and Related Provisions, 2010. Accessed August 8, 2019. https://www.taxheaven.gr/law/3863/2010.

O'Connor, Julia. "Understanding the Welfare State and Welfare States: Theoretical Perspectives". In Political Sociology: Canadian Perspectives, edited by Douglas Baer, 110–128. Oxford: Oxford University Press, 2002.

Papatheodorou, Christos. "Economic Crisis, Poverty and Deprivation in Greece. The Impact of Neoliberal Remedie". Greek Capitalism in Crisis: Marxist Analyses, edited by Stavros Mavroudeas, 179–195. London: Routledge, 2014.

Petmesidou, Maria, and Elias Mossialos, eds. Social Policy Developments in Greece. London: Routledge, 2006.

Petmesidou, Maria. "Is Social Protection in Greece at a Crossroads?". European Societies 15, no. 4 (2013): 597–616.

Petmesidou, Maria. "Social Care Services: 'Catching Up' Amidst High Fragmentation and Poor Initiatives for Change". In Social Policy Developments in Greece, edited by Maria Petmesidou, and Elias Mossialos, 319–357. Aldershot: Ashgate, 2006.

Pinker, Robert. The Idea of Welfare. London: Heinemann, 1980.

Reform of the Labor Inspectorate, Social Insurance Regulations and Other Provisions, 2011. Accessed August 8, 2019. https://www.taxheaven.gr/law/3996/2011.

Robolis, Savvas, and Vasilis Betsis. The Insurance Odyssey. Athens: Livani, 2016.

Rogne, Leah, Carroll Estes, Brian Grossman, Brooke Hollister, and Erica Solway, eds. Social Insurance and Social Justice: Social Security, Medicare and the Campaign Against Entitlements. New York: Springer, 2009.

Sakellaropoulos, Theodoros, ed. The Reform of the Social State. Athens: Kritiki, 1999.

Sakellaropoulos, Theodoros, Varvara Lalioti, and Nikos Kourachanis. "The Social Impact of the 'Social Solidarity Income' in Greece: A Qualitative Interpretation". Social Cohesion & Development 13, no. 2 (2019): 1–23.

Sakellaropoulos, Theodoros. Social Policy Issues. Athens: Dionikos, 2006.

Sotiropoulo, Dimitris, and Dimitris Bourikos. "Economic Crisis, Social Solidarity and the Voluntary Sector in Greece". Journal of Power, Politics and Governance 2, no. 2 (2014): 33–53.

Spicker, Paul. The Welfare State: A General Theory. London: Sage Publications, 2000.

Stergiou, Angelos. Social Insurance Law. Athens: Sakkoula, 2017.

Taylor-Gooby, Peter. "Postmodernism and Social Policy: A Great Leap Backwards?". Journal of Social Policy 23, no. 3 (1994): 385–404.

Turner, Bryan. "Citizenship Studies: A General Theory". Citizenship Studies 1, no. 1 (1997): 5–18.

Unified Social Security System – Reform of Insurance – Pension System – Income and Gaming Tax Arrangeemnts and Other Provisions, 2016. Accessed August 8, 2019. https://www.taxheaven.gr/law/4387/2016.

Venieris, Dimitris. Crisis Social Policy and Social Justice: The Case for Greece. GreeSE Paper no. 69. London: LSE, 2013.

Venieris, Dimitris. "The Social Insurance System in Greece: A Historical Exploration". Social Security Law Review 10, no. 442 (1995): 577–584.

Vis, Barbara, Kees van Kersbergen, and Tom Hylands. "To what Extent did the Financial Crisis Intensify the Pressure to Reform the Welfare State?". Social Policy & Administration 45, no. 4 (2011): 338–353.

Yalsin-Heckman, Lale. "Introduction: Claiming Social Citizenship". Citizenship Studies 15, no. 3–4 (2011): 433–439.

Social Security in Greece in the Aftermath of the Economic Recession: Policies and Challenges Lying Ahead

Christos Koutsampelas

1   Introduction

In 2008, the advanced economies of the western hemisphere faced one of the worst economic crises since the Great Depression of 1929. The crisis started in the United States but soon spread across Europe. Although many European countries were severely affected, Greece experienced by far the worst fiscal episode due to a spiraling public deficit that panicked investors resulting in the exclusion of Greece from international financial markets. As a consequence, the Greek state received emergency loans in the context of three consecutive bailout programs concerted by a tripartite coalition of lenders (European Union, International Monetary Fund and European Central Bank). Although the programs fended off a complete financial collapse, they came at the cost of drastic measures affecting not only the public sector, but also the real economy. Over the 2010–2016 period, three consecutive governments legislated successive rounds of austerity measures (i.e., tax increases and spending cuts) and structural reforms causing political instability, social turmoil and nationwide protests.

Official figures are very indicative of the depth of the recession, the extent of the fiscal consolidation effort and the ensuing impact on firms and households. Overall, the Greek economy recorded six consecutive years of negative real GDP growth (from 2008 to 2013) losing almost one third of its GDP, while robust growth rates started to be recorded only after 2017.[1] Over this period, Greece exerted a unique fiscal effort in modern economic history, with the government deficit shrinking from -15.1% of GDP in 2009 to 0.5% GDP in 2016.[2]

---

1   This short narrative is based on Eurostat data: Eurostat, Real GDP Growth Rate – Volume, http://appsso.eurostat.ec.europa.eu/nui/show.do?dataset=tec00115&lang=en (accessed June 18, 2019).

2   Eurostat, Government Deficit/Surplus, Debt and Associated Data, https://appsso.eurostat. ec.europa.eu/nui/show.do?dataset=gov_10dd_edpt1&lang=en (accessed June 18, 2019).

At the same time, government consolidated gross debt increased from 126.7% of GDP in 2009 to 181.1% in 2018, despite the debt restructuring program of 2012, the level of which reached almost 50% of 2012 GDP.[3] Unsurprisingly, the effect of these events on the labor market was devastating. The unemployment rate almost tripled between 2009 and 2013; from 9.6% to 27.5%.[4] Despite the improvement in the unemployment rate improved since then (mostly due to the migration of many job-seeking Greeks abroad), Greece still recorded the highest unemployment in the EU28 in the aftermath of the crisis (19.3% in 2018). Another staggering statistic regards the record level of long-term unemployment. At 19.5% in 2014,[5] it can be claimed as one of the highest levels of long-term unemployment ever recorded in post-war Europe.

As may be anticipated, the combined effect of the recession and the ensuing policy reforms on the social security system of the country was large, multiple and complex. Generally speaking, one can discern two main channels of influence. First, fiscal consolidation inevitably endangered both the redistributive capacity and the adequacy of the system. Second, the economic downturn not only increased the demand for social protection but also changed its structure by exacerbating social needs. Policymakers found themselves at an impasse, as they were incessantly called on to do more with less. Yet, there was a potentially positive aspect, as well. Hardships triggered adaptation, forcing the state to implement structural changes which otherwise would not have been politically desired or feasible. Although there was considerable controversy in the public debate concerning the necessity of these reforms, the consensus of most policy and official reports is that they may also have positive effects, especially if viewed in a long-term perspective. Typical examples are the reforms promoting the fiscal sustainability of the pension system. Obviously, they were very unpopular. Yet, in view of the rapid ageing of the population, they seem not only unavoidable but also to ensure intergenerational equity. This is a theme transcending several parts of this chapter, the main aim of which is to provide a brief, but focused overview of the social security system as crystallized in the aftermath of the recession.

The focus of the analysis is placed on three branches of the system: healthcare, pensions and minimum income protection. This choice is not coincidental.

---

3   Jeromin Zettelmayer, Christoph Trebesch and G. Mitu Gulati, "The Greek Debt Restructuring: An Autopsy", Economic Policy 28, no. 75 (2013): 513.

4   Eurostat, Unemployment by Sex and Age – Annual Data, https://appsso.eurostat.ec.europa.eu/nui/show.do?dataset=une_rt_a&lang=en (accessed June 18, 2019).

5   Eurostat, Long-term Unemployment by Sex – Annual Data, https://ec.europa.eu/eurostat/databrowser/view/une_ltu_a/default/table?lang=en (accessed June 18, 2019).

Pensions and healthcare clearly account for the largest share of social protection spending in all European countries, including Greece.[6] These branches are also expected to face significant financial pressure in the coming decades due to population ageing, implying that they must be reformed in order to become future proof. Minimum income protection, on the other hand, represents a low fraction of social spending.[7] Yet, it is a welfare program of growing importance for the European Social Model and the continuous fight against poverty and social exclusion.[8] Moreover, until recently, Greece was one of the last countries in Europe without a national minimum income scheme, thereby marking its introduction in 2016 a milestone in the history of the Greek welfare state. The chapter investigates these issues on the basis of a document analysis of legislative sources, official reports and documents and research papers on national social policy. A wide variety of quantitative evidence, derived from official statistics readily available from national and international agencies, is used to corroborate the qualitative arguments. The study is an attempt to give an answer to the question: *What are the policy challenges that the Greek social protection system faces in the aftermath of the recession?*

The structure of the chapter is as follows: the next section describes social outcomes over 2009–2017 using a wide variety of indicators. This information provides a useful quantitative background for understanding and analyzing the content of the rest of the chapter. The subsequent three sections are devoted to healthcare, pensions and minimum income protection sharing a common structure: a first subsection succinctly describing the main features of each system, a second subsection presenting reform trends mostly focusing on recent structural reforms and their underlying rationale, and a third one analyzing the main policy challenges that lie ahead. The last section concludes by deriving the common denominator of the previous sections.

---

6   The share of public pension and healthcare spending in EU28 is estimated at 70% (European System of Integrated Social Protection Statistics – ESSPROS).

7   According to ESSPROS data, social exclusion function (where minimum income schemes are classified) represented only 1.8% of total social spending in EU28 in 2015 (author's calculations using European System of Integrated Social Protection Statistics) ESSPROS: Eurostat, Tables by Functions, Aggregated Benefits and Grouped Schemes – million EUR, https://appsso.eurostat.ec.europa.eu/nui/show.do?dataset=spr_exp_eur&lang=en (accessed June 18, 2019).

8   Hugh Frazer and Eric Marlier, Minimum Income Schemes in Europe (Brussels: European Social Policy Network 2015), 5.

2   Main Social Outcomes

The 2009–2015 recession in Greece caused significant distributional changes, affecting social outcomes in multiple ways.[9] Suffice to say, although the recession has technically ended as of the time of writing this chapter, formidable economic and social challenges still remain. Understanding these changes is important for comprehending changes in policy and how the social security system adapted to cope with shifting social needs.

Figure 8.1 shows the evolution of income poverty for five population groups over the period 2009–2017. In general, the percentage of the population below the poverty threshold (i.e., persons with income below 60% of the median equivalized income) fluctuated slightly above 20% over the whole period. Yet, the stability of the average population rate hides considerable differences

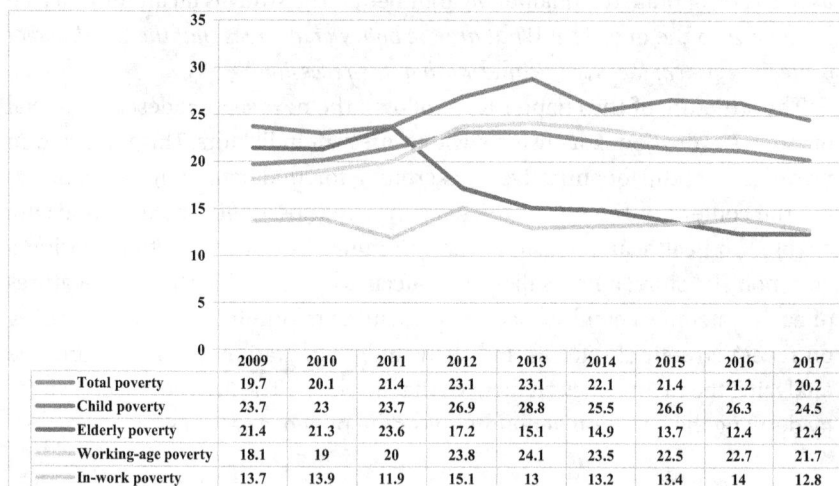

	2009	2010	2011	2012	2013	2014	2015	2016	2017
Total poverty	19.7	20.1	21.4	23.1	23.1	22.1	21.4	21.2	20.2
Child poverty	23.7	23	23.7	26.9	28.8	25.5	26.6	26.3	24.5
Elderly poverty	21.4	21.3	23.6	17.2	15.1	14.9	13.7	12.4	12.4
Working-age poverty	18.1	19	20	23.8	24.1	23.5	22.5	22.7	21.7
In-work poverty	13.7	13.9	11.9	15.1	13	13.2	13.4	14	12.8

FIGURE 8.1   Poverty in Greece (2009–2017)
   SOURCE: EUROSTAT, AT-RISK-OF-POVERTY RATE BY POVERTY THRESHOLD, AGE AND SEX – EU-SILC AND ECHP SURVEYS, HTTP://APPSSO.EUROSTAT. EC.EUROPA.EU/NUI/SHOW.DO?DATASET=ILC_LI02 (ACCESSED JUNE 18, 2019), EUROSTAT, IN-WORK AT-RISK-OF-POVERTY RATE BY AGE AND SEX – EU-SILC SURVEY, HTTPS://EC.EUROPA.EU/EUROSTAT/DATABROWSER/VIEW/ILC_ IW01$DV_407/DEFAULT/TABLE?LANG=EN (ACCESSED JUNE 18, 2019).

9   Eirini Andriopoulou, Alexandros Karakitsios and Panos Tsakloglou, "Inequality and Poverty in Greece: Changes in Times of Crisis", in Socioeconomic Fragmentation and Exclusion in Greece under the Crisis, ed. Dimitris Katsikas, Dimitri A. Sotiropoulos and Maria Zafeiropoulou (Cham: Palgrave Macmillan, 2018), 49.

among groups. The most impressive change is observed with respect to poverty in old age, which, rather counterintuitively, fell from 21.4% in 2009 to 12.4% in 2017. The main explanation for this distributional shift is that the cuts in pensions were substantially lower than the decline in average income.[10] Nevertheless, the declining trend in poverty in old age appears to have ended in 2016–2017, as the rate remained stable at 12.4% for two consecutive years. Most probably, it will increase in the coming years as reverse income dynamics are likely to dominate.

Child poverty had been increasing since the onset of the recession peaking at 28.8% in 2016. Yet, it decreased between 2015 and 2017 by 2.1 percentage points. The high levels of relative poverty among children in combination with the problem of low fertility Greece is facing today reflects and reinforces the issue of population ageing. It also gives a clear indication to what direction effective poverty-reducing policies should be directed the coming years. Poverty among the working-age population increased during the crisis, peaking at 24.1% in 2013. However, since then, the rate has been decreasing. Similarly, in-work poverty increased during 2009–2012, decreased in 2013 and increased in 2014 and 2015. One can reasonably expect that as the labor market recovers, the in-work poverty rate will record further and more substantial decreases.

Figure 8.2 reports the at risk of poverty or social exclusion (AROPE) rate, which measures not only monetary but also material deprivation and exclusion from the labor market (defined as living in a household with very low work intensity). Similar patterns to those observed in Figure 8.1 are also evident in Figure 8.2. This is largely because the poverty rate is a major element of the AROPE rate. However, the AROPE rate contains further information providing a more accurate picture of the lack of sufficient economic resources among persons. Bearing this in mind, it can be observed that the AROPE in the population stood at relatively high levels, even before the eruption of the recession, and increased substantially during the crisis years, from 27.6% in 2009 to 36% in 2014 (one of the highest in Europe in that year), only to reduce by 1.2 percentage points between 2014 and 2017. Another interesting point is that the AROPE rate is associated with age. In particular, one child in three in Greece is at risk of either poverty or social exclusion, with the indicator reaching 36.2% in 2017.

In contrast, the AROPE among the elderly reduced over the period 2009–2017; from 26.8% in 2009 to 22.8% in 2017 (nevertheless it still stands at relatively high levels). The AROPE rate among the working-age population (i.e., the

---

10   Ibid.

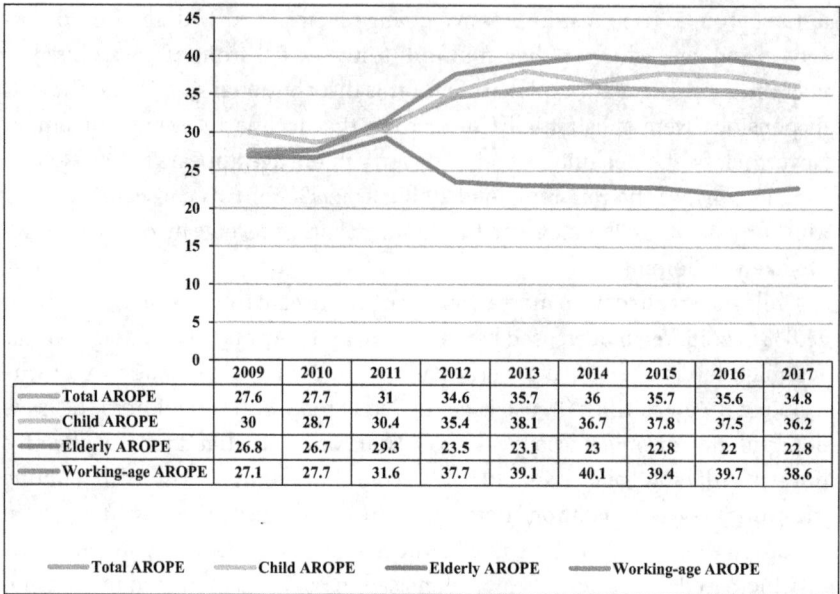

	2009	2010	2011	2012	2013	2014	2015	2016	2017
Total AROPE	27.6	27.7	31	34.6	35.7	36	35.7	35.6	34.8
Child AROPE	30	28.7	30.4	35.4	38.1	36.7	37.8	37.5	36.2
Elderly AROPE	26.8	26.7	29.3	23.5	23.1	23	22.8	22	22.8
Working-age AROPE	27.1	27.7	31.6	37.7	39.1	40.1	39.4	39.7	38.6

FIGURE 8.2   At risk of poverty or social exclusion (AROPE) in Greece (2009–2017)
SOURCE: EUROSTAT, PEOPLE AT RISK OF POVERTY OR SOCIAL EXCLUSION BY
SEX, HTTPS://EC.EUROPA.EU/EUROSTAT/WEB/PRODUCTS-DATASETS/-/TEPSR_
LM410 (ACCESSED JUNE 18, 2019).

18–65 age group) increased at unprecedented levels, reaching a record level in
2014 (40.1%). However, since then, the rate has slightly decreased, reflecting
gradual improvements in the labor market.

The overall conclusion stemming from Figures 8.1 and 8.2 is that poverty
and social exclusion stood at relatively high levels even before 2008–2009. The
recession increased everyone's risk of poverty but in an unbalanced way, as
working-age adults and children were affected disproportionately more than
pensioners.

3   Overview of the Healthcare System: Main Features, Reform Trends and Challenges

3.1   Short Description of the Current System
The health status of the Greek population stands at relatively satisfactory levels. Life expectancy at birth has increased substantially over the last decades,

reaching 81.4 years in 2017, slightly above the EU28 average.[11] There is also a considerable gender gap, with women living on average four years longer than men. Cardiovascular disease is the leading cause of death, accounting for 40% of all deaths among women and 33% among men. Cancer is the second most frequent cause of death, accounting for 20% of deaths among women and 30% among men.[12] Health inequalities are also common, with life expectancy as well as other health outcomes being associated with socioeconomic factors.[13]

Public healthcare in Greece is provided by a network of public and contracted private providers of primary, hospital and ambulatory care. The role of private providers is important especially in the areas of primary care, diagnostics and pharmaceuticals. The system is financed by general taxation, social insurance contributions and co-payments. A single public healthcare organization (i.e., the National Organization for the Provision of Health Services, whose Greek acronym is EOPYY) acts as a single purchaser of healthcare services, negotiating contracts and remunerating health professionals on the basis of a common regulation which defines the healthcare provisions for the beneficiaries of the system.

Primary healthcare is provided by contracted private providers (mostly private doctors, diagnostic centers and private clinics) or health units belonging to the National Primary Healthcare Network (PEDY), while patients may also choose to purchase services from the private sector. Hospital healthcare is provided by a network of public hospitals, which comprise the National Health System, contracted private clinics and private hospitals and clinics. Contracted private doctors provide services remunerated by EOPYY up to a predetermined ceiling, while a co-payment of 25% is imposed on pharmaceuticals.

---

11   Eurostat, Life Expectancy at Birth by Sex, http://appsso.eurostat.ec.europa.eu/nui/show
      .do?dataset=sdg_03_10&lang=en (accessed June 18, 2019).

12   OECD/European Observatory on Health Systems and Policies, Greece: Country Health
      Profile 2017, https://www.euro.who.int/__data/assets/pdf_file/0005/355982/Health
      -Profile-Greece-Eng.pdf (accessed June 18, 2019); OECD/European Observatory on
      Health Systems and Policies, State of Health in the EU (Brussels: OECD Publishing, Paris/
      European Observatory on Health Systems and Policies, 2017), 1.

13   Charalambos Economou, Daphne Kaitelidou, Marina Karanikolos and Anna Maresso,
      Greece: Health System Review. Health Systems in Transition 19, no. 5 (2017): 132; OECD/
      European Observatory on Health Systems and Policies, Greece: Country Health Profile
      2017, https://www.euro.who.int/_data/assets/pdf_file/0005/355982/Health-Profile
      -Greece-Eng.pdf (accessed June 18, 2019).

Total and public expenditure on health stood at 9.8% and 6.8% of GDP in 2013, slightly below the EU average.[14] The system is also characterized by very high levels of out-of-pocket spending, which in 2015 accounted for 35% of total health expenditure, considerably above the EU average.[15]

3.2   Reform Trends

The most important reform in the history of Greek healthcare was the establishment of the National Health System (NHS) in 1983. This pivotal reform paved the way for the development of a universal public healthcare system. The aspirations of the architects of the 1983 reform were to design a system based on the principle of universalism, which would offer equal access to all citizens, while it would be financed in a fiscally fair manner. However, the gradual development of the system deviated from its initial goals. The NHS soon evolved to a fragmented, inefficient and over-regulated system offering different services to different socioeconomic groups.[16] Widespread informal payments became a major source of corruption in the system due to patients attempting to circumvent the long waiting lists in hospitals and, in general, to receive a higher quality of services.[17] Informal payments to jump waiting lists was not the only form of corruption, with procurement corruption (i.e., favoring specific private providers) and misuse of high-level positions in the administrative hierarchy further endangering the economic soundness of the system.[18] In general, the system was characterized by many inefficiencies threatening both equity and efficiency.[19] It is not an exaggeration to claim that the inefficiency of the public healthcare sector made a certain contribution to the economic misfortune that hit the country in 2008.

---

14   European Commission, Health Care & Long-Term Care Systems: Greece. Joint Report on Health Care and Long-Term Care Systems & Fiscal Sustainability (Brussels: European Commission, 2016), 115.

15   OECD/European Observatory on Health Systems and Policies, Greece: Country Health Profile 2017, https://www.euro.who.int/__data/assets/pdf_file/0005/355982/Health -Profile-Greece-Eng.pdf (accessed June 18, 2019).

16   Elias Mossialos, Sara Allin, and Konstantina Davaki, "Analysing the Greek Health System: A Tale of Fragmentation and Inertia", Health Economics 14, (2015): 151–152.

17   Lykourgos Liaropoulos, Olga Siskou, Daphne Kaitelidou, Mamas Theodorou and Theofanis Katostaras, "Informal Payments in Public Hospitals in Greece", Health Policy 87, no. 1 (2008): 80.

18   European Commission, Health Care & Long-Term Care Systems, 112.

19   Kyriakos Souliotis, "Increasing Health Spending whilst Widening Inequalities: The Greek Paradox in Health Policy", in Health, Society and Economy: Unequal Relations – Welfare Gaps, ed. Charalampos Economou (Athens: Alexandria, 2013), 126.

The eruption of the economic crisis in 2009 fundamentally changed the healthcare landscape, as the NHS was found in the epicenter of fiscal consolidation. A series of reforms aiming at the rationalization of the system was introduced through the three Memoranda of Understanding (MoU) that were signed between Greece and its international lenders. Among the plethora of interventions and modifications, which cannot be covered in detail in this chapter, the most fundamental reforms included the establishment of the EOPYY that integrated services to all insured people including uninsured patients, the imposition of stricter control over medical prescriptions, the application of new pricing rules for pharmaceuticals and the establishment of the National Primary Health Care Network (PEDY).[20]

The establishment of EOPYY was a critical reform,[21] as it aimed at the integration of a highly fragmented system of public healthcare into a single public entity, thereby promoting efficiency and equity. Compared to the old system that offered different benefit packages to different occupational groups, EOPYY offers a common standardized benefit package covering all citizens. It is also important to note that after the legislative initiative of 2016, uninsured persons and undocumented immigrants also enjoy access to public healthcare.

Much policy effort was also exerted to reduce public spending on pharmaceuticals. This band of measures included the introduction of digital prescriptions, the imposition of ceilings for the prescription budget of each doctor and the introduction of the use of generics. Further efforts to economically rationalize the system included the integration of the system through the National Primary Health Care Network (PEDY) which aimed at creating a national primary health care network administered at the regional level. Essentially, in 2014, all primary public health care units were grouped under PEDY. Generally speaking, the upgrade of primary healthcare was seen as an important step for improving efficiency by reducing excessive reliance on costly hospital services, reducing unnecessary hospital admissions and

---

20   Dimitris Ziomas, Danai Konstantinidou and Antoinetta Capella, Inequalities in Access to
       Healthcare: Greece, 4.
21   Law No. 3918/2011 on Structural Changes to the Healthcare System and Other Provision,
       https://bit.ly/3p38KXt (accessed September 2, 2019) and Law No. 4238/2014 on the National
       Primary Health Care Network (PEDY), on the Change of Scope of the Greek National
       Health Service (EOPYY) and Other Provisions, https://www.ilo.org/dyn/natlex/natlex4
       .detail?p_lang=en&p_isn=100566&p_country=GRC&p_count=579&p_classification
       =15&p_classcount=96 (accessed September 2, 2019).

over-usage of emergency care services and counteracting the phenomenon of supply-induced demand.[22]

Yet primary care provision proved problematic, as PEDY was not enhanced with additional resources and the system remained unable to sufficiently cover the needs of the population due to staff shortages, which caused long waiting lists and limited provision of services.[23] On that basis, primary care has not proved yet successful in effectively preventing costly overreliance on specialists and inpatient care.[24] In view of this, it is not an exaggeration to add the PEDY reform to the long history of repetitive attempts to decentralize and rationalize the system of public primary healthcare.[25]

3.3   *Policy Challenges That Lie Ahead*

Before the crisis, the Greek public healthcare system was characterized by numerous inefficiencies causing not only waste of resources but also considerable socioeconomic and spatial inequalities. The policy reforms of the recessionary era undoubtedly focused on cost containment and economic rationalization, putting other policy goals, such as the reduction of health inequalities, low on the policy agenda. In fact, this policy prioritization was to a large extent inevitable due to the fiscal limitations all Greek governments encountered during the recessionary period. Additionally, one has to consider the problem of population ageing which, according to all projections, is expected to escalate, which will place extra pressure on public healthcare spending in the coming decades.[26] This means that even if the recession had never happened, some kind of economic rationalization still would have been imposed sooner or later.

That said, in the aftermath of the recession, problems relating to access, equity and quality must be addressed. Problems related to accessibility burden disproportionately vulnerable groups such as children with disabilities, the elderly, refugees, low income families, undocumented migrants, Roma, and

---

22   European Semester: Country Report – Greece (Brussels: European Commission, 2019), 37.

23   European Commission, Health Care & Long-Term Care Systems, 110; Dimitris Ziomas, Danai Konstantinidou and Antoinetta Capella. Inequalities in Access to Healthcare, 11.

24   OECD/European Observatory on Health Systems and Policies, Greece: Country Health Profile 2017, https://www.euro.who.int/_data/assets/pdf_file/0005/355982/Health-Profile -Greece-Eng.pdf (accessed June 15, 2019).

25   Athanasios Athanasiadis, Stella Kostopoulou and Anastas Philalithis, "Regional Decentralization in the Greek Health Care System: Rhetoric and Reality", Global Journal of Health Science 7, no. 6 (2015): 56.

26   European Commission, "The 2018 Ageing Report: Economic and Budgetary Projections for the EU Member States (2016–2070)", (Brussels: European Commission, 2018), 297.

persons suffering from chronic illnesses or facing hardships in accessing public healthcare services.[27] The problem of informal payments, which disproportionately affects low-income patients, seems also persistent, even though the crisis increased citizens' unwillingness to pay under-the-table.[28]

The prospect of economic growth in the coming years may allow some optimism regarding the financing of the system. Yet political will is necessary to improve the financing of the system in an efficient way, while avoiding falling into the pitfalls of the past. In any case, the policy emphasis should be on upgrading the primary healthcare infrastructure, improving hospital infrastructure, hiring health personnel, allocating human resources in a balanced way, placing an emphasis on geographically disadvantaged areas and addressing the lack of basic medical equipment.

4   Overview of the Pension System: Main Features, Reform Trends and Challenges

4.1   *Short Description of the Current System*
The backbones of the public pension system in Greece are the Unified Agency for Social Insurance (EFKA) which provides a primary pension to all persons and the Unified Fund for Auxiliary Social Insurance and Lump Sum Benefits (ETEAEP) which provides supplementary pensions and lump sum retirement benefits to salaried employees, including certain categories of the self-employed. EFKA is financed by compulsory contributions levied on the insurable earnings of all employees (with the participation of employers) and self-employed persons. The system is also financed by general taxation. There are also means-tested schemes covering uninsured persons and/or providing additional income support to low-income pensioners. The main pension provided by EFKA consists of two parts: a basic flat-rate part (i.e., national pension) financed directly by general taxation and a contributory part, which is calculated on the basis of the contribution record of the insured. The statutory retirement age is set at 67 years for both men and women, with certain

---

27   Marina Karanikolos and Alexander Kentikelenis, "Health Inequalities after Austerity in Greece", International Journal for Equity in Health 15, no.1 (2016): 83; Dimitris Ziomas, Danai Konstantinidou and Antoinetta Capella, Inequalities in Access to Healthcare: Greece, 15.
28   Kyriakos Souliotis, Christina Golna, Yiannis Tountas, Olga Siskou, Daphni Kaitelidou and Lycourgos Liaropoulos, "Informal Payments in the Greek Health Sector amid the Financial Crisis: Old Habits Die Last", The European Journal of Health Economics 17, no. 2 (2015): 159.

exceptions such as mothers with children with disabilities and workers in arduous or hazardous occupations. Early retirement is possible at 62 years, requiring at least 15 years of contributions, whereby actuarial penalties are also applied. Pensions are adjusted on the basis of a formula that takes into account inflation (as measured by the Consumer Price Index, CPI) and GDP growth. However, the rate of increase cannot exceed the CPI. Finally, starting in 2021, the minimum and statutory retirement ages will be linked with life expectancy. Expenditures on pensions have been always at relatively high levels, largely reflecting political priorities. In 2015, expenditures reached 17.7% of GDP, 4.9 percentage points above the EU28 average and 4.6 percentage points above their pre-recession levels.[29] The aggregate replacement ratio[30] (a widely used measure of pension adequacy) stood at 0.62 in 2017, slightly above the EU average and significantly above its pre-recession level (0.42).[31]

4.2   *Recent Reforms*

When the recession erupted, the Greek pension system was literally caught in the eye of the storm. Decades of clientelism and mismanagement produced a highly fragmented and economically unsustainable pension system.[32] The degree of fragmentation was extreme, with different rules and entitlements applying across several sectors of employment and a plethora of occupational categories. The system was characterized by large variation in regard to the statutory retirement age, contribution rates, minimum length of contribution periods and replacement rates.[33] Rules governing pensions were marred by a bewildering complexity, which also contributed to economic mismanagement. In parallel, pension expenditures were on the rise during the '00s, with most projections showing further increases in the coming decades due

---

29   Eurostat, Expenditure on Pensions, https://ec.europa.eu/eurostat/databrowser/view/spr_exp_pens/default /table?lang=en (accessed June 18, 2019).
30   The aggregate replacement ratio is measured as the gross median pension income of persons aged 65–74 relative to gross median earnings from work of persons aged 50–59, excluding other social benefits.
31   Eurostat, Aggregate Replacement Ration for Pensions (Excluding Other Social Benefits) by Sex, https://ec.europa.eu/eurostat/databrowser/view/tespno70/default/table?lang=en (accessed June 18, 2019).
32   Platon Tinios, "Pension Reform in Greece: 'Reform by Instalments', a Blocked Process", West European Politics 28, no. 2 (2005): 402–403; Platon Tinios, "Vacillations around a Pension Reform Trajectory: Time for a Change?", in The Challenge of Reform in Greece, 1974–2009: Assemssment and Prospects, ed. Stathis Kalyvas, George Pagoulatos, and Haris Tsoukas (New York: Columbia University Press, 2011), 3.
33   Manos Matsaganis, "The Welfare State and the Crisis: The Case of Greece", Journal of European Social Policy 21, no. 5 (2011): 4.

to population ageing.[34] In short, the combination of mismanagement, fragmentation, population ageing along with the notorious fiscal irresponsibility
of successive Greek governments created an explosive cocktail which fell heavily on pensioners. Pensions were severely cut after a long series of austerity
measures,[35] causing unprecedented social turmoil and a heavy political cost
upon the successive governments which imposed them over 2010–2016. The
ultimate aim of these measures was to safeguard the fiscal sustainability not
only of the pension system but also of the government itself as pensions were,
and still are, heavily subsidized by the state budget.

The extensive reforms of the period did not only include pension cuts. As
was also discussed above in the section devoted to healthcare, several structural reforms were deemed necessary for the rationalization of the system.
Most recently, in 2016, the government integrated all the main public pension
funds into a single entity (EFKA), while all supplementary pensions and lump
sum benefits were integrated into another single entity (ETEAEP) within the
framework of the third Memorandum of Understanding.[36] The aim of this
reform was to improve governance and equity through applying uniform
rules to eligibility conditions and benefit entitlements. Of course, the merger
of small social insurance agencies into a single one does not automatically

---

34   European Commission, The 2018 Ageing Report: Economic and Budgetary Projections for
      the EU Member States (2016–2070), 297.
35   For example, in 2011 and 2012 several legislative actions imposed pension cuts (Law No.
      4024 of 2011 Issues of Retirement Pensions, of Unified Wage System – Grading System,
      Employment Reserves and Other Provisions concerning the Mid-Term Framework of Fiscal
      Strategy 2012–2015), http://ilo.org/dyn/natlex/natlex4.detail?p_lang=en&p_isn=89634&p_
      country=GRC&p_count=610 (accessed September 2, 2019), Law No. 4051 of 2012 Introducing
      Retirement Adjustments and Other Emergency Regulations in Apllication of Memoran-
      dum of Understanding, https://www.ilo.org/dyn/natlex/natlex4.detail?p_lang=en&p_
      isn=99834 (accessed September 2, 2019), and Law No. 4093 of 2012 Approving Medium-
      Term Fiscal Strategy 2013-2016 and Introducing Emergency Measures Implementing Law
      No. 4046 of 2012 and the Medium-Term Fiscal Strategy 2013–2016, https://www.ilo.org/
      dyn/natlex/natlex4.detail?p_lang=en&p_isn=99876 (accessed September 2, 2019), while
      the 13th and 14th pension were substituted by an allowance, which thereafter was abol-
      ished (National Actuarial Authority, 2015); Law No. 4093 of 2012 approving the Medium-
      Term Fiscal Strategy 2013-2016 and Introducing Emergency Measures Implementing
      Law No. 4046/2012 and the medium-term fiscal strategy 2013–2016, https://www.ilo
      .org/dyn/natlex/natlex4.detail?p_lang=&p_isn=99876&p_country=GRC&p_count=702
      (accessed September 2, 2019).
36   Law No. 4387 of 2016 introducing the Unified System of Social Insurance, providing for
      the reform of the social protection system and pension scheme and regulating the tax
      income and taxation for chance-games and inserting other provisions, https://www.ilo
      .org/dyn/natlex/natlex4.detail?p_lang=en&p_isn=104502 (accessed September 2, 2019).

guarantee uniformity, as the acquired rights of the past pensioners will be protected for a transitory period.[37] However, it is reasonable to expect that if new forms of fragmentation are avoided in the future, Greece will gradually acquire a pension system aligned with the principles of horizontal and vertical equity.

The structural pension reforms extend beyond the establishment of the single social security agency and included the establishment of a national non-contributory minimum pension, the gradual phase-out of the Pensioners' Social Solidarity Benefit (EKAS), the introduction of a statutory linkage between life expectancy and retirement age, the tightening of the eligibility criteria for several old-age benefits as well as other reforms, which to present and describe is far beyond the limited scope of this chapter.

4.3   Policy Challenges Lying Ahead

Although severe cuts were imposed on pensions, an oxymoron occurred: poverty among pensioners did not increase but actually declined significantly in recent years. Specifically, the poverty rate for pensioners fell from 18.4% in 2009 to 9.5% in 2017. In 2017, Greece recorded one of the lowest poverty rates among pensioners in the EU (EU28: 14.2%).[38] This income phenomenon has been also observed in other recessionary contexts[39] and its explanation is simple. The sharp decline of the risk of poverty among the elderly during a recession reflects a relative (i.e., *vis à vis* the income of other age groups) improvement in their position. In particular, it appears that during recessions, the income of the working age population is more vulnerable to reductions.[40] Yet this trend also reflects the political willingness to protect pensioners (or certain groups of pensioners), at least in relative terms.

Overall, it appears that the current adequacy and the economic sustainability of the system have been achieved, at least for the present time. Several of the very unpopular measures and reforms implemented over 2010 – 2016 appear less unattractive in retrospect. To give an obvious example, increasing statutory retirement ages and linking them with life expectancy is not an unreasonable option for a country with a rapidly greying population. Indeed,

---

37   Manos Matsaganis, The Welfare State and the Crisis: The Case of Greece, 503.

38   Eurostat, At-risk-of-poverty Rate for Pensioners – EU-SILC survey, https://ec.europa.eu/eurostat/databrowser/view/tespn100/default/table?lang=en (accessed June 18, 2019).

39   Christos Koutsampelas, "Aspects of Elderly Poverty in Cyprus", Cyprus Economic Policy Review 6, no. 1 (2012): 82–83.

40   Ibid., Andriopoulou Eirini, Karakitsios Alexandros and Panos Tsakloglou. Inequality and Poverty in Greece: Changes in Times of Crisis (Bonn: Institute of Labor Economics, 2017), 24–25.

according to the European Commission,[41] Greece faces one of the highest rates of population ageing in the EU28, with the old-age dependency ratio reaching 34.1 in 2018; 3.6 percentage points above the EU28 average.[42] This demographic trend is accompanied by persistently high unemployment rates and the strong waves of emigration of young Greeks still may place the sustainability of the system in the future in doubt. Thus, the policy challenge in the case of pensions is straightforward: to continuously monitor the economic viability of the system, making interventions when necessary, while simultaneously safeguarding pension adequacy.

5   Overview of the Minimum Income System: Main Features, Reform Trends and Challenges

5.1   *Short Description of the Current System*
Minimum income protection is provided by the Social Solidarity Income (SSI) scheme. The scheme, which is financed by general taxation, provides a means-tested top-up cash benefit, the aim of which is to guarantee that all eligible persons do not receive an income below a specified guaranteed minimum income, which is assumed to ensure a minimum accepted standard of living. The cash benefit is supplemented by certain in-kind benefits (such as free medical treatment) and access to several social and activation services deemed necessary for recipients' social and labor-market integration. The scheme also provides for a Social Solidarity Allowance for Uninsured Elders, which targets persons over age 67 living in poverty and without (sufficient) pension income.

The guaranteed minimum income varies according to the household structure (i.e., the number and age of household members) on the basis of the modified OECD equivalence scale (while special provisions hold for families with disabled members and single-parent families). In particular, the minimum threshold is currently set at €200 per month for a single person, plus €100 per month for each additional adult member in the household and another €50 per month for each additional child. However, the maximum guaranteed amount cannot exceed €900 per month, regardless of the household composition. As is typical in most minimum income schemes, eligibility requires the fulfilment

41   European Commission, The 2018 Ageing Report: Economic and Budgetary Projections for the EU Member States (2016–2070), 297.
42   Eurostat, Old-age-Dependency Ratio, http://appsso.eurostat.ec.europa.eu/nui/show.do?-dataset=tps00198&lang=en (accessed June 18, 2019).

234

KOUTSAMPELAS

of certain job conditionalities (only for working-age adults) such as registering with Public Employment Services and accepting suitable jobs if offered.[43]

5.2   *Recent Reforms*

Until 2016, Greece was among the very few EU countries lacking a comprehensive national minimum income scheme.[44] This was not entirely coincidental, as it reflected the orientation of the Greek social welfare state towards contributory and occupational-based benefits, while non-contributory social assistance found little political support. In general, the marginal role of social assistance has been historically understood as a defining feature of the southern welfare states stemming from their unique political and institutional characteristics.[45] Nevertheless, the constantly deteriorating socioeconomic conditions of 2009–2014 created the necessary pressure for the design of a minimum income scheme.[46]

Initially, a pilot scheme was operated in thirteen municipalities in 2014 to 'test the waters' before implementing the scheme at the national level.[47] The pilot program operated for six months. In 2016, the gradual implementation of the national SSI launched,[48] following two joint Ministerial Decisions regulating the first and second phase of implementation.[49] It is important to note

---

43   Hugh Frazer and Eric Marlier, Minimum Income Schemes in Europe (Brussels: European Social Policy Network, 2015), 17.

44   Ibid.

45   Manos Matsaganis, Mauricio Ferrera, Luis Capucha, and Luis Moreno, "Mending Nets in the South: Anti-poverty Policies in Greece, Italy, Portugal and Spain", Social Policy and Administration 37, no. 6 (2003): 641.

46   It is interesting that a major minimum income reform took also place in Cyprus in 2014. In that period Cyprus also experienced a deep economic recession and harsh socioeconomic conditions that created the necessary political pressure for reforming the national minimum income scheme, see Christos Koutsampelas, "The Cypriot GMI Scheme and Comparison with other European Countries", Cyprus Economic Policy Review 10, no. 1 (2016): 3–26.

47   Varvara Lalioti, "The curious Case of the Guaranteed Minimum (GMI): Highlighting Greek 'Exceptionalism' in a Southern European Context", Journal of European Social Policy 26, no. 1 (2016): 88.

48   Law No. 4389 of 2016, Introducing Emergency Provisions for the Implementation of the Agreement on Fiscal Objectives and Structural Reform and Other Provisions, Article 235, https://www.ilo.org/dyn/natlex/natlex4.detail?p_lang=en&p_isn=104600&p_count=15&p_classification=01 (accessed September 2, 2019).

49   Joint Ministerial Decision No. D23/oik.30299/2377, https://data2.unhcr.org/en/documents/download/49869 (accessed September 2, 2019) and Joint Ministerial Decision C.D.5 oik.2961–10, https://bit.ly/3wFiObC (accessed September 2, 2019).

that the ssi is very similar to the pilot scheme with only few minor changes pertaining to technical issues and modifications of the eligibility criteria.

The ssi scheme is based upon three pillars: (i) financial assistance for eligible persons/families, (ii) access to social services and goods and (iii) provision of supportive services for their (re-) integration into the labor market. The fact that financial assistance is linked to the other two pillars of the active inclusion policy (namely inclusive labor markets and access to services) is considered a step in the right direction and very close to what prevails in other European welfare states. According to official data, in June 2017, 246,529 households (or 559,621 persons) were benefiting from the scheme, with the average monthly expenditure fluctuating at around €55 million.[50]

5.3   Policy Challenges Lying Ahead

The Greek ssi is a new welfare program whose coverage, take-up and impact has not been yet thoroughly evaluated. Nevertheless, a first assessment of the 2014 pilot program showed that the scheme is inadequate, providing income support far below the poverty threshold.[51] At its current levels, it can only be expected to reduce acute poverty and provide some relief to marginalized groups suffering from severe material deprivation and social exclusion. Even so, the establishment of a national minimum income scheme for the first time in the history of the Greek welfare state is a very positive step, filling a significant void in social protection. It also justifies authors[52] who had already observed in the 2000s a marked progress of South European countries towards "mending their social safety nets" and gradually developing fully fledged minimum income schemes. Obviously, the main policy challenge lying ahead is to improve the adequacy of ssi. It is not unreasonable to expect that as the economy embarks on a robust growth trajectory in the coming decade and public finances improve, properly funding minimum income protection will become a priority in the social policy agenda. The active inclusion of ssi beneficiaries also poses a formidable challenge, endangered not only by the long-standing dysfunctionality of the Greek labor market but also by the lack of adequate and properly trained personnel characterizing social and employment services in Greece.

---

50   Dimitris Ziomas, Antoinetta Capella and Konstantinidou Danai, The National Roll-out of the "Social Solidarity Income" Scheme in Greece (Brussels: European Social Policy Network, 2017), 1.

51   Ibid.

52   Manos Matsaganis, Mauricio Ferrera, Luis Capucha, and Luis Moreno, "Mending Nets in the South: Anti-Poverty Policies in Greece, Italy, Portugal and Spain", 651–653.

6   Conclusion

The aim of this chapter is to provide a short overview of public healthcare, pensions and minimum income support in Greece in the aftermath of the recession. By drawing upon a growing literature on social policy studies in Greece and including further evidence and analysis from official reports, legislative sources and statistical agencies, the chapter also aims to outline the most important policy challenges that lie ahead for the social security system. Reflecting upon policies and reforms is undoubtedly a timely task after a long and harsh economic recession. Furthermore, policy lessons derived from the case of Greece might be useful for countries experiencing similar structural problems and economic challenges.

In a wider context, an intriguing question is whether economic recession and austerity should be understood as threats or opportunities for reform.[53] In other words, did the reforms of 2010–2016 erode the foundations of the welfare system, or were they necessary for its sustainability, thereby strengthening it in the long run? Does the Nietzschean "whatever does not kill you, makes you stronger" aphorism apply to welfare state policies? Inevitably, budgetary cuts of unprecedented magnitude weaken the redistributive capacity of the system and are in contrast to the declared national and EU goals to reduce poverty and social exclusion.[54] On the other hand, as numerous scholars and official reports already demonstrated in the pre-crisis period, the social security system of the country was not only expensive and inefficient, but also inequitable. Social expenditures had been constantly increasing before 2009 and they were mostly directed to the pension system with the purpose of actuarially over-compensating pensions.[55] Similar patterns were observed with respect to public healthcare, where inefficiency and inequity went hand in hand. Official data are indicative: total spending on social protection increased from 17.9% to 24.4% of GDP in 2001–2009, with pensions and healthcare accounting for almost three quarters of the total

---

53   Maria Petmesidou and Ana M. Guillén, "Can the Welfare State as We Know It Survive? A View from the Crisis-Ridden South European Periphery", South European Society and Politics, no. 19 (2014): 296.

54   Andreas Feronas, "The 'New Face' of Europeanization in Times of Crisis: Imposing the EU 'Recipe' on the Greek Welfare State Reforms", in The Impact and Implications of Crisis: A Comprehensive Approach Combining Elements of Health and Society, ed. Maria Saridi and Kyriakos Souliotis (New York: Nova Science Publishers, 2018), 179–180.

55   Eirini Andriopoulou, Alexandros Karakitsios and Panos Tsakloglou, Inequality and Poverty in Greece: Changes in Times of Crisis (Bonn: Institute of Labor Economics, 2017), 23–24.

spending.[56] At the same time, the redistributive effect of public spending was rather limited in comparison to other European countries equipped with more effective welfare states and the level of inequality persistently stood among the highest in Europe.[57] Moreover, all projections showed a further escalation of costs due to demographic factors. In light of this evidence, it is difficult to deny, regardless of one's ideological predisposition, that an economic rationalization of the system was inescapable. Yet it is sensible to wonder: did retrenchment go too far? Did these reforms lead to an irreversible path towards diminishing social rights in the context of a welfare system that has retreated substantially? Providing definite answers to these complex questions requires a substantial analytical and research effort, extending far beyond the modest aims of this chapter.

That said, one must admit that although the focus of the chapter concerned a major recession and its repercussions, the tone of the narrative was not intended to be pessimistic at all. Indeed, leaving aside simplistic austerity measures (e.g. benefit cuts), several structural reforms, although far from perfectly implemented, can be viewed as laying positive foundations for a sound social security system. An obvious example is the policy effort to unify public pensions into a single entity on the basis of common rules, which not only promotes economic efficiency but also is important for equity. Measures to safeguard the long-term sustainability of the pension system (such as taking life expectancy into account in determining statutory retirement age) are understandably unpopular, yet quite valuable for maintaining intergenerational fairness. The introduction of the national minimum income system has also been a crucial reform. As some first policy assessments have indicated, its levels are inadequate, mostly useful for eradicating extreme forms of poverty and in need of formidable revisions in the coming years so as to provide more substantial poverty relief as well as effective links to active inclusion. Still, the scheme has been implemented, filling a long-standing gap in social protection. Similarly, the attempt to integrate healthcare delivery and rationalize the various aspects of the health system has been also substantial, although much more effort is needed and admittedly several policy initiatives (i.e., primary care reform)

---

56   Eurostat, Tables by Functions, Aggregated Benefits and Grouped Schemes – million EUR, https://appsso.eurostat.ec.europa.eu/nui/show.do?dataset=spr_exp_eur&lang=en (accessed June 18, 2019).

57   Eirini Andriopoulou, Alexandros Karakitsios and Panos Tsakloglou, "Inequality and Poverty in Greece: Changes in Times of Crisis", in Socioeconomic fragmentation and exclusion in Greece under the crisis, ed. Dimitris Katsikas, Dimitri A. Sotiropoulos and Maria Zafeiropoulou (Cham: Palgrave Macmillan, 2018), 50.

have been incomplete, with dubious outcomes. Taken all together, it remains to be seen whether the post-recession governments will utilize the hopefully increased fiscal space of the coming years to strengthen a social security system which, compared to its pre-recession state, is certainly much less generous but at least more sustainable. Toward this aim, considerable policy effort is needed to address the demographic challenges as well as striking a balance between efficiency and equity.

Bibliography

Andriopoulou, Eirini, Alexandros Karakitsios, and Panos Tsakloglou. "Inequality and Poverty in Greece: Changes in Times of Crisis". In Socioeconomic Fragmentation and Exclusion in Greece under the Crisis, edited by Dimitris Katsikas, Dimitri A. Sotiropoulos, and Maria Zafeiropoulou, 23–54. Cham: Palgrave Macmillan, 2018.

Athanasiadis, Athanasios, Stella Kostopoulou, and Anastas Philalithis. "Regional Decentralization in the Greek Health Care System: Rhetoric and Reality". Global Journal of Health Science 7, no. 6 (2015): 55–67.

Economou, Charalambos, Daphne Kaitelidou, Marina Karanikolos, and Anna Maresso. "Greece: Health System Review". Health Systems in Transition 19, no. 5 (2017): 1–192.

European Commission. Health Care & Long-Term Care Systems: Greece. Joint Report on Health Care and Long-Term Care Systems & Fiscal Sustainability. Brussels: European Commission, 2016.

European Commission. The 2018 Ageing Report: Economic and Budgetary Projections for the EU Member States (2016–2070). Brussels: European Commission, 2018.

European Semester: Country Report – Greece. Brussels: European Commission, 2019.

Eurostat. Long-Term Unemployment by Sex - Annual Data. Accessed June 18, 2019. https://ec.europa.eu/eurostat/databrowser/view/une_ltu_a/default/table?lang=en.

Eurostat. Aggregate Replacement Ratio for Pensions (Excluding Other Social Benefits) by Sex. Accessed June 18, 2019. https://ec.europa.eu/eurostat/databrowser/view/tespn070/default/table?lang=en.

Eurostat. At-risk-of-poverty Rate by Poverty Threshold, Age and Sex – EU-SILC and ECHP Surveys. Accessed June 18, 2019. http://appsso.eurostat.ec.europa.eu/nui/show.do?dataset=ilc_li02.

Eurostat. At-risk-of-poverty Rate for Pensioners – EU-SILC Survey. Accessed June 18, 2019. https://ec.europa.eu/eurostat/databrowser/view/tespn100/default/table?lang=en.

Eurostat. Expenditure on Pensions. Accessed June 18, 2019. https://ec.europa.eu/eurostat/databrowser/view/spr_exp_pens/default/table?lang=en.

Eurostat. Government Deficit/Surplus, Debt and Associated Data. Accessed June 18, 2019. https://appsso.eurostat.ec.europa.eu/nui/show.do?dataset=gov_10dd_edpt1&lang=en.

Eurostat. In-work at-risk-of-poverty Rate by Age and Sex – EU-SILC Survey. Accessed June 18, 2019. https://ec.europa.eu/eurostat/databrowser/view/ilc_iw01$DV_407/default/table?lang=en.

Eurostat. Life Expectancy at Birth by Sex. Accessed June 18, 2019. http://appsso.eurostat.ec.europa.eu/nui/show.do?dataset=sdg_03_10&lang=en.

Eurostat. Old-age-dependency Ratio. Accessed June 18, 2019. http://appsso.eurostat.ec.europa.eu/nui/show.do?dataset=tps00198&lang=en.

Eurostat. People at Risk of Poverty or Social Exclusion by Sex. Accessed June 18, 2019. https://ec.europa.eu/eurostat/web/products-datasets/-/tepsr_lm410.

Eurostat. Real GDP Growth Rate – Volume. Accessed June 18, 2019. http://appsso.eurostat.ec.europa.eu/nui/show.do?dataset=tec00115&lang=en.

Eurostat. Tables by Functions, Aggregated Benefits and Grouped Schemes – million EUR. Accessed June 18, 2019. https://appsso.eurostat.ec.europa.eu/nui/show.do?-dataset=spr_exp_eur&lang=en.

Eurostat. Unemployment by Sex and Age – Annual Data. Accessed June 18, 2019. https://appsso.eurostat.ec.europa.eu/nui/show.do?dataset=une_rt_a&lang=en.

Feronas, Andreas. "The 'New Face' of Europeanization in Times of Crisis: Imposing the EU 'Recipe' on the Greek Welfare State Reforms". In The Impact and Implications of Crisis: A Comprehensive Approach Combining Elements of Health and Society, edited by Maria Saridi, and Kyriakos Souliotis, 169–190. New York: Nova Science Publishers, 2018.

Frazer, Hugh, and Eric Marlier. Minimum Income Schemes in Europe. Brussels: European Commission. European Social Policy Network, 2015.

Joint Ministerial Decision C.D.5 oik.2961–10, 2017. Accessed September 2, 2019. https://bit.ly/3wFiObC.

Joint Ministerial Decision D23/oik.30299/2377, 2016. Accessed September 2, 2020. https://data2.unhcr.org/en/documents/download/49869.

Karanikolos, Marina, and Alexander Kentikelenis. "Health Inequalities after Austerity in Greece". International Journal for Equity in Health 15, no. 1 (2016): 83.

Koutsampelas, Christos. "Aspects of Elderly Poverty in Cyprus". Cyprus Economic Policy Review 6, no. 1 (2012): 69–89.

Koutsampelas, Christos. "The Cypriot GMI Scheme and Comparisons with Other European Countries". Cyprus Economic Policy Review 10, no. 1 (2016): 3–26.

Lalioti, Varvara. "The Curious Case of the Guaranteed Minimum (GMI): Highlighting Greek 'Exceptionalism' in a Southern European Context". Journal of European Social Policy 26, no. 1 (2016): 80–93.

Law No. 3918 of 2011 on Structural Changes to the Healthcare System and Other Provision. Accessed September 2, 2019. https://bit.ly/3p38KXt.

Law No. 4024 of 2011 concerning Issues of Retirement Pensions, of Unified Wage System – Grading System, Employment Reserves and Other Provisions concerning the Mid-Term Framework of Fiscal Strategy. Accessed September 2, 2019. http://ilo.org/dyn/natlex/natlex4.detail?p_lang=en&p_isn=89634&p_country=GRC&p_count=610.

Law No. 4051 of 2012 Introducing Retirement Adjustments and Other Emergency Regulations in Application of Memorandum of Understanding. Accessed September 2, 2019. https://www.ilo.org/dyn/natlex/natlex4.detail?p_lang=en&p_isn=99834.

Law No. 4093 of 2012 Approving the Medium-Term Fiscal Strategy 2013-2016 and Introducing Emergency Measures Implementing Law No. 4046 of 2012 and the Medium-Term Fiscal Strategy 2013–2016. Accessed September 2, 2019. https://www.ilo.org/dyn/natlex/natlex4.detail?p_lang=en&p_isn=99876.

Law No. 4387 of 2016 Introducing the Unified System of Social Insurance, Providing for the Reform of the Social Protection System and Pension Scheme and Regulating the Tax Income and Taxation for Chance-Games and Inserting Other Provisions. Accessed September 2, 2019. https://www.ilo.org/dyn/natlex/natlex4.detail?p_lang=en&p_isn=104502.

Law No. 4389 of 2016 Introducing Emergency Provisions for the Implementation of the Agreement on Fiscal Objectives and Structural Reform and Other Provisions. Accessed September 2, 2019. https://www.ilo.org/dyn/natlex/natlex4.detail?p_lang=en&p_isn=104600&p_count=15&p_classification=01.

Law No. 4238 of 2014 on the National Primary Health Care Network (PEDY), on the Change of Scope of the Greek National Health Service (EOPYY) and Other Provisions. Accessed September 2, 2019. https://www.ilo.org/dyn/natlex/natlex4.detail?p_lang=en&p_isn=100566&p_country=GRC&p_count=579&p_classification=15&p_classcount=96 .

Liaropoulos, Lykourgos, Olga Siskou, Daphne Kaitelidou, Mamas Theodorou, and Theofanis Katostaras. "Informal Payments in Public Hospitals in Greece". Health Policy 87, no. 1 (2008): 72–81.

Matsaganis, Manos. "The Welfare State and the Crisis: The Case of Greece". Journal of European Social Policy 21, no. 5 (2011): 501–512.

Matsaganis, Manos, Maurizio Ferrera, Luis Capucha, and Luis Moreno. "Mending Nets in the South: Anti-Poverty Policies in Greece, Italy, Portugal and Spain". Social Policy and Administration 37, no. 6 (2003): 639–655.

Mossialos, Elias, Sara Allin, and Konstantina Davaki. "Analysing the Greek Health System: A Tale of Fragmentation and Inertia". Health Economics 14 (2015): S151–S168.

National Actuarial Authority. Greek Pension System Fiche. European Commission, Economic Policy Committee, Ageing Working Group, 2015. Accessed September

2, 2020. https://ec.europa.eu/info/sites/info/files/economy-finance/final_country_fiche_el.pdf.

OECD/European Observatory on Health Systems and Policies. State of Health in the EU. Brussels: OECD Publishing, Paris/European Observatory on Health Systems and Policies, 2017.

OECD/European Observatory on Health Systems and Policies. Greece: Country Health Profile 2017. Accessed June 15, 2019. https://www.euro.who.int/_data/assets/pdf_file/0005/ 355982/Health-Profile-Greece-Eng.pdf.

Petmesidou Maria and Ana M. Guillén. "Can the Welfare State as We Know It Survive? A View from the Crisis-Ridden South European Periphery". South European Society and Politics, no. 19 (2014): 295–307. https://doi.org/10.1080/13608746.2014.950369.

Souliotis, Kyriakos, Christina Golna, Yiannis Tountas, Olga Siskou, Daphni Kaitelidou, and Lycourgos Liaropoulos. "Informal Payments in the Greek Health Sector amid the Financial Crisis: Old Habits Die Last". The European Journal of Health Economics 17, no. 2 (2015): 159–170.

Souliotis, Kyriakos. "Increasing Health Spending whilst Widening Inequalities: The Greek Paradox in Health Policy". In Health, Society and Economy: Unequal Relations – Welfare Gaps, edited by Charalambos Economou, 125–144. Athens: Alexandria, 2013.

The 2018 Ageing Report: Economic and Budgetary Projections for the EU Member States (2016–2070). Brussels: European Commission, 2018.

Tinios, Platon. "Pension Reform in Greece: 'Reform by Instalments', a Blocked Process". West European Politics 28, no. 2 (2005): 402–419.

Tinios, Platon. "Vacillations around a Pension Reform Trajectory: Time for a Change?". In The Challenge of Reform in Greece, 1974–2009: Assessment and Prospects, edited by Stathis Kalyvas, George Pagoulatos, and Haris Tsoukas. New York: Columbia University Press, 2011.

Zettelmayer, Jeromin, Christoph Trebesch, and G. Mitu Gulati. "The Greek Debt Restructuring: An Autopsy". Economic Policy 28, no. 75 (2013): 513–563.

Ziomas, Dimitris, Antoinetta Capella, and Danai Konstantinidou, The National Roll-out of the "Social Solidarity Income" Scheme in Greece. Brussels: European Social Policy Network, European Commission, 2017.

Ziomas, Dimitris, Danai Konstantinidou, and Antoinetta Capella. Inequalities in Access to Healthcare: Greece. Brussels: European Social Policy Network, European Commission, 2017.

Index

CPSIA information can be obtained
at www.ICGtesting.com
Printed in the USA
JSHW011731290822
29834JS00006B/7

9 781642 597950